Political Theology for a Plural Age

Political Theology for a Plural Age

Edited by

MICHAEL JON KESSLER

OXFORD
UNIVERSITY PRESS

OXFORD
UNIVERSITY PRESS

Oxford University Press is a department of the University of Oxford.
It furthers the University's objective of excellence in research, scholarship,
and education by publishing worldwide.

Oxford   New York
Auckland   Cape Town   Dar es Salaam   Hong Kong   Karachi
Kuala Lumpur   Madrid   Melbourne   Mexico City   Nairobi
New Delhi   Shanghai   Taipei   Toronto

With offices in
Argentina   Austria   Brazil   Chile   Czech Republic   France   Greece
Guatemala   Hungary   Italy   Japan   Poland   Portugal   Singapore
South Korea   Switzerland   Thailand   Turkey   Ukraine   Vietnam

Oxford is a registered trademark of Oxford University Press
in the UK in certain other countries.

Published in the United States of America by
Oxford University Press
198 Madison Avenue, New York, NY 10016

© Oxford University Press 2013

Portions of Elizabeth Bucar's essay in chapter 7, "Gauging the Status of Public Theologies:
Rhetorical Analysis of the Media Construction of Political Islam," appear in Elizabeth
Bucar, "Speaking of Motherhood: The Epideictic Rhetoric of John Paul II and Ayatollah
Khomeini," *Journal of the Society of Christian Ethics* 26, no. 2 (2006): 93–123.
Reprinted by permission of the publisher, all rights reserved.

Portions of Charles Mathewes's essay in chapter 10, "Augustinian Christian Republican
Citizenship" appear in Charles Mathewes, *The Republic of Grace* © 2010 Wm. B. Eerdmans
Publishing Company, Grand Rapids, Michigan. Reprinted by permission of the publisher,
all rights reserved.

Library of Congress Cataloging-in-Publication Data
Political theology for a plural age / edited by Michael Jon Kessler.
p. cm.
Based on a conference held in Oct. 2008 at Georgetown University.
Includes index.
ISBN 978–0–19–976927–8 (pbk. : alk. paper)—
ISBN 978–0–19–976928–5 (hardcover : alk. paper)   1. Political theology—
Congresses.   2. Public theology—Congresses.   I. Kessler, Michael (Michael Jon)
BT83.59.P645 2013 261.7—dc23
2012030250

1 3 5 7 9 8 6 4 2
Printed in the United States of America
on acid-free paper

Contents

PART THREE: *Confronting Pluralism: Main Trends in*
Political Theologies Today

Acknowledgments

THIS VOLUME WAS made possible through the support of the Berkley Center for Religion, Peace, and World Affairs at Georgetown University. The book emerged from an October 2008 conference featuring a keynote conversation with John Milbank and Mark Lilla and three public sessions. Besides the authors included in this volume, I wish to thank Jacques Berlinerblau (Georgetown University), Damon Linker (University of Pennsylvania), Erik Owens (Boston College), and Hent de Vries (Johns Hopkins University) for their thoughtful participation in the conference and encouragement of this project.

The Berkley Center has been a supportive and engaging home for encouraging this and other work. In particular, Thomas Banchoff's direction, support, and guidance were essential to the project. My faculty and staff colleagues made the work easy and pleasant, in particular I wish to thank Melody Fox Ahmed, Jamie Scott, Erin Coleman, Erin Taylor, Annie Hunt, Abby Waldrip, Eric Patterson, Tom Farr, Katherine Marshall, Paul Elie, Chet Gillis, and José Casanova.

I was graced with an editor who was patient, insightful, and encouraging—many thanks to Theo Calderara for his constant good advice, Charlotte Steinhardt for her diligence at every stage, and the other staff and members of Oxford University Press who shepherded this project.

Finally, a number of friends were the source of inspiration, confidence and, at times, the right amount of prodding during the years in which this project came to fruition. In particular, I thank Jerome Copulsky, Charles Mathewes, William Schweiker, Mark Lilla, and Thomas Banchoff. Finally, thanks especially to the person who sustains and enlivens me in all my pursuits, Kara Ward.

Contributors

Elizabeth Bucar is Associate Professor of Philosophy and Religion at Northeastern University.

José Casanova is Professor in the Department of Sociology at Georgetown University and a Senior Fellow at the Berkley Center for Religion, Peace, and World Affairs.

Jocelyne Cesari is Director of the Islam in the West Program at Harvard University, an Associate at the Center for Middle Eastern Studies and at the Center for European Studies, and teaches at the Harvard Divinity School and Government Department.

Jerome Copulsky is Assistant Professor of Philosophy and Religion and Director of Judaic Studies at Goucher College.

Patrick J. Deneen is David A. Potenziani Memorial Associate Professor of Constitutional Studies at the University of Notre Dame.

Eric Gregory is Professor in the Department of Religion at Princeton University.

Paul Heck is Associate Professor of Islamic Studies in Georgetown University's Department of Theology and founding Director of the Center for the Study of Religions across Civilizations.

Michael Jon Kessler is Visiting Assistant Professor of Government, Adjunct Professor of Law, and Associate Director of the Berkley Center for Religion, Peace, and World Affairs at Georgetown University.

Mark Lilla is Professor of Humanities at Columbia University.

Robin Lovin is Cary M. Maguire University Professor of Ethics at Southern Methodist University.

Charles Mathewes is Carolyn M. Barbour Professor of Religious Studies at the University of Virginia, Director of the Virginia Center for the Study of Religion, and Co-Principal of Brown College at UVA.

John Milbank is Professor in Religion, Politics, and Ethics, in the Department of Theology and Religious Studies at the University of Nottingham.

David Novak holds the J. Richard and Dorothy Shiff Chair of Jewish Studies as Professor of the Study of Religion and Professor of Philosophy at the University of Toronto.

Political Theology for a Plural Age

Introduction

POLITICAL THEOLOGY IN A PLURAL CONTEXT

Michael Jon Kessler

POLITICAL THEOLOGY IS, among other things, the collection of stories we tell ourselves about our nature as humans, our aspirations for order and justice in light of the sacred, and what, thereby, constitutes and limits legitimate rule over our collective lives. The classic questions of political theology have always been characterized by a plurality of viewpoints and competing stories. Indeed, different theological-political worldviews constantly wrestled for supremacy in the political arena, sometimes sanctioning the official use of power, other times prophetically resisting the reigning powers, often imagining new possibilities for collective life and insisting on a horizon of hope and value wider than the civil order.

Different definitions of political theology abound.[1] Mark Lilla notes in a recent exploration of modern political theology, "Political life revolves around disputes over authority: who may legitimately exercise power over others, to what ends, and under what conditions. In such disputes it might be enough to appeal to something in human nature that legitimizes the exercise of authority, and leave the matter there."[2] Yet humans also travel up the chain of causes, ascribing to God intentions for, and control over, our political ideas, power, and goals. On Lilla's account, political theology is the name for this "discourse about political authority based on a revealed divine nexus."[3] Lilla contrasts political theology with political philosophy, wherein humans developed "habits of thinking and talking about politics exclusively in human terms, without appeal to divine revelation or cosmological speculation."[4]

Other contemporary accounts of political theology expand the scope of how religious worldviews infuse and animate our accounts of political orders. For instance, the editors of a recent collection of essays on political theology define the term broadly: "The analysis and criticism of political arrangements (including cultural-psychological, social and economic aspects) from the perspective of differing interpretations of God's ways with the world."[5] In this regard, political theology is based on more than accounts of revelation, encompassing a wider swath of normative inquiries into how the political order ought to be arranged.

Paul Kahn has argued that political theology is a descriptive phenomenological method used to "identify and describe the presence of the sacred, wherever it appears."[6] Such a method can "pierce the [modern liberal] state's self-presentation as an efficient means of justly advancing individual welfare and look to the *experience* of the political" that, at its core, is imbued with the "*mysterium tremendum* of the sacred, with its tremendous power for both destruction and construction," a reality that political theory in general misses in its analysis.[7] The infamous definition of Carl Schmitt lurks in the background of this approach: "All significant concepts of the modern theory of the state are secularized theological concepts not only because of their historical development—in which they are transferred from theology to the theory of the state...—but also because of their systematic structure."[8] In this phenomenological reading, the "sacred" can appear in the political order as a latent holdover from a premodern era, and political theology seeks to identify its appearances. At the same time, even naturalistic accounts of politics may expose dynamic forces at play in human lives and interactions, forces that can only be understood through theological and religious categories and concepts.

Political theology has enjoyed something of a renaissance in the past decade. Recent projects in political thought have had to recognize that even late-modern enlightened people do not neatly follow the imperatives of the grand narrative of modernity wherein they desacralize their justifications for political life, leaving behind thick accounts of moral and religious being. Religions—both traditional and emergent—persist and play a significant role in moral motivation, social integration, and political will formation, even as late-modern tendencies of political thought have wanted to sequester religious influence from official policy debates.[9] Indeed, many have explored how the classic thesis of modern secularization has increasingly unraveled on many fronts.[10] Political life—its legitimacy, its goals, its supposed necessity—is rooted all the way down into our deepest conceptions of being and our ultimate concerns.

A feature of late modern political orders is that these ultimate concerns clash as the diverse tapestry of humans approach political issues from starkly different background assumptions. The horizon of political theology was thus long ago transformed by the widespread recognition of epistemological pluralism and the linguistic basis of reason and cognition. Most political theorists recognize that modern societies are grounded without a shared consensus about moral and political values and cohere (if they cohere at all) without a common stock of theoretical and tradition-based resources. Knowledge of public matters is increasingly evidence-based, and religious claims are met with skepticism. Any serious political theology must navigate this landscape and somehow reconcile the many viewpoints arising when ideologically diverse citizens contest one another's claims.

Questions of political formation, legitimation, and collective policy are thereby intensified and complicated for any political society of persons formed and shaped through diverse cultural, ethnic, religious, and ideological lines. The "many" who join together within a political society also find themselves formed as agents and joined together in myriad ways, through ties that arise beyond and apart from their political bonds. We live more deeply than our politics, a fact which imposes challenges for any politico-theological account of political authority. How can political legitimacy be reconciled when different actors within the same political space relate to political authority in vastly diverse ways? More than reconciling competing claims and principles, this requires political society to negotiate sometimes radically different goals, hopes, fears, aspirations, and values. How does accounting for and analyzing the diversity of gods and religions help or hinder figuring out how these many citizens (and tribes, and communities, and nations), animated by different norms and worldviews, can come to live peacefully in proximity? What has been needed, and is now emerging as a crucial aspect of study in political theology, is how to navigate the *actual, lived* pluralism of citizens of different religions, cultures, and ethnicities trying to live together as fellow citizens.

Recent modes of political theology have responded divergently to this new pluralistic horizon, ranging from, on the one hand, acquiescence and accommodation to maintain religion within a private sphere and reframe religious arguments within publicly available conceptual vocabulary to, on the other hand, forcefully proclaiming the legitimate power to marshal religious arguments to justify political and legal stances and activities, to, in a different vein, redeveloping visions of the prophetic (but not necessarily political) public presence of the *ecclesia*.[11]

This volume is not framed by any one of these particular, oft-debated tendencies. Some authors are concerned with advancing the thought of their own traditions within the pluralistic landscape. Others investigate the empirical phenomena of religion's role in political legitimation and policy formation across various political societies, trying to tease out the implications of that thought within a pluralistic political system. Some directly challenge the predominant implications of pluralism, while others take these implications for granted. This plurality of approaches, views, and methods is intrinsic to the task of political theology. As such, the various essays are related at a general level through a recognition that the horizon for political theology must engage a diverse and plural world.

A number of the essays, across traditions, explore the implications of the relativization of the political sphere in light of the primacy of the religious. This move makes it easier to accommodate pluralism in the political sphere because the civil state does not need to reflect any single ontology or religious worldview. While many of the essays reflect theological-political stances in which ultimate reconciliation cannot be attained in this present life, the particular resources religions bring to bear for constructing the political institutions and ideas of justice, hope, and legitimacy vary across traditions. At the same time, a surprising number of these configurations lead to some confirmation of the democratic order, even while they insist on a wider horizon of human meaning and value and limits on the appropriate aspirations of political orders.

This collection of essays is also connected by a focus on some of the main trends and challenges for Christian, Jewish, and Islamic political theologies today. The volume, implicitly, explores whether there is a common discourse across the three Abrahamic traditions about how political power is legitimated and relates to other modes of life. The Abrahamic context is a purely editorial choice. One could envision a thousand more essays across the vast phenomena of human thinking about politics that arise from other religious worldviews and confront other material and institutional realities. This work is already undertaken in thoughtful ways, and I hope this volume helps encourage more work that explores how political theologies have adapted, and may yet further adapt, to the shared global challenges of the twenty-first century.

The first chapter is a compilation of a series of dialogues Michael Kessler convened between Mark Lilla, José Casanova, and John Milbank held at Georgetown University during 2008 to 2009. In part a discussion of Lilla's recent book *The Stillborn God*, these distinguished scholars lay the groundwork for thinking about how our present configurations of the intersection of politics and religion came to be and the challenges posed to Western political theologies today. What is the task and scope of political theology, and does it still matter in an age of pluralism and suspicion about religion? How, if at all, can religious claims about the nature and legitimacy of the political order still resonate? How do immigration, pluralism, secularism, and new models of consumerism and economics affect how religion legitimates politics?

The essays in part II, "Domesticating Religion: The Abrahamic Faiths and the Democratic State," aim to elucidate how contemporary Abrahamic political theologies have developed in relation to historic and modern pressures. In the Christian and Jewish contexts, political theologies emerged in their modern form in response to the wars of religion, the rise of rationalism, the emergence of the nation-state, the challenges of totalitarianism, and the development of democracy. The Islamic tradition critically inherited some of these traditions and sought new models for political order under colonial rule and in the postcolonial context. In Christianity, the emergence of the individual subject leads, in some ways, to the rights-bearing individual subject of the modern nation-state. Was this a rejection of Christian theology or one example of its modern flowering? In Judaism, the experience of Diaspora and semi-autonomy was reconfigured with the Emancipation and the development of Zionist movements. In Islam, the encounter with colonialism in the nineteenth and early twentieth centuries decisively shaped the reception of democratic ideas in the postcolonial era. The essays in part II are explorations of the genealogy and development of political theology within Abrahamic traditions, with special attention to the legitimation of political power in the historical and contemporary context.

Patrick Deneen (chapter 2) wages a historically based theoretical argument for the reevaluation of the Christian political-theological project. He argues against the predominant narrative of post-Enlightenment political theologies, most recently espoused by Mark Lilla in *The Stillborn God*. Deneen disavows Augustine's "Great Separation" between religion and politics, which was an effort to remove appeals to "the divine nexus" in connection to political authority, instead vesting political authority wholly in rational and secular terms, therefore rendering religion an affair of private life, individual conscience, and voluntary association. On the contrary, Deneen argues that modern political thinkers tried to overcome the "Great Separation" by means of two distinct "Great Combinations." Each corresponds roughly with a development within liberal theory; one in its classical conception, enunciated most clearly by Hobbes and Locke, and the other in its progressive period, represented by thinkers such as Rousseau and J. S. Mill. These Great Combinations of the modern project have led to depletion and destruction because of the rearrangement of the human relation to the created order. Instead of finding our place and meaning from a preexisting created order, the modern project has transformed this relation into mastery over a world that is subject to human dominion. Deneen calls for a new, true separation—an acknowledgment that humans are not divine and are created subjects, not sovereigns.

Jerome Copulsky (chapter 3) argues that the question of the political nature and meaning of Judaism is central to the development of and debates within modern Jewish religious thought in the West. In order to adapt to their new situation in the modern nation-state, Jewish thinkers tried to transform the political structure of Judaism: its conceptions of peoplehood, law, and messianic hope. The *halakhah* was the very heart of premodern Judaism, the framework for Jewish norms and behavior. The eclipse of the law, the turn to belief as the heart of Judaism, was to render Judaism liberal, humanistic, and "Protestant," that is, a confessional rather than "political" religion. When Jewish belief and practice were detached from the practice of *halakhah* and conceptions of peoplehood, theology became more significant to Jewish self-understanding. In the context of the collapse of Christendom and the rise of the Enlightenment, these moves allowed for the political integration of the Jews, yet forced the modern theological-political question for Jewish theology.

Eric Gregory (chapter 4) explores different strands of political theology and articulates a position of ambivalent acceptance of democracy as an earthly instrument of justice. He argues that while today most Christian political theology finds itself in an ambivalent relation to modern configurations of rights, equality, and the power of the democratic state, prophetic critiques of modern democracies usually reflect fundamental features of the democratic tradition. Christian political theology has a creative role in imagining anew the inherited traditions and the insistence on social virtues necessary to face an ambiguous future.

Paul Heck (chapter 5) explores the democratic side of contemporary politics in Morocco by examining the Islamic religious principles that shape understandings of the polity. He focuses on how the rulers in the constitutional monarchy recognize, through Islam, that rule exists for the sake of the interests of society as a whole directed to the common good. He articulates how Islam supports a view by the people that they have self-determinative freedom and the inherent capacity to govern themselves and serves as a source of stability and coherence even while democratic aspirations emerge among the people.

The essays in part III, "Confronting Pluralism: Main Trends in Political Theologies Today," address how the contemporary pluralism of religion and worldviews in the public sphere poses a shared set of challenges to adherents of Abrahamic traditions as they seek to organize and participate within political institutions and the public sphere. Religious communities are grappling with economic and cultural globalization and its powerful secular and individualist ethos. At the same time, they are operating amid unprecedented religious pluralism, which creates both friction—especially through immigration—and opportunities for collaboration. Theologians and religious actors are developing new modes of political theology for public action and political participation while trying to navigate old and new models of understanding their own traditions, beliefs, and practices.

In chapter 6, I explore how political theology is, in a plural age, a necessarily comparative enterprise. Reflection about political practices and norms and political engagement require encounters with those of different normative viewpoints and those who are citizens of other political orders, necessitating communicative clarity across divergent background assumptions, worldviews, and legitimating norms. Political theology as a discipline has not yet developed a robust justification for the comparative enterprise. I explore the challenges in the related field of comparative religious ethics; a field from which lessons can be drawn about the need for systematic and methodological clarity about the goals for and possibilities of comparative political theology.

Elizabeth Bucar (chapter 7) argues that the status of specific theologies in national politics can be accurately gauged through analysis of media coverage. She posits that the media simultaneously serves as proxy for and source of mainstream logics about the proper public role for religion. She develops a method of analysis that focuses on three rhetorical categories of assumptions and applies this method to a case study of the media construction of political Islam in the United States, specifically offering a close reading of media coverage of (1) rumors in 2008 that Barack Obama was a Muslim and (2) Iranian president Mahmoud Ahmadinejad's 2007 visit to the United States. Bucar uncovers a number of assumptions grounding a public mistrust of Islam. This case study reveals that coverage of "Obama's Muslim Problem" makes it clear that the public does not know sufficient facts about Islam and Muslims and that many presumptions exist. The mainstream media's presentation of Ahmadinejad demonstrates assumptions about Islam that are widespread and no longer explained by the media. Exposing this media rhetoric about political figures can usefully serve to elucidate the public perception of political theologies, a methodology Bucar argues has broad applicability in comparative perspective.

Robin Lovin (chapter 8) argues for a pluralistic political theology based on the common pursuit of a diversity of human goods. He argues that an approach to political theology that can engage the problems of modern constitutional democracies must transcend the tired debate between public reason and theology and develop a framework for understanding democracy that maintains the integrity of both politics and theology. Regardless of the rules of public reason, public life will be filled with the ideas about human goods that people use for guiding social life and creation of institutions. He develops a pluralist political theology concerned with balancing between the various contexts where the human good is sought based on a realist attention to proximate justice and balancing power in all spheres of politics, not just in the politics of nations.

David Novak (chapter 9) explores how political theology is pitted against the theological control of politics, the antithesis to democracy. The task of political theology—which he holds as advocating political policies from a decidedly theological perspective—is to rescue the project of political theology from the suspicions of those, on the one hand, who would sever all relation between theology and politics under a secularist model and, on the other hand, those who would identify theology and politics. Novak examines whether the privatization of religions is the best way to prevent one religious community from attempting to dominate the state at the expense of others but shows that no religious community can accept being so privatized. He concludes by arguing for a way to do authentic political theology in a pluralistic, multicultural society through a revitalization of natural law theory, in which even nonreligious persons can come to a good-faith understanding about what biblical revelation presupposes in order to be morally intelligible, even if they themselves cannot affirm it in good faith.

Charles Mathewes (chapter 10) develops an account of Christian political theology that aims to be authentically liberal, even while it is deeply ambivalent about the liberal situation. Mathewes shows that Christian political theology—inspired by Augustine among others—bears the ability to criticize and undo the inevitable tendency toward "political idolatry." On his account, there is an affinity between the self-limitation that liberal democracy with its constitutionalism and defense of personal privacy maintains and the theological injunction. There is, he says, "a salutary suspicion at the root of liberalism" of the "potential of any and every political (and, by extension, cultural) system...to reduce people to a role in some immanent system of political or cultural power"—liberalism does not equate the state with the *summum bonum*, with "the final frame of human's moral identity"—just as there is, in liberalism, a healthy fear of "the absolutization of the state—its theologization." Mathewes argues that a pluralistic setting undercuts religious belief's "taken for grantedness" and makes such belief no longer an unquestioned background assumption but transparently contingent.

Finally, Jocelyne Cesari (chapter 11) argues that Islam's many forms at the international level demonstrate that the opposition between modern secularism and Islam is insufficient to account for the complex relationship of religion generated by cultural globalization. Islam is too easily essentialized in typical international relations discourse; the reality is far more complicated, both for contemporary Muslim polities and for historic predecessors. Cesari demonstrates through discussion of Iran, Pakistan, and Turkey that various manifestations of political Islam have developed in the postcolonial nation-building and modernization processes of Muslim societies, and these are inherently part of the modernization and secularization of Muslim-majority states. The standard narrative of secularity, by which secularism leads to the decline of public religion, fails to grasp this fundamental phenomenon.

Notes

1. Eric Gregory's essay in this volume offers a helpful four-part typology of different types of political theology.
2. Mark Lilla, *The Stillborn God: Religion, Politics, and the Modern West* (New York: Alfred A. Knopf, 2007), 22.
3. Ibid., 23.
4. Ibid., 2–5.
5. William Cavanaugh and Peter Scott, introduction to *The Blackwell Companion to Political Theology*, ed. Peter Scott and William Cavanaugh (Malden, MA: Blackwell, 2007), 1.
6. Paul Kahn, *Political Theology: Four New Chapters on the Concept of Sovereignty* (New York: Columbia University Press, 2011), 25.

7. Ibid., 26–7.

8. Carl Schmitt, *Political Theology: Four Chapters on the Concept of Sovereignty*, trans. George Schwab (Chicago: University of Chicago Press, 2005), 36.

9. See, for instance, John Rawls, *Political Liberalism* (New York: Columbia University Press, 1996), and Jürgen Habermas, "'The Political': The Rational Meaning of a Questionable Inheritance of Political Theology," in *The Power of Religion in the Public Sphere*, ed. Eduardo Mendieta and Jonathan VanAntwerpen (New York: Columbia University Press, 2011).

10. See, for instance, José Casanova, *Public Religions in the Modern World* (Chicago: University of Chicago Press, 1994), and Peter Berger, ed., *The Desecularization of the World: Resurgent Religion and World Politics* (Grand Rapids, MI: Eerdmans, 1999).

11. As Charles Mathewes put this: "What has actually happened in the last few decades is that those religious voices attuned to the complexity of religion in public life have effectively ceded the rhetorical high ground of thick discourse to extremist and often reactionary (whether right-wing or left-wing) voices" in *A Theology of Public Life* (Cambridge: Cambridge University Press, 2007), 7. For an excellent and concise overview of some of these recent trajectories, see Luke Bretherton, *Christianity and Contemporary Politics* (Oxford: Wiley-Blackwell, 2010), 10–18 and 45–53.

PART ONE

Theologies of the Political

I

A Conversation

José Casanova, Michael Jon Kessler, John Milbank,
and Mark Lilla

DURING A SERIES of conversations in 2008 and 2009 at Georgetown University, Michael Kessler engaged in dialogue with José Casanova, Mark Lilla, and John Milbank about current issues and challenges in political theology. The following essay is an edited compilation of these conversations.

Michael Kessler: In *The Stillborn God*, Mark Lilla describes how humans, in seeking to explain the "conditions of political life and political judgment...seem compelled to travel up and out: up toward those things that transcend human existence, and outward to encompass the whole of that existence."[1] And yet, in spite of these transcendent and messianic tendencies, the overwhelming number of Western political thinkers in the past four centuries have tried to constrain our wandering minds and wills, so as "to separate the basic questions of politics from questions of theology and cosmology."[2]

There are few more pressing questions confronting our contemporary situation than the relation of theological worldviews with our collective political orders. Mark, how did you develop this argument?

Mark Lilla: Originally, I thought I was going to write a book on the counter-Enlightenment down into the twentieth century. This led me to study the revival of messianic theology and political theology during the Weimar years following on the works of Karl Barth, which in turn set me on an even more unusual path, back through the nineteenth century to study liberal theology, both Protestant and Jewish. None of this is on the standard curriculum of political theory, which is what I studied in graduate school.

But it did give me a different perspective on thinkers we normally do study, like Kant and Hegel. Looking anew at Rousseau and his views on religion gave me a different view of Hobbes. This in turn led me to think about a problem I had never really thought seriously enough about: the theological-political problematic of Christianity. That is, I was driven further back to think about the theological preconditions that seemed to make necessary the break with Christian political theology at a certain historical juncture.

So this backward tour through the history of political theory led me to write *The Stillborn God* as a kind of intellectual passion play about how we get from Hobbes to thinkers like Hermann Cohen and Karl Barth. The connection is political theology.

Michael Kessler: Political theology is a term that has reemerged to capture a complex set of phenomena about the relationship between politics and religion. It is not clear what the term means or if it is the best term to use to capture these intersections. John, do you find the term fruitful?

John Milbank: I think that it is important to stress that political theology is not a traditional term at all—that fact alone is significant. There are theological treatments of the area of politics, and so I much prefer to describe this as "theologies of the political." The term "political theology" in its more recent incarnation tended to suggest theologies whose entire horizon is political, and here I am thinking of someone like Johann Baptist Metz. This is an approach that I would strongly reject, not least because I think that if you decide that the entire horizon is political, then you are left with a less, rather than a more, radical and critical approach to politics.

I am far more interested in the first incarnation of the term in Carl Schmitt's usage, the criticism of Schmitt by Erik Peterson, and the conversations they were both having with Ernst Kantorowicz. I think that this body of work is of far greater significance to understanding the legacy of political theology.

But this was not political theology in the later sense so much as it was an attempt to talk about the way in which our discourse in the West about politics is far more theological than we imagine, particularly in the way that Schmitt asserted that the entire theory of sovereignty is irreducibly theological in character. Of course, Peterson replied by saying, "Yes, but it is based on heterodox Christianity, and it relates to voluntaristic deviations, and this notion is incompatible with Trinitarian theology." And then Kantorowicz joined in by talking about the ways in which the models of rule in the West were not just theological but also Christological, most notably in his book *The King's Two Bodies*. This work is now being revived, notably by Giorgio Agamben, who has suggested that the entire obsession with the economic in the West is, in the end Christian, although (in a Peterson-like response), I would want to add that it is also a distortion of the Christian idea. This tradition undermines the idea that we are living in a conceptual terrain of pure secularity.

Michael Kessler: Mark, what terrain does the term "political theology" map in your book?

Mark Lilla: In the book, I define political theology narrowly as a doctrine that legitimates the use of public authority by appeal to divine revelation. The term "political theology" is very much in fashion right now, but I want to insist on this narrow definition because I want to find a concept that helps us to understand the distinctiveness of Western political thought since the seventeenth century. I wanted to focus on how the exercise of authority gets legitimated intellectually in political theology and then on the modern alternatives, beginning with Thomas Hobbes, who self-consciously set out to break with Christian political theology and, more deeply, with political theology as such.

Michael Kessler: How does this alternative tradition originating in Hobbes accomplish a break with political theology?

Mark Lilla: Well, I've come up with the term "the Great Separation." With Hobbes, what changes is not all of the things that we usually pay attention to in Hobbes, such as the image of the Leviathan; who the sovereign is and how much authority he has; life being nasty, brutish, and short; and so forth. Rather, I focus on what Hobbes doesn't talk about. Hobbes manages in the *Leviathan* to change the subject of Western political discourse. Up until that point, a large part of Western political discourse took the form of discerning God's intentions from his nature and revelations, and then asking how those intentions work themselves out in political life. In order to understand what we are supposed to do here on earth, we need to understand something about the nexus between God, man, and the world.

What Hobbes did was change the subject, from God to why human beings believe in God, and why they think God has commands for us in political life. Now Hobbes couldn't refute political theology because there is no way to refute revelation. But what he managed to do was to cast enough suspicion on those who appealed to revelation that he simply took our eye off the ball, so to speak, and got us instead asking why it is that people come to believe these things about religion and politics. Why is it that religion seems to initiate, and then perpetuate, a cycle of religious and political violence and fear? And how might we short-circuit this cycle? [He] does this all without saying anything (or much) about God himself. He says he'll get back to us, but never does. Hobbes did the most revolutionary thing a thinker can ever do: not refute somebody, but change the subject.

The story then goes on. We pass through Rousseau and his concerns about Hobbes's political anthropology; we go from political theology to political anthropology. I then talk about how liberal political theology gets reborn on an anthropological basis, and the rest of the passion play then plays out until we get down to Weimar.

I want to insist on my definition of political theology because I think it helps us see that the fundamental distinction we need to understand is not between religion and politics, or between church and state, because religion always plays a role in social life and political life. Rather, the fundamental question is whether the basic institutions of a political regime are legitimated by appeal to revelation or not. Even in regimes that are not legitimated that way, people have religious views, and laws have to be made about what you do about religious institutions. Religion is always present, but it is vitally important to understand how the basic institutions are legitimated.

Michael Kessler: So what is the major conclusion of *The Stillborn God?*

Mark Lilla: Well, the most fundamental conclusion for me is that there is no third way between political theology and a modern political philosophy that makes no appeal to divine revelation. The "stillborn God," from which the book draws its title, was the attempt in the nineteenth century to have it both ways. That is, to somehow imagine that by repristinizing and reforming Protestant Christianity and Judaism you could not only make it possible to be religious in modern society, but that religion could be the moral foundation of, and a legitimating force in, modern political life.

Perhaps even more importantly, I wanted to argue that political theology is always a live, intellectual possibility, and there is, at least potentially, a political possibility for human beings. Nothing has happened in modern history to extinguish that possibility. This is the bone I have to pick with the concept of secularization, and all the books that are coming out now about this secular age, and the rest. I am deeply skeptical of all of that.

Those books seem like fairy tales to me, "just-so" stories about how we got where we are now, stories that might look very different fifty or one hundred years from now. It seems to me that recent history has shown us that the trinkets of the modern economy and modern society are really impotent amulets against the power of the idea of redemption, even political redemption.

Some have read the book, oddly, as a kind of triumphalist book about the modern West. The lesson I draw from it, on the contrary, is that the modern West, historically speaking, in the history of world civilizations, is a very unusual exception. Most societies in most times and places have legitimated public authority by some sort of appeal to revelation loosely conceived. And we have somehow managed this trick of not doing that.

This seems to me a fragile experiment because it turns out that human beings are theotropic creatures, and that it is only through a certain kind of training that they cease to try connecting up the basic political institutions of their societies to some larger story about God, man, and world. That's what we should focus on. I think we need to be less concerned about issues like the church and state separation, since, in fact, there is tremendous variety among Western nations in the way they handle this.

Michael Kessler: How is your account about the legitimation of political authority different from a tradition-based thinker like John?

Mark Lilla: I actually find common ground with thinkers like John. I think there is recognition on both our sides that there is a significant break in modern thought, and I use a metaphor of the two shores to describe our respective positions. Theorists like John and theorists like me are standing on opposite shores looking at each other with a mutual disdain for those who think that they can somehow negotiate the middle by developing a liberal theology. I think we agree entirely on that picture.

I am not interested in secularization. I have nothing to say about that. I am not interested in secular society. And I look at all the genealogy junkies who write books that say, "Well, we've got a contemporary problem, but to explain that, let me go back to the eleventh century." And then they have to spin out a whole story, which then replaces someone else's story. These are just stories, even fairy tales, which we use to orient ourselves in the present. So I have got nothing to say about how society got secularized, whether the term is appropriate or not.

I am interested in one thing only, and that is how we have come to legitimate the public authority that we exercise today.

Michael Kessler: José, you have written a somewhat critical review of the book on *The Immanent Frame*.[3] Do you think Mark was successful in articulating this change in legitimation?

José Casanova: My critique was not a critique of the main text, which I have found a fascinating episodic and analytic history of ideas, but with the pretext and the context of the book, as it was portrayed schematically in the Sunday *Times Magazine*'s article, "The Great Separation."[4]

I first read it as I had just returned from the Salzburg Trilogue. The Trilogue, held in the midst of the Salzburg Festival, is an attempt by Austrians to bring together the Abrahamic traditions, Judaism, Christianity, and Islam, which are at loggerheads in the Middle East into a tri-logical conversation.

And the message of those at the Trilogue was that we Europeans also had problems with religion in the past. Once upon a time, so the narrative went, we also had not learnt yet to separate religion and politics. But then the religious pluralization brought by the Protestant Reformation brought all those terrible religious wars of the early modern era. Felicitously, however, out of the catastrophe of the religious wars, we happily learned to secularize the state; we learned to tolerate one another; and we accepted religious freedom, religious pluralism; and this is the lesson that we Europeans can teach to the rest of the world.

This is the founding myth of modern European secularism. When I saw Mark's thesis of the Great Separation that he offers in *The Stillborn God*, which supposedly begins with Hobbes, I just read it as the same thesis that one hears all the time in Europe, about precisely how we became secular, freed ourselves from the myth of divine revelation, and can therefore constitute rational political orders freed from religion.

My problem with Mark's narrative is not so much with the history of ideas he traces, but rather with the beginning and the end, that is, what comes before and after his narrative. I have difficulties viewing Hobbes as the great hero and founding father of the Great Separation, and I have difficulties viewing nineteenth-century liberal Protestant and Jewish theologies as "the stillborn God," which in their failing provoke the return of messianic and political theology in the work of Karl Barth and Franz Rosenzweig, which through their disciples, Friedrich Gogarten and Ernst Bloch, leads directly to the totalitarianisms of National Socialism and Bolshevism.

What unites the beginning and the end of Mark's story is "the myth of religious violence," so aptly deconstructed by William Cavanaugh. Why is it that, as Mark puts it, religion tends to lead to violence in the extreme, undergirding a cycle of religious and political violence and fear, and then (Hobbes) poses the question about how we might short-circuit that. This

Hobbesian question of how to short-circuit the cycle of religious and political violence is indeed pervasive in European public opinion and in European public debates.

This secularist premise was in my view typified by the staging of *Idomeneo* (the Mozart opera cancelled in 2006 in Berlin after threats against the director who added an epilogue of the decapitation of all the founders of religion, symbolically to get rid of violence). The idea is, symbolically, if you get rid of religion then you get rid of violence in the world because war and violence enter history through religion. Seventy-five percent of the population of almost every European country agrees that religion is intolerant and that religion is violent. I find this a rather striking phenomenon given the European experience of violence in the twentieth century. No other century in the history of humanity has been as violent, as catastrophic, or as genocidal as the twentieth century. Yet none of these catastrophes—WWI (out of which came the reaction of liberalisms that is the subject of *The Stillborn God*), the Holocaust, and Nazism, and Bolshevism—none of them have anything to do with religious passions or with actual political theology in the Christian sense of the term. Yet when Europeans are confronted with renewed experiences of cycles of violence at the end of the twentieth century around the world, they do not remember the history of European violence of the twentieth century, but rather retrieve the forgotten histories of the wars of religion of early modern Europe, finding a ready-made answer to the question. Religion is the cause of violence, and, fortunately, we have freed ourselves from such an irrational violent and intolerant force.

This is the context within which I read *The Stillborn God*, and this is the context within which the summary of his argument in the Sunday *Times Magazine* was received by American secularists, because this is the way they view religion.

My critique challenged these two assumptions. The first is the assumption that religion is really the reason for violence and especially messianic religion, and if you get rid of it, then you have peace. The other assumption is this myth of the Great Separation.

As to the question of violence, one could, of course, understand the wars of religion not so much as wars of religion but rather as wars of state formation, of modern state formation. If so, then one sees that the real beginning of the story is the formation of the Catholic kingdom of Spain, in particular the expulsion of Jews and Muslims and the formation of a homogenous Catholic confessional territorial state. And this was actually the model established in the Peace of Westphalia by every continental European state, that is, absolutist confessional states where both religion and people were territorialized.

This is the way in which the modern absolutist Leviathan solved the problem of religion, through the principle *cuius regio eius religio*, by which the sovereign determined the religion of his subjects.

People in continental Europe were not offered freedom of religion or toleration but the freedom to leave their countries, and this model of religious homogeneity has continued in Europe for four hundred years. The confessional boundaries that were established then, the territorial boundaries between Catholic and Protestant, between Lutheran and Calvinist, have remained practically frozen for four hundred years in Europe. Interestingly enough, the transition from royal to popular and national sovereignty did not alter the dynamics of ethno-religious homogeneity in Europe.

As a sociologist, I am looking at the dynamics of sociopolitical institutionalization rather than at the history of ideas, and from this perspective, "the Great Separation," in my view, happens later with the modern democratic revolutions on both sides of the Atlantic. That's why on the eve of the democratic revolutions Rousseau was still struggling with the idea of "civil religion," without which he could not conceive the viability of a democratic republic.

It is the self-constituting constitutional regimes which for me mark the Great Separation, and in this sense I am somewhat skeptical about the relevance of Mark's history of ideas. And my fundamental question is, How relevant is Hobbes for this task of trying to see the Great Separation as the achievement of a self-constituting constitutional regime which guarantees civil and political rights to its citizens?

In so far as Locke responds to Hobbes—and Locke is undoubtedly very important for the foundation of modern liberalism, and for the founding fathers, and for the establishment of the American Republic—then Hobbes is at least indirectly important to this development. But in my view, the spread of Deism was much more important in undermining doctrines that legitimate the use of public authority based on divine revelation than the ideas of Hobbes. Here I would side with Charles Taylor's story and his focus on the societal changes in social imaginary throughout broader social strata.

But I would even go further in arguing that it was actually the religious fanatics, the enthusiasts, the sectarians, who were as important in establishing the separation of church and state and the foundations of our constitutional structure as were the Deists. Madison, in my view, is the key figure here, mediating between the Deist Jefferson and the sectarian Baptists in Virginia. The theological arguments they offered for the freedom of religion from church and state truly ushered in the Great Separation.

Michael Kessler: How are sectarians central to this narrative of separation?

José Casanova: The sectarians are the first ones to offer arguments for the freedom of religion, their own, not only from ecclesiastical institutions, that is, from any visible church, but also from the state. Their truly revolutionary argument is that the state has no business and no jurisdiction in the religious sphere, and therefore much less can base its legitimacy on any doctrine of divine revelation. But most importantly, they do not only offer arguments but are ready to mobilize and to defend these dissenting arguments against the established political authorities through civil disobedience and at the cost of imprisonment. They are the first ones ready to secularize the state and to create modern political structures based not on the liberal principle of toleration but on their own nonnegotiable principle of religious freedom as an inalienable right. Roger Williams's settlement of Providence was the first modern political structure to restrict government to "only civil things." The "town agreement" was signed by all the male head of households in 1637, fourteen years before the publication of *Leviathan* and fifty-two years before the publication of Locke's *Letter on Toleration*. Baptist Rhode Island and Quaker Pennsylvania are the first colonies to institute the Great Separation. The Baptists in Virginia were instrumental in aiding Jefferson and Madison in defeating the attempt of the other founding fathers to institute some kind of nondenominational Christian establishment in Virginia. Madison's "Memorial and Remonstrance" remains the most articulate defense ever written of the Great Separation on religious grounds. Georg Jellinek showed convincingly, over a century ago, that the language of the Declaration of the Rights of Man by the National Constituent Assembly, the second historical instance of the institutionalization of the Great Separation, was heavily indebted to the Bills of Rights of the American colonies.

Michael Kessler: And why do you argue that the Great Separation is a myth, and a false one at that?

José Casanova: Well, the first aspect to this question has to do with the extent to which political structures prior to the Great Separation were actually legitimated on the basis of divine revelation. Charles Taylor is, I think, right on this issue. If one retraces the history of the concept of political theology, the modern emergence of the concept is 1922 with Carl Schmitt. Eric Peterson answers against Schmitt with the theological argument, using Barth, that there can be no real Christian political theology. Granted, the argument here is limited: there can be no Augustinian political theology.

But the central question is, What do we mean by divine revelation? In the Bible, if anything, the truly prophetic political theology is precisely against any attempt to sacralize any form of politics here as having anything to do with God. We are dealing here more with the issue of a transcendental structure than an eschatological messianic one. One could even go further and argue that this is the common contribution of the so-called axial breakthroughs. All of them bring a certain de-sacralization of sacred or divine kingship, which is now subjected to transcendent ethical principles. I am not convinced that the issue of divine revelation is the key one here. It is undeniable that under medieval Christendom there is a re-sacralization of kingship and political authority under the dual influence of the theocratic impulse of the papal revolution and the Germanic pre-axial tradition of charismatic kingship. But the protracted investiture conflict clearly indicates that the medieval system of temporal rule was more complex than Mark's image of the Great Separation would tend to indicate. Certainly, as Harold Berman has in my view conclusively shown in *Law and Revolution*, dualistic principles of separation were well institutionalized throughout the legal-political structures of medieval Christendom.

The second aspect of the question which leads me to speak of the myth of the Great Separation is the one that dovetails with what I've referred to as the foundational myth of European secularism. It has its origins in the Enlightenment critique of religion and in the argument put forth by Voltaire and others that the Great Separation was the felicitous outcome of the catastrophic experience of the wars of religion. Indeed, the model that became institutionalized throughout Europe after the Peace of Westphalia was not that of the Great Separation but rather that of absolutist royal control of ecclesiastical institutions. The fact that absolutist rulers may not have based their legitimacy any more on principles of divine revelation is, in my view, not that relevant. Certainly Marc Bloch and many others after him showed conclusively that there was a pronounced re-sacralization of kingship under absolutism.

Michael Kessler: Mark, how do you reply to these arguments that your narrative is incomplete or that you focus on the wrong thinkers?

Mark Lilla: There are so many things you cannot say in a single book or article. But I certainly should have said that we have to remember that the greatest political crimes of recent historical memory took place by regimes that observed the Great Separation. One could go further—the Great Separation is partially responsible for fascism, and communism, and all these modern ideologies that do not appeal to revelation.

In fact, that argument was made after WWII by a number of religious thinkers, many proto-existentialist, who insisted that what the West had just experienced was the culmination of this atheist, humanist tradition. That could only mean that we had to reconsider political theology. So they were aware of the distinction I make and aware of what had happened on our watch. There is truth in this position, but it's not the whole story. Hobbes reminds us of what human beings can do to each other in political life no matter what, and shows, convincingly to me, that revelation throws gasoline onto the fire. That is Hobbes's argument: religion has the potential to make things worse. Though I realize there are arguments against that, put forward by theologians who say, "No, on the contrary, we are the ones who are holding *all* of this violence back."

Why did I write the book as I did and not discuss these other issues? Why did I write what I called an "episodic history of ideas." Because I wanted to try to write a kind of intellectual history that would follow the implication of ideas as they reveal themselves in the history of the argument, doing something similar to those chess reports you see in newspapers for chess games. You know, "queen to rook three," or "here you see what happens when you use the Sicilian strategy."

I faced a problem. Given that modern political thought begins with Hobbes, was there a logical path (and I mean logically, not socially) that led us from Hobbes to messianic thinkers like Bloch and Gogarten? How could that have happened? By focusing on strategies, I wanted to show how it's possible for the human mind by beginning with one assumption to end up somewhere quite different.

The reason Hobbes is important is that when Hobbes shifted the focus of Western political discourse from God and his commands to human beliefs about God, that put the ball in the court, so to speak, of political anthropology.

But Hobbes only had one idea about how religious faith gets generated, and that is through this combustive combination of ignorance and fear. This, I think, explains the ultimate weakness of modern political thought about religion in the West. It was a weakness that someone like Rousseau saw right away. I choose Rousseau, not because everyone read him, but because he made the next logical move in response to Hobbes, specifically in stating that Hobbes got our religious nature wrong. He paints a picture of religious behavior that shows that it can be moral, rational, and noble.

Once you make that move, then people start saying, well, if that's the case, if Hobbes got religion wrong, might it not be possible to exploit religion for political life by reforming it in a way that it would be rational, moral, and noble rather than base, violent, and corrupting? And if we did that, wouldn't it then be possible to reconcile revelation with regimes that seem to be legitimate on the basis of popular consent? That is what produced the dream of liberal theology. Then political messianism comes about through the collapse of this liberal theology.

I think of *The Stillborn God* as a methodical mind experiment. It is drawn from history, but it does not explain history. That is a misunderstanding that I probably should have guarded myself against more clearly in the book.

Michael Kessler: What are the origins of this collapse of liberal theology—the basis of the so-called stillborn God?

Mark Lilla: Many of our modern political regimes, especially the United States, were made possible by a transformation of Protestantism that opened up a new space for people to argue *theologically* that human beings legitimately govern themselves. The stillborn God is the God of a liberal theology that thought that it could somehow fudge the issue of who legitimately exercises authority.

What brought about the collapse of liberal theology was WWI. Both Christian and Jewish liberal-political theology in Germany gave their benediction to the Western European civilization that melted and collapsed before everyone's eyes. It was very difficult to be a liberal theologian in the wake of that catastrophe, because liberals had linked their destiny to this particular civilization and these particular forms of government, all of which collapsed.

But a deeper cause of liberal theology's weakness, in my view, is that it never gave members of these faiths reasons for why they should be Protestants, or why they should be Jews. Liberal theology prescribed many duties: why you should be a moral human being, why you should be charitable, why you should be reasonable, why you should be a good citizen, why you should buy tickets to the opera. But it didn't say why you had to accept this particular tradition and this particular revelation.

This is why, just leading up to WWI, there were intellectuals who fled liberal Christianity, liberal Protestantism, and liberal Judaism. That's the drama of the Franz Rosenzweig story. Going into WWI, he was planning on converting to Protestantism; he has cousins who already converted who were saying, "Hey, join the winning side here. It has everything Judaism does but it's more rational, it makes more sense, none of all that crazy stuff." The famous story then goes that he went to Yom Kippur services, experienced a kind of counter-conversion, went back home, and decided to start taking his Judaism more seriously. Liberal Judaism could not answer the question, "Why should I be a Jew?"

Michael Kessler: So, has liberal Judaism, Protestantism, or Catholicism since WWII been able to answer that question?

Mark Lilla: No.

And that is why they have been overtaken by evangelicalism and other forms of spirituality, because they can't answer that question. Because they want to efface all differences in the name of toleration or understanding. If you cannot make distinctions you are not going to be able to form adhesions. And if people are not persuaded of their faiths then, in a moment of crisis, they will leave.

Michael Kessler: One thing that happens consistently in many of the political theologians that you talk about that come at the end of the nineteenth century, such as Troeltsch and Cohen, and those in the twentieth century, such as Niebuhr and Tillich, is that all of them say that reason in some way is necessary but insufficient.

And this is also something that is apparent in the Catholic tradition, particularly in the most serious political statement of the nineteenth century, Leo the XIII's *Rerum Novarum,* a Lockean- and Marxian-inspired piece of political theology.

All of these thinkers say that autonomous reason is necessary, that we must work to use reason to achieve a better political order, but also they insist that reason alone is insufficient for our final good. We need revelation, yet it is an open question whether this divine aid comes to shatter human categories of experience or works in and through them.

The event of Christ on this account is then something that unlocks for the political community a deeper awareness of "human dignity," and that this revelation is the only way that the full expression of human dignity can be manifest in human experience. The political task of the church is to remind and instruct about this message Christianity brings, a kairotic statement about the fact that value and meaning, especially the value of human dignity, are not reducible simply to rational concepts.

The separated, autonomous institution of the state is important and crucial to human well-being, but without this deeper notion of dignity rooted in revelation, the state will end up as the iron cage of technical reason.

Mark Lilla: I recognize that argument. And it stirs different thoughts.

One is, Why do you need the church for that? Why don't we just appoint a group of elders or throw dice or take turns or something? The assumption seems to be that somehow the church sees something others don't see, otherwise we wouldn't need the church to articulate it.

But let's say reason is not sufficient. It does not follow from that fact that anything else is sufficient. Maybe nothing is sufficient. All we have is reason; live with it. If you are not willing to accept that that, that means that somewhere knocking around your head is the idea that someone else sees something you don't see.

So, either this argument presumes that the church is the holder of some revelation, or it is just an appeal for prudence, call it conservatism, call it pragmatism, call it lucidity. But we don't necessarily need a church for that, we just need someone conservative, pragmatic, and lucid.

No, I think the serious intellectual challenge is posed by the messianic theology that emerged at the time of the collapse of liberal theologies.

Michael Kessler: What is the political nature of these so-called messianic faiths?

Mark Lilla: Not all political theology legitimates the exercise of public authority. On the contrary, as Peterson pointed out, Christianity delegitimizes claims to authority by human rulers who claim to stand in for God and claim his authority on earth. And Karl Barth, in his commentary on the Epistle to the Romans, is very firm in deflating human pretense in the political sphere.

But that kind of thinking in the end, seems to me, does one of two things. It either tells the believer that he has to become a citizen without qualities—that he is just passing through, because there is no way he can take seriously his commitment to political life, given that life is elsewhere. Or, on the other hand, he becomes some kind of uncontrolled prophet who does not have to be responsible for what actually happens politically, because he is always just throwing down his thunderbolts and then going off. That is very much what Karl Barth was like throughout his career, even when it was in the service of the angels, like his Barmen Declaration against the Nazi church.

In contrast, someone like Reinhold Niebuhr rejects this refusal to engage the political. Niebuhr took seriously Barth's critique of politics and also took seriously the fallenness, in an Augustinian way, of human nature. But just for that reason he felt that it was necessary to think through human political nature, much the way Hobbes did in his tradition, on the theological assumption that we are much as Hobbes describes us, because of the fall. This led him to take full responsibility for the political sphere, including the exercise of power.

Niebuhr went as far as you could on the side of political theology to making sense of the way we live now in modern political regimes. But nonetheless, his fundamental assumption remains a political-theological one, and it's not the assumption that we make today when we legitimate the exercise of authority in the United States.

Michael Kessler: So we are back to Hobbes who provides insight into each of these moves?

Mark Lilla: Some human religious behavior has to do with talking about God or the gods, some has to do with sacralizing the state. Hobbes gives you a point of view for understanding both.

John Milbank: One question I raise to Mark is whether he is ignoring the fact that Hobbes is, actually, a political theologian, in spite of Mark's insistence that Hobbes represents the end of political theology. On my reading, on the contrary, one could say that Hobbes begins to reinvent political theology because he reads the Bible entirely within a political horizon. A substantial part of the point of the *Leviathan* is that he is insisting that the message of the Bible is political and not a spiritual message at all. So Hobbes's political position is not quite as yet an outright secular argument. This is another example of the claim that we are not as secular as we appear because we are still recycling bric-a-brac from the theological past.

Many of my endeavors have been arguing that the secular is not as secular as it appears; it's extremely difficult to have the purely secular. And in fact, I would further enunciate the paradox that only if you have the church and acceptance of the role of the church, do you have the secular, because it was the social reality of the church in the Christian realms that relativized the political and made it secular. Once you don't have the church playing a publicly recognized role, then what you tend to have is a re-sacralization of the political order, rather than simply secularity. I tend to think this is the strongest part of Mark's thesis.

Mark Lilla: I couldn't agree more! As for Hobbes, though, I don't take his theology seriously as theology. Whether he believes all the biblical citations and theological arguments he presents or not, his own argument stands alone. That's all I'm concerned with.

Michael Kessler: In a Festschrift for Jean-Luc Marion, John wrote an essay accusing Marion of having a bleakly Pascalian view of love which requires handing the physical world, political society, and positive and humane science over to an inevitable lovelessness.[5]

And again in "Christ the Exception," a small essay, John wrote, "We are to imitate Christ and to love ecstatically through exchange, losing our lives in order to gain them. But if only Christ reconciles us to each other, nation to nation, race to race, sex to sex, ruler to subordinate and person to person, then this can only mean that the specific shape of Christ's body in his reconciled life and its continued renewal in the church provides for us the true aesthetic example for our reshaping of our social existence."[6]

Could you clarify—given this apparent resignation about the world and the turn to renewal only through the church—what you view as the contribution of radical orthodoxy to theologies of the political?

John Milbank: I think that what you've just said shows that it is not quite right to say that I am against the mediating role of culture with respect to religion. I'm not a Barthian at all. In fact, I think Barth is a kind of inverted liberal. I actually agree with Mark Lilla that he represents a sort of deranged apocalypticism, and he never quite gets rid of that. In Barth, there is really no mediation at all between God and world. So in a strange kind of way, Barth lets everything in the world stand on its own.

And another manner in which I would like to relate what I have done to political theology is through reflecting on the idea of reconciliation. The thrust of Christian ideas about reconciliation is the point where it is not simply otherworldly, and yet also includes something substantial that goes beyond the political. For those of us in radical orthodoxy, ecclesiology is for this reason much more important than in most political theologies, certainly, for instance, in the case of liberation theology.

The idea that the church itself is, as the anticipation of the kingdom of God, tasked with the true project of creating a real society, goes beyond political purposes for two reasons. First of all, because it posits what I call an "ontology of peace." Thus I agree with Pierre Manent, who hovers, I think, in the background of Mark's work, in holding that liberalism actually assumes the priority of evil. I think this is very, very important: liberalism is reactive and it ironically assumes the worst about human nature—it is egotistic and selfish, etc. I think that Christianity, on the contrary, is committed to a counter-ontology of an original harmony and peacefulness, which is ruptured by the Fall. The important thing to remember about the Fall is that it does not ontologize evil. The idea of the Fall makes evil all-pervasive, but not coincident with being as such. Evil is, rather, contingent, even though it is omnipresent.

Mark Lilla: I do not know what makes you say that liberalism ontologizes evil. The account I would give is closer to something I suppose Niebuhr would say: politics copes with our interaction by assuming the worst. Modern political thought puts evil first because it puts first preventing the worst things that we can do to each other.

Now, you can say that this is a thin way to think about ourselves, but liberalism is not committed to a robust ontology. Rather, it holds that for the purposes of this part of human interaction, we should focus on preventing the worst harms. The family is another matter.

John Milbank: Mark, I think that's a very American pragmatist take on European liberalism. Consider Hobbes as a counterexample. Hobbes clearly links politics to an ontology, to an atomistic and nominalistic ontology, and this is linked to a theory of human nature which prioritizes the individual.

Mark Lilla: Then what do you do about Montesquieu? There is no ontology in Montesquieu. With Hobbes I will grant that you could make your argument. However, the figure that really matters in the development of liberalism, particularly French liberalism, is the strand of thought from Montesquieu to Tocqueville. It is too easy to be selective in crafting these ideal narratives.

John Milbank: Well, I think there are ontological assumptions in all of these positions. However, if for the sake of argument we say that these accounts are completely pragmatic, there is still something being said about human nature, and therefore an implied ontology after all.

In the modern narrative, when it comes to the collective dimension, we have to focus on negative things and this relates always to some kind of individualism, whether the primary thing is that people are struggling against each other, or the primary thing is that people are pursuing economic self-interest, and so forth. This lands you with a suspension between the individual on the one hand and the absolute sovereign state on the other hand, because all these doctrines tend to be linked to arguments for why you must have an absolute monopoly of power at the center.

So these approaches are definitely ruling out higher purposes for politics of the classical kind. Of course there were all kinds of problems about those, that they sacralized city-states, they excluded most people from citizenship and so on.

But this is where I think that the Christian invention of ecclesia makes a significant difference. I think the Christian project involves something like the paradoxical democratizing of the noble, whereas antique democracy could only think in terms of the lowest common denominator. In fact, I think this is a problem for the Left even today—it tends in effect to say, "Let's just have equality in mediocrity."

Whereas the whole point about ecclesia is that Paul writes to everybody in the churches and says, "Have I not said that you are all kings?"

Thus the Christian event declares that nobility, and the virtues redefined around love, can be radically achievable by all. At the same time, a hierarchy remains, because some people are more virtuous than others, and some are more fit to exercise a general influence and promote the good. This is why, increasingly, I insist that Christian politics cuts across all our secular categories including our Left-Right categories—for without the promotion of the good there can be no possible critique of a generalized pursuit of mere abstract wealth and egoistic contentment.

I think people are increasingly critical of capitalism now, and I believe we have to go beyond capitalism; yet, as Jean-Claude Michéa argues, we also have to go beyond the Left, because the whole essentially liberal (as he shows) idea of the Left is not critical enough. We have to face up to the fact that the Left as liberal and secular has not managed to sustain the critique of capitalism in practice because the Left does not have a deep enough theoretical account of the human, including a human teleology. Because it can't say what we're here for; it can't criticize a system based upon a senseless pursuit of abstract wealth and promoting a game of competing egos.

This is why I think Christianity is moving back into the center of political thinking and is reviving the notion of the public role of the ecclesia. The latter, beyond antiquity, is able to orientate the political (which antiquity sought but finally failed to do) since the ecclesia as a community of reconciliation exceeds the political. For within the church everything to do with coercion (war, punishment, policing) is regarded with semi-suspicion. What is sought is not just forced agreement, nor "live and let live," but real harmony and possibility of individual fulfillment in many different roles which are complementary.

Here I talk about the aesthetic to mark out that there is something about community and its goal of just harmony that is ineffable. The sense of this goal can only be conveyed by an elusive tradition; somehow the Catholic tradition is a tradition of how you bind lots of different concrete cultures into a universal seen as a greater concreteness, a greater ineffability without surrendering their concreteness. The Catholic project is the only one that does this, so it seems to me.

Mark Lilla: I am trying to figure out just what you mean by ecclesiology. Let me re-create the steps of the argument properly.

To begin with, you say that Christian theology must be ecclesiology. Second, you deny that there is an ontological reality to the church/state distinction. And then you make the argument for the eventual withering away of the state.

Let me read you something you wrote: "The good ruler must reduce the scope of the political precisely in so far as he is a good ruler," and you call the state the "anti-church."

That leaves me with the conclusion that you are thinking about a new postpolitical community with a mission of salvation. And I will quote something else. "The Church enacts the vision of paradisal community or else it promotes a hellish society beyond all tenors known to antiquity: *corruptio, optimi, pessima.*" What can go wrong will go wrong. Do I have you right?

John Milbank: In summary, you have me right.

I am most concerned—in the wake of Ivan Illich—that when the project of reconciliation becomes a kind of institutionalized, even over-institutionalized, disciplinary project, then it does lead to something sinister. I think Charles Taylor is right, as well, that this is a big factor in secularization, that such a drift to the disciplinary starts to suggest that the heart of what matters is the ethical and that the religious elements can slip away. But you are right in the sense that what I am arguing for is again something Augustinian and Gelasian, rather than something medieval in the wake of Bishop Jonas of Orleans, in that I think that the state is both outside and in the church—whereas after Jonas the bounds of both were seen as coinciding. Ultimately, the state needs to be regarded as outside of the church because it necessarily aims for compromises and has to use dubious solutions and so forth in order to keep a second-rate, but indispensable, sort of peace.

But at the same time, in Augustinian terms, the very validity of the politics concerns its subservience to the project of reconciliation, and this is where I insist that we do need to carry on in the West recognizing the social and political primacy of the Christian church.

I think Tocqueville's reading of America exemplifies this and is actually a very Catholic reading. He claims in effect that America works not on account of the Constitution alone but because that there is something sustaining intermediate institutions between the individual and the state, and this is the church space.

Mark Lilla: Well, I think that this makes it more clear to me that there is a kind of elision for you between the ambition of theology to *think* the whole and the ambition of the ecclesia to *be* the whole.

For me, the task of philosophy is to understand the whole. But, as someone who is committed to liberalism, the task of philosophy is to understand from the point of view of the whole why liberalism works.

One can want reconciliation in thought and not want reconciliation in life. You, however, want both. I do not, because I have come to be suspicious, not of reconciling things in thought, but in trying to do so in history. This is why I would be interested to hear you talk less about the references going back in the tradition, and more about the present and future. What would politics look like in your vision? I actually don't know. You even speak of "Eucharistic anarchism." I have no idea what that means.

John Milbank: Well, it seems to me that when you are talking about Rousseau, you are recognizing the importance of the question about what actually psychologically motivates people, and the way in which people bind together to form societies under shared visions and so on. But this is something that is not completely liberal; Rousseau is a bizarre mixture in the sense that for him initially the isolated individual has primacy but then when he or she encounters other people, he recognizes the primacy of relationality and the way the social is then the prime source of both evil and good—of terrible rivalry but also of a higher sort of freedom.

And most of the nineteenth-century French liberals, including Tocqueville, recognized that you have to qualify liberalism in terms of this question of why do people really act in social formations? Even the Scottish tradition about sympathy at times qualifies liberalism because it asks the question about what in reality binds people together.

But I think the real difficulty arises once one has a kind of ersatz version of this—when religion in the nineteenth century gets associated strongly with nationalism. Part of the problem is the absolutely sovereign state which evolves into the nation-state which, to be candid, is a racist state and an inevitable instigator of war. If we focused on real religion, if we talked about the real church community, this might actually be less dangerous to politics because of the powerful religious idea of the actual transcendence of the political, which opens up a realm that is continuously self-critical.

Now, the West continues this negative critique of power Christianity started, but the secular version inevitably turns critical for the sake of critique: critical without any positive exit. It is not in favor of "anything else" and, so becomes like a negative theology that has become nihilistic because it no longer inhabits or tries to craft the ecclesial space of something we haven't yet fully got but are trying to get toward by cultivating existing seeds. One needs something like the cultivation of this sort of space if one is to be able to achieve a far greater distribution of property and power, since this requires an agreement in ends and values to be distributed. Such an attempt would include ending the artificial separation between the economic and the political on which liberalism is built—the pretense that money is neutral in relation to power and power in relation to each other. Through this separation they exist secretly only for the sake of each other. By contrast, if it is admitted that money is political and politics economic, then we can truly ask what is the combined money-power operation actually *for?*

At this juncture it is worth saying that I am not so sure that we inhabit modernity. We have never been modern, we just live in one medieval project: that of the Franciscans whose theology supported individualism, nascent capitalism, absolute sovereign power and the separation of economics from politics on the basis of a certain theology. Instead, we need today to live in a different Middle Ages, or a different modern development of a different Middle Ages, essentially a Dominican one in continuity with the Fathers—the way of Aquinas of Eckhart and of Cusanus. Because we have chosen one medieval trajectory rather than another, the modernity we have found ourselves in is not fated, not inevitable.

Mark Lilla: I do not see how you can hold both of these things together. On the one hand you say that to understand history you cannot say, "Stuff happens." But rather that this is the working out of the logic of the theological debate in the eleventh century.

John Milbank: No, genealogy isn't inevitable like that. I am just trying to dig out what are the hidden presuppositions because I am a historicist in that sense, and I do not think that I have got a grosser genealogical disease than you have Mark. I just think your genealogy is truncated because you are saying that secularity has come about because of the wars of religion and because of religious fanaticism, and I think it is not as simple as that and that it comes about because of all sorts of stuff going on previously in the Middle Ages, and that Hobbes could only have done what he had done because all the intellectual tools were ready prepared for him by people like William of Ockham.

Nor do I think that religion is, as such, fanatical. I do think that Protestantism is fanatical in certain degrees, as it is iconoclastic in certain degrees. I think also that members of a faith who do not have explicitly authorized doctrines, such as in the case of Islam, can have an inherent tendency to be fanatical, where this lack is not balanced by other factors—such as an integrally mystical vision and practice as with Sufism and mystical Shi'ism. W. H. Auden had this right: if you do not have doctrines, then any old trivial stuff becomes important. Headscarves become important (for God's sake!), whether you are for them or against them; you cannot distinguish what matters any longer. So it is a particular kind of religion that is fanatical and especially it has to do with smashing images and people who think that God cannot be mediated by symbols and images whereas, as the Rhineland mystic Henry Suso put it, "only images cast out images," only symbols destroy idols, not hammers. If you smash images, you are also likely to be more prepared to smash people's faces, and you think you have a direct line to God, which we do not, because you have forgotten the need for analogy and approximation. So, I just reject this idea of religion itself being the problem. The problem is the breakdown of Catholic Christendom. The problem is heterodoxy.

Mark Lilla: But one of the consequences of this breakdown is that, out of it, the idea was born that people legitimately govern themselves, and that all the other questions that haunted us for so long don't matter for the purposes of politics.

Now, I understand that out of this new idea came many other ideas, and we can discuss which ones we consider to be true liberalism, which ones are deviations from liberalism, and all the rest. But this idea does seem to me to be a real break. This is a genuinely new conception of politics.

However, if you do not accept this narrative about politics, which you do not, then it seems to me you are obliged to say more than you have about what politics in your terms might look like. On this question you slide around in your writings. This sliding is evident even in the way you describe the exercise of authority—*the* fundamental political question from the point of view of liberalism. You talk about the exercise of authority as a tragic reality.

In fact, when you discuss Augustine and how to deal with the state, you insist that the Christian has to be both in and out. It seems to me there is an unsustainable dualism here. You do not want to separate out politics, but in fact, you do not follow the logic of your thought, which would be to insist that the state and the ecclesia are one. There are not, in your view, tragic realities and nontragic realities; rather, there is only reality. And politics is part of this reality, and this is the whole that Christians should think. Now, that does seem to me to be, as you say, a Catholic alternative.

This vision of a whole—that you seem to shy away from ultimately—is the real alternative to what I am talking about. Your view, on the opposite shore from me, so to speak, is a much more respectable one, than trying to be in the middle, because it provides an alternative to and highlights what is different about liberalism.

My view is that, for liberalism, the task is to somehow make its two fundamental insights into one. On the one hand, Hobbes got politics right while getting the anthropology wrong. Rousseau got the anthropology right while getting the politics wrong. Solve.

John Milbank: I absolutely agree. I am interested in you saying this, because I thought that in your book you were siding with Hobbes and yet the whole book was building up to this aporia. And this is why I am suggesting the solution to this aporia is clearly a Catholic solution.

To repeat, we have to sustain in the West, and beyond, the notion and practice of a transpolitical community. In other words, of a community whose purposes exceed the purposes of politics—the coercive pursuit of an imperfect peace—since it aims for total reconciliation and the fulfilled flourishing of each in harmony with the fulfilled flourishing of all. It is clear that both Rousseau and many secular socialisms attempt problematic versions of this ecclesial notion.

But at the same time, this is a critical enterprise because you know we are not quite getting there yet, so there is an eschatological dimension. That is precisely the way you resolve your aporia.

Mark Lilla: But you have not solved my problem, which is, more precisely, how can you as a Christian hold onto what we have achieved with liberal politics? I feel you simply are not saying enough. How do you hold onto the politics that Hobbes commences, in spite of the fact that it is based on a crazy anthropology, with a wider, richer anthropology that Rousseau offers, without all these political problems?

John Milbank: There is always a kind of disappointment because this liberalism always has to do with the *libido dominandi* in an Augustinian sense. I am not committed to naturalizing individualism and selfishness,

I am more with Rousseau that this is a kind of choice, although at the same time I think we are more corrupted than Rousseau is saying. But I am saying that by not naturalizing individualism one is holding open the possibility for something else in the political realm, or something that the political can imperfectly point us toward. And, if you like, what we are seeing in the present crisis is that where you allow the *libido dominandi* to run riot, when individuals are reduced to making calculations, eventually they start to do insane things, like treating debt as if it is an asset and make apparent money out of debt, and it turns out that actually there is no invisible hand saving this process at all. And at that point you have to start thinking again about the root questions: why do we have finance? In what way does the economy serve society and the political? When the crunch comes, in the real political sense, it turns out that nations after all have to reassert themselves; they can't just let the economy dominate because this threatens human political existence.

Mark Lilla: But you can do all of this reconsidering while still assuming that human beings legitimately rule themselves. Because what you talk about in *Theology and Social Theory* is not a richer anthropology; instead, you talk about supernaturalizing the natural.[7]

John Milbank: Well, that is correct because I think if we inquire into what is authoritative, or what is the good, then we are inevitably invoking something like a mythical, transcendent dimension. The heart of what makes all these signifiers work is, as Lévi-Strauss said, an *X* that does not have an immediate reference. This is the space of the mythical and the transcendent.

I think this idea that you can have pure self-government is untrue. For one thing, it is a kind of formalism that suggests that nothing is ruling. Somehow out of the mere formal rules we can distill a kind of order. The problem about that is that the formalism is in reality backing the arbitrary content of arbitrary power, because the idea of "no content" at all is impossible. The people who rule then are those who cream off the bureaucratic surplus value of those rules or cream off the surplus value of economy, to put this in Marxist terms. At the same time, I think that something ideologically extra—to make a sort of Schmittean point—or something mythical, will always fill in the heart of this empty formalism.

Mark Lilla: My view is that those are withdrawal symptoms. For me, that is what your whole line of thinking is. You want to say, "You can't see it, you can't smell it, you can't touch it, but trust me, political theology is there. If we send the canary into the mine it will die. It is this secret thing holding the whole together." You do this instead of just admitting the obvious that nothing holds it together anymore and we get by.

John Milbank: But what do you do about the biopolitical problematic: is this self-ruling thing natural, or is it cultural and constructed? Surely it turns out to be aporetically both at once. As Bruno Latour and Marshall Sahlins say, modernity tries to divide off the natural and the cultural whereas, in fact, they are always already blended.

Mark Lilla: Well, for the reason Aristotle gave: Man is the creature that by nature departs from his nature.

John Milbank: Aristotle said we are a political animal, which the liberal takes reductively to mean that the human is biopolitical in the sense of a precultural nature, about which we cannot really say anything, because we have decided already in cultural terms that man is naturally fearful or economical or something like this.

But Aristotle is saying something quite different: in our very animal nature, we are political, we are teleologically intended to live in cities. This is not what liberals interpret him to mean.

Mark Lilla: No, but you can have a view that man is a political animal and sustain that one of the things he can do as a political animal is say, "For the purposes of exercising political authority, this is what we are going to do. We are going to limit ourselves to these things, to protecting ourselves against the worst harms, and we will either leave people in their other social relations or individually to cope with the remainder."

But I agree with you that what is lacking in the little story I tell, is someone who solves the problem. Someone who gives us a new account of man as a political creature that makes sense of the fact of what is, from my point of view, the success of liberal government.'

John Milbank: Well, I think that it tends to turn into a kind of relentlessly disciplinary project, that Foucault's right about this, because once you've said, "Oh, the worst harms," these turn out not to be finance, and you get endlessly worried about what is inhibiting somebody else's freedom, or you start to see all interference by somebody with somebody else as a kind of violence.

Mark Lilla: Well that was before Foucault went to California and discovered that it is not all discipline, it is also fun. He got a whole lot less gloomy after he went to California.

John Milbank: I have no idea what you're talking about! But to elaborate, even to interact with anybody in any manner whatsoever is to impose stuff on them, and so if one tries to outlaw interpersonal imposition (as in ordinary conversation), you are doomed to endless policing, so that liberalism it turns out not to be merely a formal, contractualist thing, but to have such a disciplinary process at its very heart, combined with the cult of civility—of acceptable (because predictable and teleologically neutral rather than honorable) behavior. Political correctness was always on the horizon of liberalism, if you will.

Michael Kessler: Mark, you end the book in a very curious way, which is to point us back to what you describe as our own lucidity, which in some sense makes possible the West's success in achieving our self-constraint.

You describe a couple of times in *The Stillborn God* that we are able in the West to separate religion from politics or this theological speculation from our legitimations of politics because it is an exercise of self-constraint.

And then, at the very end, what we have leftover in order to build our political orders and also to prevent us from moving in this direction once again and get carried away by biblical prophetism and messianism is our own lucidity.

Could you talk about what you mean by lucidity?

Mark Lilla: I am saying that there is a fundamental weakness in the Hobbesian tradition, and for liberalism to keep working, we need to think a lot harder about what religion is, what it can and cannot contribute to the public good, even if we don't use it to found the basic political order. That's accomplished. We now have to be lucid about which religious things do and do not threaten that basic order.

Michael Kessler: Archbishop of Canterbury Rowan Williams stirred up a tempest when he said that the UK may need to find a place for Muslim law, shari'a, within its larger legal order, and he said in the way that the UK has already accommodated other religious law.[8] I am curious John, now that we are on the other shore, now that we are in the state with plural religions, what is your response to Williams as a thinker coming from his same country and religious tradition.

John Milbank: The problem with Rowan's speech, which incidentally all his advisors told him not to deliver, was that he appeared to be saying that shari'a law could actually be in conflict with British law, say in relation to marriage law, and you could sort of choose which one to use. And people immediately said, including a lot of Muslim women, "Well, you know, we would not have a free choice, we would be under huge internal pressure to go for shari'a law, even though we did not really like it."

And soon after that Rowan retracted and said, no, he was only talking about instances where things like marriage negotiations or Islamic ways of conducting mortgages are not incompatible with British law—the procedures are a little different, but they are compatible, and they could actually be useful. And this already goes on in relation to Judaism, it has been going on for a hundred years under British law, that certain things are dealt with internally. Yet earlier Rowan appeared to be talking about a kind of choice of jurisdictions, and I think at that point a kind of multiculturalist legalism had entered into his thinking, which he seemed to quite quickly forswear, and quite rightly, in my view.

The only kind of pluralism that can work here is a much more organicist pluralism, where we recognize that there are certain goods pursued by Islamic communities, certain kinds of tacit modes of self-control. Then you can connect how this contributes to the overall good of the country, so that shari'a could have a role in certain areas. But in some instances people are demanding legalized polygamy and other things that do challenge the principles of our Western way of life. In this regard, I think it is very clear to me living in the UK, far clearer than when I lived in America, that Islam is a problem unless it reinvents itself in a more depoliticized form, because historically it *just is* a political religion in a way that is just not compatible with our Western ideas. We need Islam to go Western and not Oriental—though nearly all that the U.S. and the UK has done and not done since 9/11 has been counterproductive in this respect.

Mark Lilla: Well, I am glad we agree about that, and glad that you said we have been doing this for a hundred years in relation to the Jewish community. In fact, the state limits itself. A liberal state can limit itself and it can say, while the law extends this far, it can be silent about other things as long as those other things aren't incompatible with the core of a liberal order. If not, we don't care about that stuff. The only thing that matters, and this was unclear in Williams's statement, is whether shari'a should have standing in the legal system. This is the line, from the point of view of liberalism, that you cannot cross.

But, you know, let us take a lesson from this. It reminds us that we don't think about how every religious practice does or doesn't contribute to the human good. We can actually lower the bar a little bit and let lots of things go on.

John Milbank: I think it is sort of pragmatic, but it means there is some kind of shared notion. I think that what was really firing Rowan was much more the issue of the rights of collective bodies. He was returning to an old question, "Do corporate bodies have rights?" For example, Catholic adoption agencies in Britain have had to shut down because they are not

accepting gay adoption, even though they argued for exemptions and pluralism, and so on. I think Rowan was partially addressing that situation
because on the horizon there are people who are saying you should, in
effect, outlaw churches who say you can't have women priests, etc. Now I
am in favor of women priests, but I am not in favor of the state saying that
churches have to do that. This can be quite a tricky issue for liberalism
because I think that the ultimate logic of liberalism always tends to favor
the priority of the individual. But the idea of rights for corporate bodies—
truly a crucial aspect of "civil liberty"—tends to involve more a notion of
how they are contributing to the public good.

Notes

1. Mark Lilla, *The Stillborn God: Religion, Politics, and the Modern West* (New York: Alfred A. Knopf, 2007), 307.
2. Ibid.
3. José Casanova, "The Great Separation," *The Immanent Frame*, Social Science Research Council, http://blogs.ssrc.org/tif/2007/12/07/the-great-separation/ (accessed July 5, 2011).
4. Mark Lilla, "The Politics of God," *New York Times Magazine*, August 19, 2007.
5. John Milbank, "The Gift and the Mirror: On the Philosophy of Love," in *Counter-Experiences: Reading Jean-Luc Marion*, ed. Kevin Hart (Notre Dame, IN: University of Notre Dame Press, 2007), 254.
6. John Milbank, "Christ the Exception," *New Blackfriars*, 82 (2001): 541–556.
7. John Milbank, *Theology and Social Theory: Beyond Secular Reason* (Malden, MA: Blackwell, 1993).
8. The speech was delivered on February 7, 2008. The text of the speech is available at http://www.guardian.co.uk/uk/2008/feb/07/religion.world2 (accessed July 5, 2011).

PART TWO

Domesticating Religion

The Abrahamic Faiths and the

Democratic State

2

The Great Combination

MODERN POLITICAL THOUGHT AND THE COLLAPSE
OF THE TWO CITIES

Patrick J. Deneen

POLITICAL THEOLOGY, Mark Lilla instructs us, "is discourse about political authority based on a revealed divine nexus."[1] That is, political theology is the effort to associate or affiliate political authority with appeal or reference to a comprehensive doctrine of a divine being or beings. It thus represents an intermingling not only of church and state, but also theology and politics in the deepest sense—a condition in which political authority and legitimacy derives its force and definition from the society's understanding of the divine.

According to Lilla, political theology was, for the most part, *the* basis for political authority for most of human history (at least in the West, the area about which he is concerned), until the inauguration of the "Great Separation" in the early modern period by Thomas Hobbes, and subsequently developed by thinkers such as Locke, Rousseau, Kant, and Hegel. The Great Separation was an effort to remove appeals to the divine nexus in connection to political authority, instead vesting political authority wholly in terms that are rational, secular, and therefore separate from religious understandings. The Great Separation thereby removed religious concerns from the basis of political life, rendering it an affair of private life, individual conscience, and voluntary association. The hope, as Lilla suggests, was to foster a condition over time in which "modern men and women [would] have less need of religion—a need they [could] satisfy privately, so long as they [did] not enter the public sphere."[2] On the basis of this Great Separation, Hobbes and others not only hoped that the wars of religion would cease but also hoped the need to assuage human fears and longings through recourse to religious belief would fade and be replaced by concerns that were wholly secular and worldly. The world would become more like the one that many perceive, or hope, comes daily into existence: a world of societies composed of individuals who are toler-ant, peaceful, commercial, secular, reasonable, replete with plural views that do not violently conflict; and who are governed by liberal regimes that are impartial to ends and efficient at promoting political and juridical solutions to problems while also encouraging prosperity that undergirds individual fulfillment.

Such was the dream of the Great Separation, one that was at least par-tially fulfilled. However, when Lilla views the record of recent years—a record left somewhat unspecified but implicitly pointing to the rise of the Religious Right in the United States and radical Islam around the globe—he acknowledges that "the twilight of the idols has been postponed" and that "we are again fighting the battles of the sixteenth century."[3] Lilla asserts that the effort to achieve the Great Separation was always threatened by human longing for contact with the divine nexus and for the affirmation and assurance that it supplies.[4] The Great Separation was itself "the still-born God," a possibility, it appears, which has been as yet unrealized, even while remaining a hope. It was an experiment, and one whose outcome is contingent, fragile, and uncertain.

Thus goes Lilla's grand and ambitious—if somewhat well-worn—thesis. It is the thesis of the Enlightenment, the hope of the great *philosophes* and, more recently, the narrative of renowned academic liberals from Rawls to Dworkin to nearly every mainstream liberal legal and political theorist. It is the official narrative of liberal modernity. Yet this story obscures from liberal modernity the truth about itself, as Lilla has obscured the truth about the tradition he lauds in the narrative he provides about the Great Separation. Because what he argues constitutes the Great Separation is actually the Great Combination, the true *politicized* theology of the West. What liberalism was premised upon, at base, was an effort to overcome the actual Great Separation that had been effectuated by St. Augustine in his West-shaping work, *City of God*. That separation forbade a practice of political theology—understood to be the direct legitimation of political regimes by appeal to the divine nexus—recognizing that the City of Man and the City of God were governed by two loves that were opposite and incompatible. If anything, Augustine's Great Separation *undermined* all claims to ultimate political legitimacy—observing that *all* cities are robber bands, to some extent—and rejected the ultimate authority of political leaders in light of their investment in the City of Man. (Thus, Augustine would reject Hobbes's formulation that a sovereign could be considered to be "a Mortall God.") Augustine precariously placed Christians between two cities—as famously criticized by such thinkers as Machiavelli and Rousseau—making them only uneasily loyal to the City of Man and aware of their status as pilgrims in this place and hopeful citizens of the next. Such a division—a separation—in fact necessarily forestalled any form of assurance that Lilla believes to be the result of reflection or contemplation on humanity's place in the divine nexus.[5] Augustine's Great Separation left his pilgrims supremely *unassured* about their place in the divine nexus and supremely aware that the hopes and ambitions that all previous humanity may have invested in their cities were misdirected and evanescent. Augustine urged a form of epistemological humility about our capacity to know ourselves (much less God).[6] This humility further undermines the claim that theological aspirations result in a kind of "assurance" of the form that Lilla suggests results from a somewhat infantile craving for certainty about an uncertain world. Lilla's summary of the theological impulse bears little resemblance to the particulars of the main theological tradition in Western Christianity, especially that established by Augustine.

Lilla's version of the development of modern liberalism is even less on the mark than his passing and inaccurate portrait of political theology. He writes that early modern thought sought to separate considerations of the divine nexus from political considerations.

> Those who established the principles of the Great Separation did not disprove the existence of a divine nexus, nor did they try to extinguish reflection about it. They taught a new art of thinking about politics without reference to such matters so that we could conceive, discuss, and then build a decent political order free from religious violence.[7]

Lilla repeats with different iterations that the liberal order was built "without reference to such matters," arguing that its constitutive thinkers sought to emphasize solely secular grounds for politics, "wishing the extinction of political theology," and concluding that these thinkers sought the separation of "political discourse from theological discourse."[8] Yet, this claim does not correspond to the deepest theological underpinnings of liberalism in its early modern and progressive forms (roughly the two periods Lilla treats in the two respective chapters of part II of *The Stillborn God*). Instead, looking squarely at the evidence, what one sees is an effort to overcome Augustine's Great Separation by means of two distinct Great Combinations, each corresponding roughly with a development within liberal theory, from its classical conception, enunciated most clearly by Hobbes and Locke, and its progressive period, witnessed in such thinkers such as Rousseau and J. S. Mill. This Great Combination represents a true form of political theology, collapsing what Augustine had sought to hold apart, seeking fulfillment in the temporal world by combining the two cities. This combination manifests in divergent configurations, either putting the City of God in service of the City of Man or transforming the City of Man into the City of God. However this combination is rendered, it is actually intrinsically a part of the origins of the liberal tradition—that tradition that Lilla mistakenly believes to comprise the "Great Separation."

Liberalism's Two Waves

The Great Combination was effectuated within liberalism in two distinct ways that closely track how Leo Strauss outlined the development of modernity in his seminal essay "The Three Waves of Modernity."[9] In particular, liberalism's two phases are described as the first two waves of modernity, championed by Hobbes and Locke in the first wave, and Rousseau and Mill in the second wave. They also have counterparts in America, namely a number of the founders in the eighteenth century who reflect first-wave, early modern liberalism, and late nineteenth and early twentieth century thinkers, such as John Dewey, who reflect the progressive liberalism of the second wave.

Strauss begins his essay by describing the first wave of modernity, a "wave" initiated by Machiavelli and further developed by Thomas Hobbes and John Locke. This first wave represented a major break with antiquity, and, in particular, a fundamental change in how humanity viewed nature. Modern political thought is marked, perhaps above all, by a growing confidence in human powers of understanding and an admonition to exert those powers in the control of nature. Modernity was inaugurated by a transformation of scientific understanding, from viewing science as the mere observation of natural phenomena to envisioning science as the active effort to employ knowledge of natural operations in the service of controlling those operations to achieve "the relief of the human estate."

The move toward modernity was initially directed to controlling chance, or "fortune." Rejecting classical or Christian conceptions of nature—of which humanity was a part and thereby subject to its limits—modern thought began with the effort to exert control over nature's dominion and, in effect, to put humans on the course of controlling nature. One of modernity's major figures, Francis Bacon, argued that nature was comparable to a prisoner who withheld his secrets, and the scientist was like a jailer who sought to extract those secrets, by torture if necessary. The image of a recalcitrant and niggardly nature was continued by Bacon's one-time secretary, Thomas Hobbes, and John Locke in their arguments on behalf of the human conquest of nature to improve the conditions of human life and achieve ever-increasing and limitless economic growth.

Strauss argued that this "first wave" of modernity heralded modern natural rights. These rights were understood to be based on a conception of human nature, understood to be driven above all by self-interest and the pursuit of material comfort, what Hobbes called "commodious living." The first wave was thus a political philosophy that included an understanding of limits: namely, that human nature was fixed—by nature we are self-interested—and thus that political efforts to transform human nature were destined to be deeply disfiguring and ultimately unsuccessful. Human nature was self-interested and self-seeking, and, most important, it was unchangeable. As such, human nature represented a known and reliable form of motivation that could be both utilized and controlled. It could be utilized by steering its productive and competitive energies toward economic concerns, and it could be controlled by creating institutions that channeled and curtailed its potentially destructive energies through legal limits on its expression. A strong state was therefore necessary both to control the worst aspects of the citizen's natural tendencies and to provide the setting for an expansion of economic activity. This first-wave modernity—early modern liberalism—underlay the political philosophy of the founding fathers of America, most notably Madison, who understood that "men were not angels" and that "religious and moral motives" could not be relied on in politics.[10] Politics in the new modern era was not the realm of redemption and human perfection, but the domain of productive channeling of the enormous energies of self-interest toward the mastery of nature.

The "second wave" of modernity took the basic insight of the philosophers of the first wave—that nature was subject to human control—and extended this insight to human nature itself. If external nature were subject to human dominion, why not human nature, too? Thinkers like Rousseau, Condorcet, Comte, and later, John Stuart Mill—and in America, nineteenth-century thinkers like Emerson and Whitman and twentieth-century philosophers like John Dewey and Richard Rorty—developed the idea of human perfectibility, of the human ability to not only master external nature but also to improve human nature as well. Human nature—if you could still call it that—is now seen as malleable and plastic. If philosophers of the first wave argued that human nature was unalterable, philosophers of the second wave argued that human nature could be improved morally concurrent with progressive changes in the material domain. The concept of moral progress became a central feature in second-wave philosophy, a progress in historical time that was believed to culminate in man's perfection, even an ascent to a godlike condition.

Especially for post-Darwinian thinkers of the second wave, human nature could no longer be understood as a fixed and unalterable condition any more than the natural world could be understood as unchangeable. Mill writes in *On Liberty* of the "permanent interest of man as a progressive being"—that is, the only thing that is permanent about humans is our capacity to progress, or change—while Emerson speaks in his lecture "The Fortune of the Republic" of "men of elastic" and of "new times" that need "a new man."[11] In his book *Democracy and Education* John Dewey speaks of human "plasticity" and of the unlimited prospects for human growth, while more recently Richard Rorty wrote in *Achieving Our Country* that democratic peoples "have 'more being' than predemocratic humanity."[12] No essence of humanity can be posited in advance: the very definition of democracy includes a dynamic process within which not only physical and economic but also moral and intellectual progress occurs, in which human beings are transformed into different creatures—as Rorty argues, "Democracy is the principle means by which a more evolved form of humanity will come into existence."[13]

The differences between these two waves are immediately obvious and not merely in theory. Modern America, and the modern world more broadly, has been largely defined politically through battles between adherents of the first wave and disciples of the second wave. Internationally, liberal democracy combated successive waves of fascism and communism in the twentieth century, and successfully defended its beliefs that politics was not the realm of human transformation and salvation, and that freedom—particularly in the form of market economies—was the appropriate aspiration of human life. Domestically, "conservatives" are most often adherents of the first-wave philosophy—defenders of original-ism, of the founders' vision, of free markets, and of individual liberties. By contrast, those on the Left—often called liberals, but whom we might do better to call "progressives"—are more often acolytes of second-wave philosophy, believers in moral progress and human transformation, who stress the positive role of government in effecting this transformation. The two camps have been locked in a constant battle since the advent of the modern age, and they could not seem to be further apart.

However, what contemporary politics can too often obscure is what Strauss's analysis reveals, that is, a deep similarity between these two camps. Both espouse versions of modernity and, further, are species of liberalism—the one manifesting a "natural rights" liberalism and the other manifesting progressive liberalism. As such, both are deeply suspicious of claims of tradition and are hostile to a teleological conception of nature that derives from an Aristotelian, Thomistic understanding. Both seek human mastery over the external world and especially economic growth, although the second wave is less cognizant of how extensively its belief in human transformation rests upon the base of economic expansion, growth, and mastery (this tends to be more true of nineteenth-century thinkers, while thinkers such as Dewey and Rorty acknowledge what they believe to be the close connection between material and moral progress). Both embrace a concept of progress and foreground the goal of "growth," although for first-wave philosophy, progress is limited to the material realm. Above all, both philosophies share the most basic presupposition of modern thought—both are based upon a deep, profound, and pervasive antago-nism toward Augustinian theology that posits a distinction between the cities of Man and God. To that end, both seek to bridge that divide through a "Great Combination"—different in each case, but each sharing a fun-damental rejection of a permanent divide between the two. Each seeks to bring together what Augustine (and Christianity) had put asunder.

Early Modern Liberalism's Political Theology: God in the Service of Men

This first wave of modernity necessarily required a fundamental shift in thinking about religion; as Lilla persuasively argues (echoing other thinkers, such as Bryan Garsten in his masterful book *Saving Persuasion*), Hobbes's political project was motivated by the ambition to reduce violence that resulted from religious differences.[14] However, Lilla goes astray in supposing that this project aimed at a Great Separation. Instead, Hobbes aspired to achieve a Great Combination of religion and politics, of church and state, with the aim that religion and the church would serve as reinforcement and would lend legitimation to the ruling apparatus of the Leviathan. A glance at the frontispiece of *Leviathan* confirms that Hobbes's ambition was to create a true *political* theology: It portrays the sovereign (composed of the populace, looking up to his face) holding the sword in one hand and the crozier in the other. (See figure 2.1.) In him, church and state, theology and politics are combined, a combination reinforced in the pictures that line both sides of the page below the main illustration, which portray the aspects of life and world that come under the sovereign's governance, ranging from the art of war to religious disputation and doctrine. Under a single head, church and state, religion and politics are brought together. Hobbes was among the most effective and celebrated inaugurators of the Great Combination that marked early modern liberalism at the outset.

Thinkers like Machiavelli and Hobbes rejected the Augustinian tradition that held there was a fundamental divide between the City of Man and the City of God and that our ultimate allegiance lay in the Eternal City. Religion in its Christian conception was criticized for dividing human loyalties, for placing our longings beyond this world and rejecting the view of human nature as most fundamentally grounded in self-interest for material comfort, what Locke called "indolency of the body" and the rewards of this world.[15] Nevertheless, *because* thinkers like Machiavelli, Hobbes, and Locke regarded humans as irremediably self-interested, they recognized that religion was a necessary feature of the natural-rights-based liberal polity, in particular, as a necessary support for solidarity, cohesion, and ultimately for social control and obedience. For thinkers in the first wave, religion was conceived as a fundamentally civil institution that served the ends of the state, particularly as a means of governing the worst effects of self-interest and guaranteeing obedience to the terms of the social contract. Thus Machiavelli argued for a form of civil religion in which the gods would be understood to support the cause of their city, and Hobbes sanctioned the frontispiece illustration of the *Leviathan* in which the sovereign is pictured holding both the sword and the crozier, pointing to the establishment of a civil religion in

FIGURE 2.1 Frontispiece from Thomas Hobbes, *Leviathan*, 1651.

which the sovereign would direct activities of both church and state. As
Michael Gillespie wrote:

> Hobbes does not favor a secular state that takes no stance on reli-
> gious issues. The failure of the sovereign to establish and main-
> tain standards of good and evil would leave the determination of

these questions to the same private judgments that produced the problem in the first place. Hobbes thus believes that all successful states must have an established form of religious practice, but with the great caveat that political and religious authority must be in the hands of one sovereign who enforces standards of public judgment in religious matters and disallows the public expression of private religious judgment.[16]

The sovereign is thereby charged with developing "a theology for a Christian commonwealth," an outcome that Gillespie shows to be a result of "a new theological vision" inaugurated by Hobbes. Far from representing an eschewal or rejection of the divine nexus and a separation of considerations of religion in assessing the possibility and success of politics, Hobbes is the unquestioned champion of the Great Combination.

Lilla recognizes that Hobbes argues in support of a form of civil religion and thus takes recourse to an appeal to religion. However, in doing so, Lilla argues that Hobbes sets into motion a philosophic revolution that leads to liberalism's supposed separation of church and state, particularly the way in which Hobbes's analysis is adapted by John Locke "without making reference to the nexus between God, man, and world."[17] Yet, extraordinarily, even while Lilla downplays the combination effected by Hobbes, he wholly ignores the ways in which Locke relies equally and extensively upon religion as a fundamental support for the liberal regime he envisions. While Locke is celebrated for inaugurating a decisive break between church and state and rejecting established religion in his *Letter Concerning Toleration*, Locke also betrays the extent to which the liberal order rests upon a necessary theological basis. For Locke in particular, obligation becomes a significant challenge (one avoided by Hobbes in insisting on the creation of the sovereign who will enforce all contracts and promises, above all the social contract itself). Lacking such an enforcement mechanism—thus creating a liberal regime, in contrast to Hobbes's authoritarian polity—Locke is forced to fall back on religion as a necessary and useful ultimate enforcer of social behavior. Thus, in the closing passages of the *Letter Concerning Toleration*, Locke forbade extending toleration to those who may, in the course of their worship, declare allegiance to a foreign power (i.e., Catholics)—undermining the idea that there is no connection between church and state—and, more revealingly, he argued against the extension of toleration to atheists because they cannot be trusted to keep their oaths and vows. Locke writes, "Those are not at all to be tolerated who deny the Being of a God. Promises, Covenants, and Oaths, which are the Bonds of Humane Society, can have no hold upon an Atheist. The taking away of God, tho but even in thought, dissolves all."[18] A salutary fear of eternal damnation is the ultimate guarantor of the terms of the social contract, a contract whose signatories, as self-interested and self-maximizing individuals, might otherwise have every desire to break at the first possible moment they believed no earthly power would punish them.

Moreover, Locke was finally unconvinced about the efficaciousness of a rationally, contractually based polity, having little confidence in the reasoning powers of most of his contemporaries. While Locke could speak of abstract humanity as capable of both knowing and protecting its own basic self-interest and ultimate sovereignty when discussing the state of nature and the foundations of government, particularly in the *Second Treatise*, it would be a mistake to assume that Locke was sanguine about the prospects of democratic rule based on his assumptions of the "reasonableness" of the populace. For Locke, reason alone was not, nor could be, a sufficient basis for morality and good judgment in politics. As he wrote in his late and important, if less-often read treatise, *The Reasonableness of Christianity*, "'Tis our mistake to think, that...we had the first certain knowledge of [truths] from [reason], and in that clear Evidence we now possess them. The contrary is manifest, in the *defective Morality of the Gentiles* before our Saviour's time...Philosophy seemed to have spent its strength, and done its utmost."[19]

Locke admired the thoroughgoing reasonableness of the ancients but still found them lacking morality, which only became possible after revelations from "our Saviour." Locke held that one might attempt to collect the wisdom of the ancients, but "the world nevertheless stood as much in need of our Saviour, and the Morality delivered by him." While Locke stated that the laws of the New Testament conform to principles discoverable by reason, he acknowledged, "the truth and *obligation* of its Precepts have their force, and are put past doubt to us, but the evidence of [Jesus Christ's] mission. He was sent by God: His miracles shew it; And the Authority of God in his Precepts cannot be questioned." Thus, Locke concluded that the unaided reason of the sort demonstrated by ancient philosophy was insufficient to discover the grounds of morality and, further, the voluntary observation of such morality, independent of religious revelation: "And we see, [reason] resolved not the doubts that had arisen amongst the Studious and Thinking Philosophers; Nor had yet been able to convince the Civilized parts of the World, that they had not given, nor could without a Crime, take away the Lives of Children, by Exposing them."[20]

Further, Locke was not optimistic about the prospects for secular liberalism. Locke continued his analysis by supposing for a moment that reason is a sufficient guide for human morality and judgment (a point which, it must be stressed, he was insufficiently confident to begin with). Thus, he wrote (wholly in the conditional):

> Or if it [i.e., rationalistic philosophy] should have gone farther, as we see it did not, and from undeniable Principles given us *Ethicks* in a Science like Mathematicks in every part demonstrable, this yet would not have been so effectual to man in this imperfect state, nor proper for the Cure. The greatest part of mankind want *leisure or capacity* for Demonstration; nor can they carry a train of Proofs; which in that way they must always depend upon for Conviction, and cannot be required to assent to till they see the Demonstration. Wherever they stick, the Teachers are always put upon Proof, and must clear the Doubt by a Thread of coherent deductions from the first Principle, how long, or how intricate soever that be. And you may as soon hope to have all the Day-Labourers and Tradesmen, the Spinsters and Dairy Maids perfect Mathematicians, as to have them perfect in *Ethicks* this way. Hearing plain Commands, is the sure and only course to bring them to Obedience and Practice. The greatest part cannot know, and therefore they must believe.[21]

He concluded that even if reason were assumed the best guide for moral judgment, nevertheless, "the Instruction of the People were best still to be left to the Precepts and Principles of the Gospel."[22]

Within the American tradition we might point to many of the founders who attested—if not to the *truth* of religion—at least to its usefulness. We might read in this light the well-known passage from George Washington's "Farewell Address" in which he rejected the notion "that morality can be maintained without religion."[23] Washington insisted that religion is crucial to the national well-being. "Whatever may be conceded to the influence of refined education on the minds of peculiar structure, reason and experience both forbid us to expect that National morality can prevail in exclusion of religious principle." In other words, people of "refined education" might be capable of perceiving the grounds for adhering to the "national morality" without the assistance of religion, thus implying that for such people religion is probably not necessary. It is the vast majority of people who lack minds of "peculiar structure" who should be encouraged to develop religious belief to ensure the health of our "national morality." In short, religion is useful to the state, and only insofar as this is held to be the case, the state has an interest in promoting salutary forms of religious belief. Whether religion has anything to do with the condition of our soul and our relation to the divine is not only an irrelevant consideration but also a dangerous one.

For Hobbes and Locke alike (and the American founders after them), religion was put in the service of the needs of the polity. This may represent a form of "separation," excavating reflection upon the relationship of the Cities of God and Man, but, more deeply, the arguments of early modern liberalism represent a form of political theology in which theology is placed wholly in the service of state legitimation and thus represents a profound combination. To this extent, early modern liberalism constitutes a form of political theology far more than supposed by Lilla, particularly if—as he states—political theology represents the effort "to connect our political discourse to theological and cosmological questions" and the recognition of religion "as politically authoritative."[24] Moreover, it represents a political philosophy in which theology no longer serves to limit, restrain, or chasten the ambitions of politics but to wholly support and undergird its modern ambitions of mastery, growth, and expansion. To this extent, Lilla seems to get the argument wrong: political theology is a modern phenomenon, and one that—in combining concerns of the state with the sanction of religion—represents a supremely dangerous and combustible mix.

Progressive Liberalism's Political Theology: Creating the City of God on Earth

In contrast to the civil religion defended by proponents of first-wave liberalism, second-wave theorists were far more explicit in their criticisms of religion, because the civil religion of first-wave theorists—not to mention traditional Christians—maintained a belief that human beings were not subject to fundamental alteration. For this reason, thinkers of the second wave exhibit an even more ferocious critique of religion, since even the residually salutary civic religion of first-wave thinkers was defended out of a belief in the inalterability of human vanity and self-interest, that is, an unchanging human nature.

Nevertheless, we are mistaken to think that the various critiques of religion evident in the work of second-wave thinkers (e.g., Rousseau, Mill, Marx, Dewey, even Rorty) amount to a form of secularism. Far from the case, these thinkers all, in one sense or another, replace traditional religious faith with a redefined progressive faith in which humankind is subject to a kind of transformation that makes possible our own condition of godliness. Rather than putting religion in the service of politics as envisioned by first-wave thinkers, second-wave theorists see politics as an avenue to a kind of new religious apotheosis, bringing into combination the Cities of Man and God.

Rousseau understood his belief in human "perfectibility" in theological terms—the sorts of terms that Lilla suggests ceased to apply after the Great Separation. While rejecting the "dividedness" which marks the Augustinian legacy of Christianity, Rousseau does not propose secularism in its place, but instead a new religion with humanity at its center. At the same time that Rousseau rejected the dream of returning to a presocial condition described in *The Second Discourse*, he argued that a "second nature" must be fashioned for mankind, one that will make the potentially deleterious effects of indifferent natural causes irrelevant to a reconceived humanity. Rousseau thus demanded a belief in a beneficent, if not omnipotent, God (much like the optimists, such as Leibniz), but he rejected the notion of the pessimists (like Voltaire, following the Lisbon earthquake) that the universe is irredeemably imperfect. God's beneficence is not one that promises redemption by divine intervention; rather, divine beneficence is deduced through a preliminary belief in thorough human agency. While God creates a creature that can potentially become human, it is in fact humankind that then creates itself. Further, humanity is the true source of the knowledge of good and evil: evil is most fundamentally the cause of ill-conceived human contrivance and can be alleviated and even overcome by means of better-conceived human contrivance. Much of Rousseau's writing describes various forms of refashioning human nature through education, laws, political institutions, family, and even a re-creation of the individual by the means of a tutor (in *Emile*) or a legislator (in the *Social Contract*).

It is unsurprising that, in an effort to support his view of such a beneficent—if otherwise indifferent—God, Rousseau concluded his letter to Voltaire describing the basic outlines of a civil religion much akin to the one found in *The Social Contract*.[25] If humanity is to be brought to the point where they will believe in a form of Providence that recommends man's mastery of his own condition by means of artifice—thus, recommending at once a belief that humanity is the cause of, and potentially a solution to, evil—then a religious artifice must serve as the first source of a renewed human belief in its own potential. A human-based religion gives rise to a belief in a beneficent but not all-powerful God that, in turn, gives rise to the belief that evil is caused and potentially eliminated by humans. Human needs dictate the shape of our God, and the limits of that God dictate the compensating power of human creation.

Such a belief—one that finally undergirds Rousseau's faith in human transformation by means of human self-fashioning—is finally a matter of chosen faith: "I believe in God just as strongly as I believe in any other truth, because to believe and not to believe are the things that least depend on me, because the state of doubt is too violent a state for my soul, because when my reason wavers, my faith cannot long remain in suspense, and decides without it; and finally because a thousand things I like better draw me toward the more consoling side and add the weight of hope to the equilibrium of reason."[26] Rousseau recognized that as a human, he cannot escape the condition of believing: the decision comes down, simply, to which belief he will embrace. Rousseau freely admitted that his faith comes about as a result of his desire for solace: his faith is an expression of pure will and the result of a human-centered calculus of preference. Reason—poised at a point of equilibrium on a scale—cannot choose between optimism and pessimism. Human will to power tips it toward the optimistic side. Yet, to conclude by elaborating on Rousseau's image, a finger already tilts the balance of the scale—the weight of human preference, human will, and human self-flattery. The resulting faith reflects the assumptions that went into its formulation. Rousseau thus endorsed a human-centered faith that follows when humanity's view of the universe is assumed a simple matter of individual choice between faith that consoles and faith that leads to despair. Rousseau's theology serves as the basis of his aspiration of human—and political—perfectibility, a possible transcendence of our imperfect and insufficient current condition. His political theology opens up the prospect of infinite human progress, accepting at once the dissatisfaction familiar to Christians who long for a perfected condition, but placing the fulfillment of that longing in the secular realm. It is a democratic faith in human redemption, by and for humans.[27]

One finds a similar form of political theology undergirding other theories of the second wave. At once one sees a severe attack upon traditional religion, but one that precedes a new, progressive theology. Having lauded all forms of experimental living in *On Liberty*, J. S. Mill reserves special scorn for Calvinism and its "narrow theory of life" that asserts the existence of original sin and human corruption.[28] One of Emerson's earliest lectures is his "Harvard Divinity School Address" in which he scorns nearly all forms of organized religion, even arguing that Jesus merely represents the divinity that is within all humans. A theme taken up in many early writings of John Dewey, who argued in an 1898 essay, "Christianity and Democracy," that the churches had become ossified and that dynamic Christian revelation was now to occur in and through democratic processes. This theme is echoed by Richard Rorty, for whom "the terms 'America' and 'democracy' are shorthand for a new conception of what it is to be human—a conception that has no room for obedience to a non-human authority."[29]

As these passages imply, while traditional religion is soundly rejected by second-wave theorists, it is replaced not by disbelief but by a new form of religion, a religion in which the divide between the City of God and the City of Man has been wholly obliterated. Invariably, these thinkers suggest a new religion—a "religion of humanity," such as that proposed by Auguste Comte and embraced by John Stuart Mill.[30] Again and again in the thought of John Dewey there is a call to achieve a kind of secular salvation. It was especially through progressive education that he believed we would reach a time when "the distinction between the spiritual and the secular has ceased...the Church and State, the divine and human organization of society are one." Stunningly, Dewey considered the teacher to be "the prophet of the true God and the usherer in of the true of God."[31] Properly organized, the school was the agent of redemption for a progressive humanity and the avenue by which the City of God could be created within the City of Man. Far from representing a "Great Separation," thinkers in the second wave envision a new religion in which humanity is its central deity and earth is heaven a-borning.

Conclusion: A New Separation?

Modern thought—particularly the two iterations of liberalism now dominant on today's political scene—represents not the legacy of separation, but combination. In spite of their many differences from one another, both liberalisms place the human will in a place of ascendance and view the world (nature, even humanity itself) as subject to human dominion, command, and manipulation. Reaching back to Hobbes's early boss, Francis Bacon, the modern project rests fundamentally upon the redirection of human negotiation with the created world, from a vision in which the world is "given" by God, whose existence we must struggle to understand, in full cognizance that complete understanding will elude us, to a vision of the created world in which all orders, natures, and powers become subject to our dominion. As Dewey wrote (admiringly) of Bacon's understanding of the human relationship to existence, we must conceive of nature as a creature akin to a prisoner and humanity as its jailor and torturer, seeking to extract from unwilling nature its secrets.

Lilla paints a dramatic portrait of an age of premodern violence born of religious warfare and a placid and peaceful condition of modern liberalism in which toleration, industriousness, and prosperity govern. Left unsaid in Lilla's account is the violent basis on which liberalism was founded. Modern life in the liberal state is lived in a world viewed through a Gnostic lens of discontent and dissatisfaction, a relationship that was made possible by a Great Combination that put humankind in a position akin to that of gods.

This is a belief that I think we can no longer afford to hold. Everywhere we are presented with evidence of depletion and destruction that our brief experiment with modernity has left us. What is needed is a true separation, an acknowledgment—returning to an Augustinian acknowledgment—that we are not God, and that we cannot treat the world as means to our individual satisfaction or aspiration to perfectibility.[32] As the author Wendell Berry has argued, the "war against nature"—inaugurated by Francis Bacon and Thomas Hobbes, if not previously by Machiavelli—is one that we are bound to lose. Our relationship to the world must change if we are to continue to derive sustenance from it, requiring an acknowledgment that we are created—not creators—and subjects, not sovereigns.[33] At the moment, Berry writes, our relationship with nature is "dictatorial or totalitarian." We need something and we take it; we want something and we exploit it. Instead, he writes, the proper relationship with nature is that of a conversation. We should ask of a place what it can offer and what we can offer in return, and listen as we express our wants. He writes:

> The conversation itself would thus assume a creaturely life, binding the place and its inhabitants together, changing and growing to no end, no final accomplishment, that can be conceived or foreseen...And if you honor the other party to the conversation, if you honor the otherness of the other party, you understand that you must not expect always to receive a reply that you foresee or that you would like. A conversation is immitigably two-sided and always to some degree mysterious; it requires faith.[34]

Such a faith begins with doubt about our self-sovereignty. Such a faith eschews "assurance," that aspiration, above all, that marks not our ancient faith, but those modern faiths that we can no longer afford. If our modern faith is marked above all by a Great Combination of religion and politics, then I can at least agree with Mark Lilla that what is needed is a new Great Separation—albeit one that truly separates what should not have been put together.

Notes

1. Mark Lilla, *The Stillborn God: Religion, Politics, and the Modern West* (New York: Alfred A. Knopf, 2007), 23.
2. Ibid., 90.
3. Ibid., 3.
4. Ibid., 7.
5. Ibid., 6.
6. See Charles Mathewes, "The Liberation of Questioning in Augustine's *Confessions*," *Journal of American Religion* 70, no. 3 (2002): 539–560.
7. Lilla, *Stillborn God*, 131.
8. Ibid., 103, 298.
9 Leo Strauss, "The Three Waves of Modernity," in *Political Philosophy: Six Essays*, ed. Hilail Gildin (Indianapolis: Bobbs-Merrill, 1975).
10. James Madison, "The Federalist No. 51: The Structure of the Government Must Furnish the Proper Checks and Balances Between the Different Departments," in *Independent Journal*, February 8, 1788, Library of Congress, http://thomas.loc.gov/home/histdox/fed_51.html (accessed July 5, 2011).
11. John Stuart Mill, *On Liberty*, ed. Gertrude Himmelfarb (New York: Penguin Books, 1985), 70; Ralph Waldo Emerson, "The Fortune of the Republic," (lecture delivered at the Old South Church, Boston, March 30, 1878), *Online Library of Liberty*, http://oll.libertyfund.org/?option=com_staticxt&staticfile=show.php%3Ftitle=1961&chapter=123132&layout=html&Itemid=27 (accessed July 5, 2011).
12. John Dewey, *Democracy and Education* (New York: Free Press, 1944). Richard Rorty, *Achieving Our Country: Leftist Thought in Twentieth-Century America* (Cambridge, MA: Harvard University Press, 1999), 143.
13. Rorty, *Achieving Our Country*, 142.
14. Bryan Garsten, *Saving Persuasion: A Defense of Rhetoric and Judgment* (Cambridge, MA: Harvard University Press, 2006).
15. John Locke, *A Letter Concerning Toleration*, ed. James Tully (Indianapolis: Hackett, 1983), 26.
16. Michael Allen Gillespie, *The Theological Origins of Modernity* (Chicago: University of Chicago Press, 2008), 245.

17. Lilla, *Stillborn God*, 86, 88.

18. Locke, *A Letter Concerning Toleration*, 51.

19. John Locke, *The Reasonableness of Christianity as Delivered in the Scriptures*, ed. John C. Higgins-Biddle (Oxford: Clarendon Press, 1999), ch. 14: 156–157.

20. Ibid., ch. 14: 150, 153, 154. For further analysis into the insufficiency of reason in the thought of Locke (and several other early modern political thinkers), see Joshua Mitchell, *Not By Reason Alone: Religion, History, and Identity in Early Modern Political Thought* (Chicago: University of Chicago Press, 1993), esp. ch. 3, "Locke: The Dialectic of Clarification and the Politics of Reason." Based on the state of contemporary ethical theory, one might conclude that Locke was correct, in particular, about reason being insufficient to prevent arguments in favor of infanticide. See the utilitarian arguments in defense of such practices in Peter Singer, *Unsanctifying Human Life* (London: Blackwell, 2002); Helga Kuhse and Peter Singer, *Should the Baby Live?* (New York: Oxford University Press, 1988); and Singer's earlier work, *Practical Ethics* (New York: Cambridge University Press, 1993).

21. Locke, *The Reasonableness of Christianity*, ch. 14: 157–158 (emphasis mine).

22. Ibid., ch. 14: 158.

23. George Washington, "Farewell Address to the People of the United States," September 19, 1796, available at http://www.access.gpo.gov/congress/senate/farewell/sd106-21.pdf (accessed July 5, 2011).

24. Lilla, *Stillborn God*, 7–8.

25. Jean-Jacques Rousseau, "Letter to Voltaire," in *The Discourses and other Early Political Writings*, ed. Victor Gourevitch (Cambridge, UK: Cambridge University Press, 1997), 245–246.

26. Ibid., 242–243.

27. For further discussion of Rousseau's "democratic faith," see chapter 5 of Patrick Deneen, *Democratic Faith* (Princeton, NJ: Princeton, 2005).

28. Mill, *On Liberty*, 126.

29. Richard Rorty, *Achieving Our Country: Leftist Thought in Twentieth-Century America* (Cambridge, MA: Harvard University Press, 1998), 18.

30. See John Gray, *Al-Qaeda and What It Means to Be Modern* (New York: New Press, 2005).

31. John Dewey, "My Pedagogic Creed," (New York: E.L. Kellogg, 1897), 18. See also my discussion of this topic in *Democratic Faith*, ch. 6.

32. See Vaclav Havel, "Forgetting We Are Not God," *First Things*, March 1995.

33. See Jean Bethke Elshtain, *Sovereignty: God, State and Self* (New York: Basic Books, 2008).

34. Wendell Berry, "Nature as Measure," in *What Are People For?* (New York: North Point Press, 1990), 209.

3

History and Essence

THE CONSTRUCTION OF A MODERN
JEWISH POLITICAL THEOLOGY

Jerome Copulsky

FOR CENTURIES JEWS were considered, by themselves and by the people they lived amongst, to be "a people apart." The Jews were living in exile, scattered among the nations of the world, practicing their own religious law and awaiting the coming of the Messiah who would gather them back and reestablish a Jewish kingdom. By the late eighteenth century, however, certain Jewish thinkers forged a new form of Judaism, a Judaism that would both facilitate the Jews' entrance into that society and serve to legitimate the social and politic order theologically.[1] This theology rejected the idea that the Jews were in exile and in an in-between time, passively waiting their reentry into history. For these Jewish thinkers, history demonstrated that Judaism had existed in a number of different dispensations. The emerging modern constitutional order would be the embodiment of the hoped-for messianic Jewish state. These theologians were not merely arguing that Jews could find their place in a modern state but, more audaciously, that the modern political order depended, indirectly but fundamentally, on Judaism. Liberal Judaism proclaimed a political theology, one which argued that the modern state was not just another possible dispensation, but its highest.

To suggest that liberal Judaism expressed itself as a political theology might at first blush appear to be a paradoxical endeavor. It is ordinarily assumed that the liberal reformers of Judaism strove to remove all political and national elements from their presentation in order to demonstrate that Judaism did not have an expressed political meaning, that it was not a state-within-a-state. Would it not be more accurate to maintain that by "cleansing" the tradition of all political and national elements, the reformers produced and promoted an expressly *apolitical* theology?

While it is certainly the case that the nineteenth-century reformers, uneasy about the theological-political critique of Judaism, denied the contemporary relevance of the ancient Jewish theocracy and much of traditional Jewish law, their work can nonetheless be seen as developing a particular form of political theology. By stressing the beliefs that orientate and stimulate ethical life (rather than the comprehensive legal and ritual praxis of premodern Judaism), the Jewish reformers signaled their political accommodation with the emerging state and their belief that Judaism had a role to play within it. They strove to present a Judaism that would not only be amenable to modern politics, but would also provide the foundation for participation in the political order. This meant dealing not only with the issues of practical reform (or the liturgy, decorum, and ritual life) but also the articulation and promulgation of a theological principle of Judaism. Such a theological principle would guide these adjustments and promote appropriate forms of religiosity and Jewish observance while providing the intellectual foundation of Jewish loyalty and devotion.

This essay surveys some significant attempts of modern liberal Jewish thinkers, responding to intellectual currents in political theory and liberal Protestant theology, and brute political facts, to construct a new political theology for the emerging Jewish bourgeois citizen. This project entailed the articulation of a new Jewish narrative, a "history" of Judaism for contemporary purposes or a "usable past" orchestrated around the theological "idea" of Judaism, detailing how it had emerged, developed, and was preserved, despite the vicissitudes of history, and affirming its contemporary and enduring meaning.[2]

To narrate this story requires first a glance at the situation of the Jews in Europe at the beginning of liberalism and at the challenges that the new order posed to Judaism.

Judaism in Modernity: A Theological-Political Predicament

A famous episode expresses, *in nunc*, the problem that the situation of traditional Judaism seemed to present to modern Jews. Standing before the French National Assembly on December 23, 1789, Count Stanislas de

Clermont-Tonnerre declared: "The Jews should be denied everything as a nation, but granted everything as individuals. They must be citizens."[3]

Clermont-Tonnerre's offer to the Jews of France succinctly expresses the conditions of political equality that the Enlightenment had to offer the Jews of Europe. The National Assembly had promulgated the Declaration of Rights of Man and of the Citizen, affirming the equality of all men in nature and before the law and the freedom of religion—so long, of course, as the activity of that religion did not prove detrimental to public order. Yet on that day it was not self-evident to the National Assembly that French Jews were to be considered citizens of the new regime. "No one," Clermont-Tonnerre reminded his audience, "shall be persecuted for his religious beliefs. Is it not profound persecution of the citizen to want to deprive him of his dearest right because of his opinions?" The count proceeded to distinguish between the realm of law and that of religion: "God wanted us to reach agreement among ourselves on issues of morality, and he has permitted us to make moral laws, but he has given to no one but himself the right to legislate dogmas and to rule over conscience." Unless the revolutionary state wished to create a "national religion" (and by doing so, he warned, "tear[ing] up your Declaration of Rights"), it was obliged to acknowledge the Jews of France as equal citizens, different from other Frenchmen only by virtue of their particular religious beliefs.[4]

But the count also argued that there was a price to be paid. To gain membership in this new society, the Jews were called upon to relinquish their traditional corporate arrangement. "It is intolerable," Clermont-Tonnerre continued, "The Jews should become a separate political formation or class in the country. Every one of them must individually become a citizen; if they do not want this, they must inform us and we shall then be compelled to expel them. The existence of a nation within a nation is unacceptable to our country."[5]

The situation in France in 1789 can be seen as a microcosm for changes that were slowly occurring throughout Western and Central Europe. The emerging order of liberty and equality seemed to offer an opportunity for the individual Jew and a challenge for Judaism. At this time, the Jews did not constitute a simple religious minority in Europe, differing from Christians merely by virtue of their doctrines, beliefs, or even outward forms of worship. The Jews also maintained that they were "a people apart," chosen by God and bound to His Law, living in exile from their land, and praying for an eventual return to it, where they would reestablish a Jewish kingdom and the Temple cult. Under the terms of the emerging political dispensation, the Jew was promised citizenship and civil rights. But in the bargain, would he be forced to relinquish his religion and law? To become a citizen of the modern state, would the Jew be required to renounce his allegiance to the Torah, the People of Israel, and the hoped-for future Jewish kingdom?

The critics of Jewish "emancipation" did not fail to pick up on the incongruity between the privileges and duties of citizenship and the nature of Judaism.[6] Some considered the Jews an alien presence in their societies, morally delinquent and economically degenerate, undeserving of toleration, and certainly unworthy of full citizenship.[7] In a classic statement during the debate of the French National Assembly, the Bishop of Nancy, Anne-Lois Henry de la Fare, rejected Count Clermont-Tonnerre's support of the Jews, stating:

> It is necessary to grant them protection, security, liberty; but must one admit into the family a tribe that is a stranger to oneself, that constantly turns its eyes toward [another] homeland, that aspires to abandon the land that supports it; a tribe that, to be faithful to its law, must forbid to the individuals who constitute it its entrance into armies, the mechanical and the liberal arts, and into the employ on the civil courts and municipalities; a tribe that, in obeying both its own law and the national law, has 108 valueless days in the year?[8]

According to de la Fare, the Jews were a "tribe" distinct from the people of France; they were not rooted to the land in which they dwelt but instead aspired to return to another; they were faithful to a law that restrained them from serving the needs of the state and integrating effectively into the economic life of the nation. In short, Judaism and the Jewish law rendered the Jews politically and economically unbeneficial, unfit for the manifold privileges of French citizenship.[9]

Aside from the predictable condemnations of the moral and economic vices of the Jews, one can perceive in de la Fare's words a *political* critique of the Jewish religion which had become commonplace during the Enlightenment. Philosophers such as Spinoza, Kant, and Fichte imagined (and disparaged) Judaism as a "political" religion.[10] For Kant, to take an influential example, Judaism was "a collection of mere statutory laws," the constitution of a defunct state, which was solely interested in external actions and the maintenance of temporal well-being.[11] Unlike a *true* religion (as Kant understood it), Judaism did not promote an inner spiritual disposition and the ethical life. Though in many ways Kant's critique reiterated long-standing Christian portrayals of Judaism as being of the body but not of the spirit, such modern views (themselves articulated in a degree of tension with Christianity) accentuated the political nature of Judaism. Judaism, so went this appraisal, was in truth not really a "religion" at all but a kind of political regime, a "theocracy" or "a state with a state," and a rigid anachronism unhappily persisting in the modern world. For Kant, this required (in a singularly unfortunate phrase) "the euthanasia of Judaism."[12] The Jews could be brought and integrated into the modern state only at the expense of their Judaism, if at all.

Critics of Jewish emancipation often charged the Jewish law with promoting social exclusivity and isolationism, and however anti-Jewish their intentions were, their assessment of the social effects of these regulations were not entirely inaccurate. The Jewish law sought to forge "a kingdom of priests," and whatever their individual meanings and intentions, the myriad commandments and prohibitions of the Hebrew Bible, expanded through the interpretations and enactments of the Jewish sages, had the consequence of forming a religious-political society differentiated from the outside "gentile" world. The law established and maintained social distance between Jews and non-Jews. It seemed then that the very possibility and future success of emancipation, the process of social, political, and cultural inclusion, would turn on a rejection of this cardinal aspect of rabbinic Judaism.

This political critique of Judaism provides a useful insight into the development of modern Jewish thought. The collapse of Christendom and the rise of the Enlightenment opened up the space for the social and political integration of the Jews, but it also exposed the theological-political question that Jewish thinkers needed to take into account. Modern Jewish thought was motivated by this new, liberating, and perplexing political and intellectual situation. Those Jews who wished to reap the benefits of an improved social and political status and who also wished to maintain some form of commitment to the ancestral faith would have to argue that Jewish belief and practice were not incompatible with the conditions of modern politics and society. This would entail a reevaluation and a reform of Judaism and the invention of what I describe as a new Jewish "political theology."

In order to accommodate themselves to its new situation, Jewish thinkers struggled to develop a liberal vision of Judaism and, in doing so, transformed its conceptions of law, peoplehood, and messianic hope.

The Jewish law, or *halakhah,* had been the very structure of premodern Judaism, the reference point of Jewish norms and behavior. Once Jewish belief and practice were detached from the practice of *halakhah* and conceptions of peoplehood, *theology* became more significant to Jewish self-understanding than it had been in previous generations. And I will argue that this theology had important political implications.

Old and New Jewish Political Theology

From the destruction of Jerusalem in the first century up until the mid-eighteenth century, the Jewish people practiced what might be called a *"galut* politics"—a politics of exile—bounded by the power of rabbinic law and sustained by messianic hope.[13] Traditionally, the Jews had considered themselves a "covenantal nation," bound together and to their God by the Torah given to Moses at Mt. Sinai. The early generations of Jewish sages recognized that the Roman occupation of the Land of Israel and the destruction of Jerusalem and the Temple meant that the Jews no longer persisted in their "normal" state. The dominant political strategy of the Jewish people was accommodation with the prevailing powers,[14] attempting to carve out of the exile a significant measure of self-administration over their own affairs.[15]

The memory of a sovereign Israelite kingdom and the Temple ritual persisted in liturgy and lore, and fastened to the messianic hope for a future redemption. Until that time, however, the Jews believed that they were not to be sovereign in the Land of Israel, possess an independent state, or rebuild the Temple. The rabbinic understanding of the Torah, of life lived in accordance with the dictates of divine law, arranged the foundation of the Jewish community and permitted the continuation and development of Judaism in the absence of sovereignty or even territorial continuity. In this conception, it was the Law of the Torah itself that had fashioned Israel. As the ninth-century theologian Saadia Gaon declared, "Our nation of the children of Israel is a nation only by virtue of its laws."[16] The law and the community were inexorably interconnected; the entire life of the Jew was subject to "the yoke of the Torah," to be lived within the "four cubits of the *halakhah.*"[17] Throughout the lands of their dispersion, the Torah functioned, in Heine's memorable phrase, as a "portable homeland," the enduring constitution of the Jewish people in exile.

One might say that this *galut* politics was not so much theorized as it was experienced and encoded in Jewish law: in legal writings such as rabbinic responsa to particular *halakhic* queries (*teshuva*) and codes, as well as occasional communal enactments (*takkanot*) of the community (*kehillah*).[18] Despite the fact that the Hebrew Bible is in many respects a meditation on political life, one finds very little sustained theoretical thinking on the problems of politics or systematic analysis of political questions in Jewish sources. Such analysis, when it exists, is occasional and brief. Most discussions of political topics in the *teshuva* literature and the promulgation of new ordinances dealt with practical matters of *halakhah*, which, while having ramifications for the structure and behavior of the Jewish communities, did not address the theoretical issues of political life as such.

In the Middle Ages, a political discourse of Judaism emerged, articulated by such thinkers as Saadia Gaon, Judah Halevi, Joseph Albo, and, most significantly, by the twelfth-century philosopher and legal codifier Moses Maimonides. Influenced by the Arabic rediscovery of Aristotle and the elucidation of Platonic political theory by such philosophers as al-Farabi, Maimonides furnished the most sustained reflection on politics in medieval Judaism. In his *Guide for the Perplexed*, Maimonides depicted the Torah as the constitution of the ideal city and Moses as its prophet-legislator. His monumental codification of rabbinic law, *Mishneh Torah*, included *The Book on Kings and their Wars*, a treatise on the nature and extent of Jewish kingship, and on the expected activities of the messianic king.[19] There is also material of interest in the biblical commentaries of Don Isaac Abravanel and the Maharal of Prague. For the most part, however, the history of Judaism lacks the kind of ongoing theological-political debate that is characteristic of Western Christianity. (The absence of such an overt literary tradition regarding politics can perhaps be partly attributed to the fact that the Jews lacked sovereign political power, and the problems associated with it, but also to the fact that, unlike Christianity, Judaism did not make a distinction between the realm of politics and earthly life and the realm of religion and faith. Jewish thinkers therefore did not need to engage with the theoretical problem of the relationship between the *sacerdotium* and the *regnum*.)

By providing theological and legal legitimation for the contemporary political situation, by possessing a way of life shaped by the divine law and imagining a future redemption which would include the restoration of a Jewish kingdom in the Land of Israel, the political theology of the exile helped to shape and maintain the coherence and distinctiveness of Jewish communities throughout centuries of exile, insecurity, and intermittent persecution. The Jewish people continued to live by their Torah, negotiated the shifting social, political, and religious boundaries with the non-Jews, and waited—mostly patiently, occasionally not—for the eventual arrival of the Messiah. But with the dawn of modernity, the first rays of a new political dispensation began to emerge. It would cast the Jews again into a theological-political crisis, one as radical and as transforming as the one faced by the Jews centuries earlier after the destruction of Jerusalem.

With the transformation of the conditions of the exile of western and central European Jewry in the mid-eighteenth century, the unity of political, religious, and national elements that had characterized this traditional Jewish existence began to unravel. A number of factors contributed to this process. The rise of the absolute state, the centralization of authority, and the bureaucratization of political life within a given territory brought about the weakening of the medieval corporations, of which the Jewish *kehillah* was but one example. As the state expanded, it encroached upon the religious affairs of the Jewish community in such matters as the training and hiring of rabbis, the exercise of the ban of excommunication, educational curricula, adjudication of internal affairs of the community, and even criminal acts committed by one Jew upon another. The *kehillah* was also beset by internal pressures—the deterioration of rabbinic authority (due to ongoing internecine conflicts in the wake of the Sabbatean debacle, an ascending and socially ambitious urban middle class, and the emergence of a secularly educated intelligentsia) intensified the crisis. In such new circumstances, the long-established political theology of *galut* became increasingly difficult to maintain. In short, as Alan Mittleman has put it, "Enlightenment, liberal notions of religion as the personal creed of individuals began to overcome inherited ideas of Judaism as the covenantal political-juridical order of a people."[20]

What were the alternatives for Judaism, then, as Jews understood them? There remained, or so it seemed, the traditional options: a stubborn clinging to the old ways, through a withdrawal into the tradition and the raising of new and higher fences around the Torah;[21] or assimilation by means of conversion to Christianity, the "entry ticket" to European civilization as Heinrich Heine famously put it. Both these options, however, avoided the hard question: the first by denying that anything had substantially changed, aside from the urgency of the problem, and the second by attempting to evade the issue altogether by leaving the fold. (The option of an ever-more trenchant traditionalism was made more difficult by the expansion of the state's interest; Jewish authorities would have to adapt to the ever-dwindling space granted by the state. The option of conversion had a high probability of failure; the ticket might not be validated, as Heine himself had bitterly experienced.[22]) Spinoza, however, had hinted at another option in his *Theological-Political Treatise*: the Jews might possibly be "chosen anew," that is, that they might find it possible to empower themselves politically and reestablish a state. This deceivingly "messianic" suggestion was not directed by traditional notions of Jewish redemption or by any belief in supernatural intervention. In Spinoza's view, the Jews would have to cultivate the virtues necessary to build a state, a task which Spinoza thought possible, given the volatile nature of human affairs, but unlikely, given the stubborn attachment of the Jews to their religion, which had rendered them "effeminate" and incapable of sober and dedicated political action.[23] As Judaism was merely the atavistic theological vestige of a defunct political entity, Spinoza did not attribute any value to its continuation in exile. Judaism as a legal constitution would have no place in the modern world, and a Judaism without its law was not Judaism at all.[24]

The Jewish theological discourse that emerged during the late eighteenth century and flourished in the nineteenth sought an alternative route, to forge a novel path between a (now defensive) traditionalism and an assimilationism that entailed the wholesale surrender of Jewish religious identity. The aspiration of this discourse was to acculturate into the general society while retaining some form of Jewish religious particularity, thus demonstrating that the Jews could successfully integrate into modern Europe without relinquishing their fundamental religious spirit.[25] It would provide a foundation for Jews who had already abandoned traditional practice and ease the transition of those still adhering to the old ways.[26] According to this view, Judaism and modern politics were not incompatible; the conflict between Jewish commitment and modern politics did not, in fact, exist.

As we shall see in the next section, these new Jewish theologians challenged the Enlightenment's political critique of Judaism by maintaining that their religion did not necessitate embodiment in an independent religious corporation or state governed by revealed law. Such a political structure had indeed been necessary to protect Judaism during difficult times, they admitted, but now that the gentile nations were coming to maturity, at last recognizing the Jews as fellow men and allowing them to participate as equal citizens in the body politic, Judaism could be purified, and the shell of law, superstition, and national identity that had built up around the ancient religious teaching could be scraped away. Liberated from a hostile environment and freed from medieval obscurantism, the true core of faith could now be recovered and reaffirmed. Judaism would emerge as a *Konfession*, proclaiming its idea of the one true God, the human being's ethical responsibility, and the prophetic appeal for the construction of a truly just social order.

The Problem of the Law and the Emergence of a New Political Theology

Often regarded as the first work of modern Jewish philosophy, Moses Mendelssohn's treatise *Jerusalem: or, On Religious Power and Judaism* (1783) is, fundamentally, an attempt to negotiate this theological-political problem and put Judaism on new footing.[27] Mendelssohn did so by articulating a liberal political theory and depicting a Judaism that would, without difficulty, find its place in the modern enlightened state. Mendelssohn's "Judaism" was fundamentally a religion of law, but of a law regarded as a form of pedagogy, inculcating correct religious ideas fully in accord with the doctrines of "rational" religion and cultivating good citizens.

Mendelssohn's effort to forge a synthesis between Judaism and philosophy subordinated Judaism's religious claims to those of the Enlightenment idea of natural religion and political aspirations to the state. "We have no doctrines that are contrary to reason," Mendelssohn wrote to his friend Elkan Herz. "We added nothing to natural religion save commandments and statutes." But for Mendelssohn, Judaism was endowed with an additional quality: by commanding actions and not beliefs, and by not sanctioning metaphysical beliefs distinct from the truths of natural religion (which are knowable by the light of reason), Judaism was the most reasonable of religions. When made aware of this conception of their faith, the Jews would develop into model citizens, capable of being integrated into the modern enlightened society, and unencumbered by any of the intellectual difficulties that arise from allegiance to irrational Christian dogmas. "The fundamental tenets of our religion rest on the foundation of reason. They are in consonance with the results of free inquiry, without any conflict or contradiction," he concluded.[28]

Though it retained a historical memory of the union of religion and politics in the Mosaic constitution, Judaism did not promote theocracy as a contemporary political option. Mendelssohn maintained that Judaism shared a set of common aims with the modern state, but so did all positive religions. If there is a political distinctiveness to modern Judaism, it did not relate to the memory of the original Mosaic constitution or the history of the Israelite state. Rather, it was the fact that Jewish law is particularly adept at fostering sociability and forging a good citizenry. In such a way, Judaism was envisioned to reinforce the moral foundations of the modern state and to aid its pedagogic goals.

In *Jerusalem,* we thus see the emergence of a new approach to Judaism's modern theological-political problem. Mendelssohn did not advocate a simple separation of spheres of politics and religion. He suggested, rather, that Judaism could work together with the state to sustain and enhance social life. He believed he had found a solution to the theological-political critique of Judaism by providing a reinterpretation of the meaning of Jewish law. In a sense, Mendelssohn's solution to the problem was to deny it. As a halakhically observant Jew, Mendelssohn could not conceive the possibility of a Judaism that was not centered in the law. His solution was to reduce Judaism to its ceremonial law and the historical beliefs that are bound up with it. In such a way, Judaism could be found compatible with both his rational philosophy and enlightened politics. By conveying the eternal truths of natural religion, reinforcing their apprehension and sociability through the performance of the *mitzvot,* and not requiring beliefs other than those disclosed by natural reason, Judaism would be seen as the modern religion par excellence.

Confident in the Enlightenment conception of natural religion, Mendelssohn argued that Judaism could be maintained through an ongoing commitment to the ceremonial law. But his contemporaries and disciples, men such as David Friedlaender (1750–1834) and Lazarus Ben David (1762–1832), understood that by providing an apologia for the law, Mendelssohn had, in effect, merely avoided the problem that confronted modern Jews. The real issue, they recognized, was not that the Jewish law had once been political law, which might interfere with the law of the modern state. Rather, the problem was the centrality of the Jewish law to Judaism itself. Mendelssohn could not conceive of a Judaism apart from the law; for him, Judaism's religious meaning was depleted in the tenets of natural religion, which all positive religions shared. Mendelssohn's radicalism on this point entailed that only the law remained as the location of Jewish particularity. He saw no problem with observant Jews integrating culturally and politically, for the Jewish law sufficiently served the moral and intellectual cultivation of the Jews, inculcating the truths of natural religion and forming good citizens. For others, however, the law seemed more a burden than a yoke; it was considered problematic for philosophical and social reasons, and appeared as an obstacle to modernization and integration and to enlightened religious attitudes and behavior.

Shortly after the publication of *Jerusalem,* a Berlin bookseller named Saul Ascher (1767–1822) published a treatise that argued the necessary modern reformation of Judaism would entail something much more radical that Mendelssohn had offered—a turn from law to theology. Ascher's provocatively titled book, *Leviathan, oder über Religion in Rücksicht des Judenthums* (1792), provides a significant example of the rejection of Mendelssohn's approach and the first shift toward basing a reform of Judaism on theology—that is, on the formulation and articulation of religious ideas.[29] Ascher criticized Mendelssohn's attempt to defend Judaism and to shape a Jewish reform by means of the law, placing Mendelssohn within a chain of thinkers who had misrepresented the essence of Judaism for polemical purposes. Maimonides had tried to adapt Judaism to Aristotelian philosophy; Spinoza, on the other hand, had attempted to sever faith from reason in order to undermine all revealed religion. In doing so, Spinoza had represented Judaism as "only a Religion for a certain constituted society," that is, it served as a state, which was the natural though unfortunate consequence of representing Judaism in "orthodox form."[30] From this discussion of Spinoza, Ascher glided into his critique of Mendelssohn, whose conception of Judaism he suggested was politically motivated. Mendelssohn had claimed that the purpose of the law was to serve as a "symbol" in order to further the apprehension of universal truths. Ascher held that this reasoning was unsatisfactory. Many things can serve as symbols of truths, not only law, and furthermore, "eternal truths" do not require any external symbols for their apprehension, as they are imprinted on the minds of all men. So Ascher returned to what Mendelssohn admitted was the original purpose of the law, the founding of a theocratic state:

If the Law has a purpose, it is completely self-evident that when the purpose becomes obsolete the Law is rendered superfluous. If the purpose of the Law in Judaism, as might be assumed from Mendelssohn, is to establish a Mosaic constitution [*mosaische Verfassung*], Judaism must cease the moment that this constitution no longer exists. If the intention of the Law, however, is to bring men to faith and to knowledge of historical and religious or eternal truths, then the Law is only a method to guide men upon a certain path. If they are already walking upon this path, then it

undoubtedly follows that they can forgo this method, and nevertheless their descendants will remain on the same path.[31]

Ascher argued that Mendelssohn's conclusion—that the Jews were obliged
to adhere to the law until it is rescinded by a voice from heaven—did not
follow from his reasoning. Mendelssohn had put forward a conception of
Judaism as law divorced from religious belief. In doing so, he had failed to
distinguish between a particular constitution and the essence of Judaism
itself, that is, its essence as a *religion*. Ascher based this critique on a distinction between "regulative" and "constitutive" religion. The former is
the essence of a religion, the latter the external forms it takes at any point
in its history. For Ascher, this essence was to be found in the religious
doctrines of Judaism. The purpose of religion, Ascher asserted, still speaking in the language of the Enlightenment, is to make people happy and
autonomous and to help them establish a just society [*Gesellschaft*]. The
law was given at a particular time and place as a means to attain this end.
It was not the essence of the religion itself. The intention of God was not
to make the Jews subservient to the law but to preserve the autonomy
of the will. "It was the highest goal of the Almighty to create of the Jews
a social body [*gesellschaftlichen Körper*]: he could unite them through the
Faith, and through it preserve their autonomy."[32]

Put another way, the *constitution* of a religion is not identical to its
essence. The constitution is merely the tool by which the religion works to
achieve its goal: for people to become happy, autonomous citizens. The
Jewish law, then, was merely a means to an end, a "method" by which the
higher purpose of religion could be achieved. Insofar as it was a method,
it was contingent, suited to a particular time and place; in other circumstances, other methods would be just as or more suitable. In the present
moment, however, the law no longer served to further faith, but rather
hindered it. Because the law is mistakenly thought of as the essence of
Judaism, when, in fact, it is only a particular constitution, its transgres-
sion is misunderstood as "an absolute abandonment of Judaism," the
process of which "threatens us with a total disintegration of our faith."[33]
Consequently, the Jews are faced with a twofold danger: externally, a critique of Judaism that resists emancipation, and internally, the danger of
disintegration of Judaism due to a misconceiving of its essence.

Why did we not understand the intention of the Almighty? Why?
Because we considered the [legal] constitution [*Constitution*] of our

faith [*Religion*] to be its essence: because by keeping the Law we neglected the entire form of our faith [*Glaubens*] [and therefore maintained the law]; because those who received the constitution of our faith from the Eternal were not capable of forming true faith and of establishing its true purpose.[34]

If faith was strong, Ascher contended, there would be no need for "symbols" such as the Mosaic law to support it. The solution to the question of Judaism is a reformation or purification [*Läuterung*] of the tradition, which will "do away with the present constitution of Judaism [*die jetzige Constitution of des Judentums aufheben*]," and the establishment of a new constitution "which will maintain in us the faith of our fathers, teach us the true essence of Judaism [*das eigenliche Weßen des Judenthums*], present in a vital way its objectives and guide us in the path upon which we can, at the same time, be good men and good citizens."[35] Such a reform would not be a rebellion against Judaism but the reassertion of its true meaning. The Jews are beholden to the enduring faith of their fathers, not to their ancient laws: "We are united among ourselves only in faith, but with all men in law."[36]

The third part of Ascher's treatise outlined this program of reformation. The old constitution of the Mosaic law would need to be replaced by a new one appropriate for the times. In the closing pages, he presented his "*Organon*" of this new constitution. Alluding to Maimonides thirteen principles of faith, Ascher now produced fourteen principles, which contained not only theological and historical claims, such as the uniqueness of God, prophecy, providence, and the giving of laws, but also the idea of the Messiah, and the obligation to perform the rite of circumcision and to celebrate the Sabbath and festival days. The law would not be completely abandoned but would be altered to suit the needs of the present. Such a reformation, thought Ascher, would bring about the reconciliation of the Jews with their neighbors and with the times:

> Our religion is for all people, for all time. Show that your religion is able to make men and by it you can build citizens, only the constitution of the religion must be reformed [*reformirt*], the religion itself cannot be lost. If we are steadfast, we will become a people worthy of divinity in all areas of life [*ein der Gottheit würdiges Volk unter allen Zonen*].[37]

Though Ascher is often regarded as a forerunner of liberal Judaism, during his lifetime, his plea to change the focus of Judaism from law to doctrine fell upon deaf ears. Rather than proclaiming a new theology, the Jewish *Maskilim* (Enlighteners) of the late eighteenth century focused instead on instituting a number of educational and cultural reforms to improve the condition of the Jews. So far as Jewish religious behavior was concerned, these early proponents of Jewish reform advocated a number of mostly aesthetic changes in synagogue worship (e.g., a stress on decorum, introduction of the German sermon intended to build up religious sentiment to replace the traditional homily [*drasha*],[38] slight modifications in the liturgy, organ music). As the historian Amos Funkenstein has observed, "Synagogal reform was a political act."[39] Such reform strove not only to demonstrate that the Jews were moderns but also to downplay problematic aspects of the tradition such as national messianic hope. Up through the middle of the nineteenth century, such reforms were driven by the laity and were for the most part resisted by the more conservative rabbinical establishment. But no coherent ideology of reform was advanced or widely accepted.

Yet by the mid-1830s, an ambitious reform movement began to emerge as a leading force in German Jewry.[40] The course of religious reform received guidance and depth by virtue of a university-trained rabbinate and a fresh historical consciousness.[41] In contrast to contemporary lay reformers, who tended toward religious radicalism, sometimes indiscriminately severing their ties to tradition and inventing new liturgies and ceremonies out of whole cloth, this new rabbinate endeavored to construct a coherent religious ideology out of the sources of the tradition, to provide a program for coherent and thoughtful reform to buttress religious practice and to maintain a unified Jewish community. Such a theological reform of Judaism was deemed necessary for the persistence of the religion and for the coherence of the Jews as a religious community after the breakdown of the *kehillah* as a political structure and the slackening of *halakhic* observance that followed. In order for Judaism to survive in the modern world, Jews needed to find a way to replace what had already been lost and what was becoming irrelevant or falling into disuse. What was required, these reformers believed, was a "religious principle" strong enough to compensate for the deterioration of communal authority and *halakhah*, dynamic enough to respond to mounting religious indifference, and savvy enough to facilitate acculturation.[42] As the historian Uriel Tal described the situation of these reformers, "The dilemma was formulated to state that while Judaism was a group identified by its religion only and its values were universal, at the same time those universal values were to identify the Jews as a peculiar group."[43]

By the mid-nineteenth century Ascher's prophecy proved true, as this generation of liberal rabbis began to articulate the *idea* of Judaism. This generation of Jewish thinkers did not develop a liberal political theory as Mendelssohn did in *Jerusalem*. For the most part, they took the form and function of the modern state and its political values for granted. Their thinking was shaped by the goal of emancipation, which implied acceptance of the political order which sponsored emancipation and into which the Jews would be integrated. They therefore did not question whether Judaism itself endorsed an alternative model of political organization. If the essence of Judaism was not found to be a particular political dispensation (such as the Mosaic theocracy, Davidic kingship, or rabbinic rule), Jewish commitment could coexist within a tolerant, constitutional state. And with the transfiguration of the messianic idea to the "mission of Israel," the reformers hoped to demonstrate the ongoing significance of Judaism, not only for the Jews but for the larger society as well. By understanding the essence of Judaism as an insight into the nature of God and the ramifications of this insight for human ethical life, the idea of revelation as establishing a particular political arrangement was abandoned. The modern political meaning of Judaism was based not on any direct claim to the state or to the institution of law, but on the indirect influence of the Jewish ethical subject.

The "Idea" of Judaism as Political Theology

Liberal Jewish theology and its program of practical reform therefore came to be grounded in the "recognition" of the *essence of Judaism*. This was a theological-ethical idea that the theologians discovered in the pronouncements of the biblical prophets of the transcendent God who demands man's moral responsibility. This idea was articulated as early as the 1820s, and it became and remained the leading idea of Jewish theology for nearly a hundred years.[44] The construction of such a modern liberal Judaism entailed the articulation of a new Jewish narrative, a "history" of Judaism for contemporary purposes or a "usable past." It would be orchestrated around the theological idea of Judaism—how it emerged, developed, and was preserved—and the affirmation of its contemporary and enduring meaning. By stressing the religious beliefs which form and stimulate ethical life (rather than the comprehensive legal and ritual praxis of premodern Judaism), the Jewish reformers signaled their political accommodation with the emerging state and their belief that Judaism had a role to play within it.

This goal of asserting the idea of Judaism marked a much deeper urge to reform than the sundry earlier attempts at ritual or aesthetic changes. In former times, such a clarification was unnecessary; Judaism entailed a life lived according to the *halakhah*. As Max Wiener argued in his seminal study of nineteenth-century Jewish thought, having been removed from the center of Jewish life, the *halakhah* needed to be replaced by another religious "life-form."[45] Early in his career, Abraham Geiger—historian, rabbi, theologian, and one of the central figures of the burgeoning liberal movement in the 1830s—declared:

> The Jew must always have something peculiarly Jewish about him since only his love for Judaism will keep him from becoming part of the multitude. It is precisely because he deviates from the majority that he must find a more solid basis for his faith which is his conviction.[46]

By successfully expressing its religious idea, Geiger believed that modern Judaism could be set on a firm theoretical foundation. Only in this manner could the future of Judaism as a religion and of the Jews as a distinct religious community be assured. As the historian Jacob Katz described this process:

> The reform movement had a double purpose. It sought a legitimate way to ease the yoke of the law for the modern Jew so that he could pursue his career, achieve his economic aims, and make his way into non-Jewish society. This was, so to speak, the practical aspect of reform. Not less important was its theoretical objective: to evolve a comprehensive philosophy of Judaism that would be in harmony with the status of the modern Jew as a citizen of the non-Jewish state and a member of non-Jewish society. This could only be effected by a thorough sifting of traditional tenets, omitting parts that seemed irreconcilable with the new position of the Jews, and introducing, or at least reemphasizing, tenets that seemed to be appropriate to the new situation.[47]

It is in this creative act of developing Judaism's peculiar theological idea that we can locate the emergence of a new *political* theology. By defining the essence of Judaism as a religious idea (distinct from the law), the reformers developed a religious strategy that would support and complement the social and political goals of emancipation.

The liberal Jewish theologians located the essence of Judaism in the concept of "ethical monotheism," that is, the notion of God and man's moral responsibility proclaimed by the prophetic voice.[48] If this essence or idea of "Judaism" could be understood as distinct from Judaism's various contingent *forms,* a coherent and effective policy of reform could emerge and flourish. Practices and beliefs such as those relating to national particularity and messianic hopes seemed to be at odds with the project of integration into the modern state and society. To resolve these issues, a good number of traditional views were reinterpreted or simply abolished. Katz has stressed how the Jewish theologians attempted "to vindicate this definition in the light of Jewish tradition," a tradition whose contents often resisted the theologian's conceptualizations. This was, as he put it, a "revolutionary trend," one that "defied three thousand years of history and tradition."[49]

The centrality and theoretical reliance on the articulation of beliefs as the center of Jewish life was a radical development, and it was modeled on Christian—in particular, on liberal Protestant—theological discourse. The hallmarks of this movement offered vital resources for the new idea of Judaism. First, liberal theology represented a "turn to the subject" in thinking on religion. The object of theological analysis is not God as such but man as a believing creature, his needs, and his feelings. Liberal theology was essentially humanistic in perspective and intent, and was less a discourse on divine subjects than a "religious anthropology." Second, liberal theology depended upon modern concepts and intellectual methods, incorporating into its discourse the enlightenment critique of religion, especially the critique of revelation, prophecy, and miracles. For example, when the issue of revelation is considered, it is done so through an analysis of the human subject, e.g., as the disclosure of moral reason, or the feeling of dependence. That is, the encounter with "transcendence" occurs only to human beings enmeshed in their own epistemic and historical categories. Third, liberal theologians tended to see religion as one of many aspects of human culture. Nonetheless, religion is not kept isolated from other human endeavors, but is a privileged dimension of human life and culture.

Though it consigned religion to a domain separate from political, economic, and legal spheres, liberal theology maintained religion as the ground of ethical life and therefore of social and political well-being. This

is where liberal theology developed its political significance. By forming
the ethical subject, liberal religion indirectly guaranteed the just political
order, which is seen as a constitutional state. Consequently, religion is
not a problem for the state, nor is the state a problem for religion. Liberal
religion did not claim the political sphere as its own domain; it did not
enunciate a political system, but rather asserted that the values inculcated
by religion and the personality which it develops are necessary for the
healthy functioning of social and political relations. Though it stood in
opposition to any direct translation of theology into politics, such as the
ongoing attempt to establish a "Christian" state or a Catholic aspiration of
papal domination, liberal theology nevertheless maintained that religion
is necessary for the social order, insofar as it built up the moral character
of the subject. In this way, religion functions as the protector and preserver
of culture, a defense against the centrifugal forces of modern life, moral
relativism, and cultural pessimism. Society and state ultimately rest on
"religious" foundations. While religion and politics are conceptually and
structurally discrete principles, and while church and state are distinct
institutions, the task of religion is to cultivate moral subjects that operate
in all realms of culture and transform the state from within into a moral
entity. It is a theology that made its peace with modernity and its politics
by taking up its appropriate station in the modern world.

The disclosure of Judaism as such a theological idea was already well
underway in the Jewish philosophical systems developed by Solomon
Formstecher and Samuel Hirsch in the early 1840s, albeit expounded
in the difficult idiom of speculative idealism, while eschewing the pan-
theistic aspects of this tradition in lieu of a strict transcendent monotheism.[50] In these dense volumes, Judaism was declared the primary form
of religion. In opposition to paganism and pantheism, Judaism stressed
the supremacy of spirit over nature, ethics over aesthetics, and freedom
over necessity. Revelation was understood as knowledge of God as spirit,
a knowledge realized through ethical activity in the world. Against Hegel,
who argued that Judaism had been sublimated by Christianity, these Jewish
idealists maintained that Judaism was not relegated to a finite moment in
the march of Spirit in history.[51] Judaism's essence was enduring, though
its outward forms (such as the state, priesthood, law, nationality, and so
forth) had been outgrown and overcome.

Composed in a highly abstract philosophical idiom, Hirsch's and
Formstecher's texts found few readers. But a more popular discourse soon
emerged. In a series of lectures entitled *Die Entwickelung der religiösen Idee*

im Judenthume, Christenthume und Islam, Ludwig Philippson (1811–1889), the founder and editor of the *Allgemeine Zeitung des Judentums*,[52] set forth his theory of the social teachings of Judaism, the foundation of which he called "Mosaism" [*Mosaismus*].[53] In these lectures, published in 1847, Philippson argued that human history was the struggle between two ideas: the "religious" idea and the "human" idea, or "heathenism." The human idea developed from man's fundamental nature—the human being is an egoist and is conscious of the world being external to him, and senses the power of external reality, which sometimes satisfies him and sometimes impedes his desires. The human being attributes this reality a force, which Philippson calls *Gottheit*. Nature therefore appears antagonistic to man and his desires, and needs to be appeased or subdued. "Heathenism," then, is essentially the conception of God that emerges from the human being's innate egoism and subjectivity, and his struggle against the external world. The social implication of this worldview is domination; the separation of humanity into castes, slavery, and domination.

Against this all-too-human idea, Philippson pitted the "religious idea." Whereas the human idea emerged subjectively with the opposition of nature and created gods, the religious idea, or "Mosaism," begins with God and the idea of unity. The doctrines of Mosaism are that God is absolute Being; the world is His creation; God is transcendent; God's absolute Being is unity; and the world is a unity, in which everything is in harmony, is necessary and good.[54] The human being is created with a dual nature—a union of body and spirit [*Leib und Seele*], and related to God through spirit. This teaching is the meaning of the Bible's claim that the human being is created in God's image. On account of his spirit, the human being has freedom, self-determination, and power over his surrounding world. The purpose of his life is to become always closer to this divine image, to dominate the egoism of one's bodily nature, "to command and to regulate it, and to resolve it into the universal by the practice of love and justice."[55] Because of this duality, an individual can sin by falling prey to his innate egoism, but Mosaism does not posit that the human being is sinful by his very nature, a conception that would undermine his ethical freedom.

Mosaism proclaimed a unique "social morality" [*sittlich-gesellschaftliche Inhalt*]. It did not separate religion from social life, but rather conceived of the unity of social life and religion. The individual was charged with the sanctification [*Heiligung*] of his practical and spiritual life, the life of devotion *in the world*, not self-annihilation, and was commanded to love his neighbor, to be just and compassionate. By means of this love, Phillipson alleged, Mosaism established a "civil society" [*bürgerliche Gesellschaft*], the general principles of which are the existence of one God, the creation of human being in His image, the commandment for holiness and the love of the neighbor. This society "establishe[d] complete equality among all members of the body-politic."[56] In such a society there was no distinction with regard to birth, occupation, or class. In ancient Israel, such equality was granted to all who lived in the land, Israelite and non-Israelite alike. (Philippson admits that there was a hereditary priesthood in Israel, but he argued that it had no real political power.) Mosaism sought to diminish the institution of slavery; conceiving the land as owned by God, it strove to produce an equality of property. It also forbade usury, and regulated charity and benevolence. In short, Mosaism "originate[d] the principles of a truly religious civil society" [*einer wahrhaft religiösen bürgerlichen Gesellschaft*].[57] All of human life is to be made holy.

The political constitution of ancient Israel, however, was established for its particular time and place. Given its fundamental standpoint of freedom, Mosaism did not require incarnation in any particular political structure. Philippson distinguished between "civil society" (shaped by the morals previously detailed) and the "constitution" of a state. The civil society is its essence, the state only the form "which must vary, not only according to the requirements of different nations, but according to the varying exigencies of different ages, in the existence of one and the same nation."[58] So the particular type of political structure is relative to the temporal needs of the society. Nevertheless, citing biblical proof-texts, Philippson suggested that the principles of Mosaism tend toward the promotion of a republican form of government, where leadership is invested in a judge, army commander, or high priest (Deut. 17:9), though it also allows for the possibility of a monarchical constitution (Deut. 17:14–15).[59]

Philippson's subsequent lectures described, in classic Hegelian fashion, the fate of this religious idea in history, in Judaism as well as in its daughter religions: Christianity and Islam. Having arisen within a heathen milieu, Mosaism had to struggle to find acceptance among the Israelites. Time and again, the Israelites abandoned the teachings of Mosaism and relapsed into heathenism. The second phase of Judaism, "Prophetism," arose to restore the idea of Mosaism to the people, but it did so in a one-sided fashion: it was able to rescue the idea but only at the expense of a form of life. "Talmudism," the third phase of Judaism, accomplished the victory of the form of life (in the shape of the Jewish ceremonial law) but only at the cost of the living idea. With the dispersion of the Jewish people, the power of the idea was suppressed by a legalism that ended up separating the Jew from his neighbors. In the meantime, the religious idea spread outward to the non-Jewish peoples of the world, through the historical mediators of Christianity and Islam. But while they were based in the idea of Mosaism, these two religions were also unable to realize the idea adequately. Both were bound to rigid dogmatism: Christianity suffered under the domination of the Church, Islam under hierarchical government.

All this was to change in the modern era, Philippson alleged. In Europe, the medieval feudal order was overcome by absolutism, which itself was now coming under assault by constitutionalism. In the realm of religion, the dogmatism of the Church had been challenged, first by the Reformation, but later and more importantly by the Enlightenment. As Christianity purified itself of its dogmas, it looked more and more to its primitive form, which brought it closer to its Jewish origins. Nonetheless, the threat of heathenism still survived in the form of modern pantheism, which Philippson claimed reduced social ideals to a basis in egoism.[60]

The situation of Judaism in the modern world was different; its struggle was not over the reign of dogma, but over the nature of observance to the rabbinic ceremonial law. The transformation of European politics, which ended the long isolation of the Jews, would bring them into the society as citizens. This transformation would necessitate the eradication of much of the ceremonial law that, Philippson claimed, had been formed for the sake of maintaining the Jews' social isolation. However, the rejection of the ceremonial law would not entail a rejection of the religious idea of Judaism: "The task of Judaism is, as it ever has been, to preserve the Religious Idea perfect and entire."[61] Judaism would be the bearer of the religious idea into the modern age: "The world will arrive, not at the specific Judaism of the Jews as it has been; but at the Religious Idea such as Judaism though all its phases has ever borne within itself unchanged, unpolluted; though brought into the world of man by Christianity and Moslemism, in an imperfect form."[62]

It is the providential design that the idea of Mosaism will enter into society's laws and institutions to form the basis of the just society, conquering the heathenism that always breeds slavery and domination. (It is not clear from Philippson's presentation exactly how the religious idea would actually work to shape these social and political structures.) It is the particular mission of Judaism, which articulates the religious idea in its purest form, to help humanity toward this messianic destiny: "to establish the unity of the Idea and Life, and in that very unity to prepare and produce the unity of the whole race of man."[63] Judaism, as the original and enduring champion of the religious idea, is, accordingly, a force in the modern world for freedom, equality, and truth.

Abraham Geiger's series of lectures, entitled *Das Judenthum und seine Geschichte,* developed from many years of specialized research, provides us with a paradigmatic example of mature liberal Jewish theology.[64] "True religion," Geiger claimed, is not to be understood as a system of metaphysical claims, but rather as the disclosure of the dual nature of man, his greatness, freedom, rational comprehension, and (here echoing Schleiermacher) his sense of dependence, finitude and limitation, his grasping for the good. In Judaism, man is disclosed as "a finite, limited, dependent being," but a being also aware of his lofty position in creation, for he is in the image and likeness of God, in the spiritual sense."[65] The idea of Judaism consequently insists upon human reason and agency, responsibility, and self-ennobling power grounded in the belief of the one unique God who exercises moral sovereignty over the world. Judaism's idea of the *love of God*—an idea of which paganism was altogether ignorant—works to turn human beings toward one another. The great commandment to love one's neighbor "runs through the whole law, whose every provision breathes love."[66] This social love is not limited to the group; the Jewish prophetic vision has a clear universalist drive—the hope for and vision of an enlightened humanity. The idea of Judaism is thus not solely for the sake of the Jews but is also directed outward to the whole world. Moreover, in contrast to religions of otherworldly or asocial piety, "energetic endeavor in the world, recognition of humanity, is the basis of Judaism."[67]

In his discussion of the concept of revelation, Geiger turned to an analysis of the classical Hebrew prophets, "the organs of that religious idea."[68] Revelation as the consciousness of the God-idea and its ethical implications was "manifested in the whole nation."[69] Here, Geiger radically democratized the idea of prophecy—while the prophets were exemplary for their powerful literary expression, the consciousness of the God-idea arose within the "religious genius" of the Jewish people as a whole. This genius, Geiger tells us, was an

aboriginal power [*ursprüngliche Kraft*] that illuminated its eyes so that they could see deeper into the higher life of the spirit, could feel more deeply and recognize more vividly the close relation between the spirit of man [*Menschengeist*] and the Supreme Spirit [*Allgeist*], that they could more distinctly and clearly behold the real nature of the Moral in man [*die tiefere Natur des Sittlichen im Menschen*], and then present to the world the result of that inborn knowledge.[70]

Yet only the nation of Israel had been endowed with this religious trait. The tension between the particularity of the Jews regarding revelation and the universal implications of the Jewish idea is left unanalyzed; Geiger provides no account of why Israel was chosen, how Israel was able to attain this prophetic consciousness. In fact, even as it occurs within the history of a nation, Geiger pulls the concept of revelation out of history. The prophetic insight into the nature of God and ethical implications "has had its history and has it yet farther on, but it is independent according to its inmost essence, always accepted for its development only what was homogeneous to that essence and what could not grow into it as foreign substance, it owes at most the stimulation to more growth to external impulses."[71] By placing this religious idea, rather than the revelation of the commandments, at the center of Judaism, Geiger undermined the authority of the legal tradition at its very foundation. The essence of Judaism is the religious idea and its ethical implications, not its *halakhic* structure.

Geiger admitted that the Jewish people began their history as a nation, for in the ancient world there was a compelling need for Jews to understand themselves in national terms. Since the religious idea was novel, it relied on protective coverings to guard it from the dangers and "seductive influences" of the pagan world, and to permit it to achieve clarity and power.[72] But the idea itself was the true bond of the people; what Geiger regarded as "hostile nationality and national pride" must be understood as merely a temporary means to protect an enduring idea in its infancy and young life.[73]

The period of Jewish statehood was therefore only an instrument; it was necessary in order to provide shelter for the prophetic idea of monotheism, in its early stages of development, from the detrimental effects of the pagan environment. The destruction of the kingdom of Judah and the First Temple and the Babylonian exile proved to be not a disaster, but the beginning of a providential mission. By that time, monotheism had so deeply penetrated the consciousness of the Jewish people that such a political artifice was no longer necessary for its future preservation.[74] The persistence of Jewish peoplehood was accordingly not to be thought of in political terms. The Jews were a people only by virtue of the fact that they were practitioners of a particular religious confession; their vocation was religious, not political. As Geiger put it, "The establishment of a nationality was not Israel's mission."[75] Even during the Babylonian exile, "Fervent attachment to their faith was united with love for their new home, although but a short time, hardly two generations, had elapsed since they had settled in their new country"[76]—a striking use of history to deal with the contemporary political issue. Geiger conceded that, following the Babylonian exile, the Jews were able to reestablish a state, but by this time "they were more than a nation, they were a community united by the bond of an idea."[77]

Throughout his depiction of the late Second Temple period, Geiger strives to recuperate the reputation of the Pharisees, which had been so maligned by centuries of Christian propaganda.[78] For Geiger, the Pharisees are inspired religious democrats, standing for a regenerated, spiritual Judaism.[79] The sage Hillel is the religious genius of the age who disclosed that "the essence of Judaism consists in the love of man and the equality of all men; the rest is commentary."[80]

The prospect of the Pharisaic reform under Hillel was influenced by two events, which together mark a "turning point" in the history of Judaism and its "world-historic transformation": the emergence of Christianity and the destruction of the Second Jewish commonwealth by the Romans in 70 C.E.[81] In the aftermath, "the people's bands were dissolved, nationality was to cease, the state was broken up, the confessors of Judaism became and should become members of that people among whom they lived and citizens of the state within the sovereignty of which they resided."[82] As they had during the period of Babylonian captivity, the Jews tried to make the lands of their dispersion into new homelands. Where they were given opportunity to settle in peace, they were filled with sentiments of devotion to their new homes, and Jewish culture and spirituality thrived. Geiger believed that this fact is demonstrated by the novel Talmudic teaching of *dina de-malkutha dina* [the law of the kingdom is the law], which recognized the laws of the "new country … as perfectly correct and valid."[83] Geiger did not discuss the actual juridical expanse of that dictum or its interpretation in Jewish legal discussions. In these lectures, he simply let the teaching stand, alongside the Jews' acquisition of new languages, as evidence of their integrationist tendency, loyalty to the lands in which they resided, and lack of ambition for sovereignty. The Jews were not eternal wanderers, but settlers who always and everywhere attempted to establish roots and to integrate into the societies in which they resided.

Judaism flourished and merged with the spiritual products of the age, and disclosed itself as a dynamic and creative force.

Unfortunately, during the medieval period, the rulers of those communities continued to regard the Jews as a separate nation, and, exposed to the irrational hatred of their neighbors, Jewish populations were forced to leave their adopted fatherlands or were compelled to turn inward, developing a deepening obsession with the law; Judaism came to regard only a vision of the past as authentic and enveloped itself in a brittle legalism [*Gesetzlichkeit*], obscuring the purity of the Jewish idea.

But with the institution of a policy of toleration in the modern era, Judaism could finally emerge from its ghetto, peel off the contingent elements that had formed as a hard crust, and reassert its true self. The armor of *halakhah* was no longer necessary in a society that allowed the Jews to integrate without first relinquishing their religion.[84] By illuminating the permanent ethical core of Jewish monotheism and describing its various historical manifestations, Geiger had believed he had proven that Judaism was indeed a rational and moral religion, a religion always permeated by science, a religion—the religion—for the modern world.

How was one to connect this theological idea to the contemporary social situation of the Jews? If Judaism had adapted in the past, it could adapt in the future; it could adapt for the present moment. What Judaism needed now, Geiger declared, was "a new Hillel" (not, we should note, a "new Moses") to usher in the new age, to help Judaism rid itself of the now inessential (and indeed reactionary) elements, and to labor toward its yet uncompleted mission. In a *drash* on Hillel's famous dictum (Mishnah *Avot* 1:14), Geiger imagined the instruction of that coming Sage:

> Whenever he shall appear—and surely he will not fail us—he will again pronounce, perhaps in another form, his old maxim *"If I do not for myself, who will do for me?* Beloved pilgrim, do not continually look backwards," he will say, "do not continually keep your eyes on the past. Jerusalem is a tomb; you must draw from the living present and labor in it. If we do not labor and produce from the innate Spirit within us as it is linked with the spirit of Revelation, who shall do it? *And if I do for myself alone, what am I then?* If we do not identify ourselves with mankind, we do not do our duty... *And if not now, when then?* If not now, while the spirit of Judaism yet animates its members, if nothing is done now, if no space is cleared whence the knowledge of ancient times may fertilize the world and new seeds

be sown for the future; if indifference increases in Israel and throws away old treasures as worthless; if the understanding of truly Jewish knowledge, the illumination of the idea of Revelation, the draft from that eternal fountain is not encouraged now—what then?"[85]

Contemporary Jews, Geiger demanded, must apply their spirit to the present and identify with humanity, and must do this in the present moment. Judaism "should guide man to walk in the ways of God, in the ways of the highest wisdom and the highest moral freedom."[86]

Geiger's theological-historical account of Judaism allowed for a self-consciousness of and program for religious reform. With the distinction between the Jewish idea and the forms it took in history in hand, modern Jews could understand ritual in an instrumental fashion, as a means to develop and heighten religious consciousness and moral responsibility. Those ceremonies and rituals that manifested contemporary "religious value" would be retained; others could be abandoned to the dust heap of history or to the scholar's study. The moral value of the Jewish law, however, served as a means to critique Christianity, particularly the Pauline conception of original sin, which destroyed the moral autonomy of the human being. The Jewish commandments did not impede moral autonomy, but presupposed human freedom and rationality. The law no longer served as the fixed structure of contemporary Jewish life; it was deployed as a principle of Judaism's rationality vis-à-vis Christianity.

By understanding the Jewish idea as an insight into the nature of God and the ramifications of this insight for human ethical life, the idea of revelation as establishing a particular political arrangement could be abandoned. The thinkers that we have considered here expressed no interest in the possibility of a future Jewish state. All the political conditions and structures of the Jewish past—the nationality of the Jews, theocracy, state, law—were relegated to the heap of contingent and outmoded external forms, which had served to protect the Jews as a people and their religious idea through the vicissitudes of history. The contemporary political meaning of Judaism would be based on the indirect influence of the Jewish ethical subject.

Conclusion

Directed toward an audience eager for increasing social integration and economic opportunity, liberal Jewish theology disclosed Judaism as the ethical religion of modernity and to inscribe Judaism into the master narrative of Western culture. Judaism was not a political but an ethical religion. But it was an ethical religion with important political *implications*. By fashioning the modern subject, Judaism pushes for the materialization of the just social order wherever its adherents dwell. Through the lives of the Jews, the teaching of Judaism would become actualized in the world, shaping and becoming embodied in social and political institutions. Judaism, therefore, had a contemporary political program—to further human freedom and the ethical life within the modern constitutional order. In such a way, a vision of progress and modernity was endowed with religious sanction. For these liberal theologians, Judaism was the religion of modernity, a religion rational in its outlook and universal in its implications. Insofar as the political order incorporated these ethical ideals, the state would become "Jewish." It was with the advent of the modern period that Judaism could at last fulfill its promise and its mission to the nations. Judaism provided the fundamental values that would support and maintain the modern constitutional polity. Thus, the Jew could find himself at home in the modern state. The Diaspora persisted, but the exile—*galut*—had ended. Emancipation harkened the dawn of the Messianic Age.

Deploying a hermeneutical strategy in which the timeless authority of revelation held only for the religious truths of the Bible while the political and legal claims were held to be historically conditioned, the liberal theologians envisioned a politics based not on the political authority of revelation (a divine institution of law), but on the ethical subject (formed by the religious idea). This political theology would rest on the distinction between the "essence" of Judaism and its historical "forms," historicizing away the political and national elements that might disturb achieving their goal. The thinkers that we have surveyed did not attempt, as Mendelssohn did, to construct a liberal political theory and then argue for the place of Judaism within it. Nor did they articulate just how these Jewish values would find their way into social and political institutions. They assumed, rather, that the modern constitutional state was the final and highest political form. As the pure form of monotheism, Judaism was the religion of modernity, the religion most conducive to the progress of science, knowledge, and freedom. This was a decisive shift in the political understanding of Jewish commitment, one that relinquished claims of a particular Jewish political authority to the state. Jewish religious belief would underwrite the universal political order of the state rather than a covenantal politics of a nation dwelling in exile.

During the second half of the nineteenth century, liberal Judaism consolidated its position as the leading form of Jewish commitment in Germany, and made considerable advances elsewhere in Europe and especially in America. However, as Jacob Katz has argued, in Europe "the conception of Jews as a congregation existing merely by virtue of a common confession of faith functioned only on the theoretical level. In reality they retained the characteristics of a subgroup in society, recognizable by its ethnic origin, its economic concentration, its comparative social isolation, and by its nonconformist minority religion."[87] Despite the invention and reception of this new theology, the hopes of emancipation, of creating a full, robust, and unproblematic integration of the Jews in state and society, had not been achieved.

Notes

1. On the experience of the Jews in "the age of emancipation," the forms of religious adjustment, the origins and development of the reform movement, and the relationship of its development to the social and political pressures of its time, see Michael A. Meyer, *The Origins of the Modern Jew: Jewish Identity and European Culture in Germany, 1749–1824* (Detroit: Wayne State University Press, 1967); *Response to Modernity: A History of the Reform Movement in Judaism* (Oxford: Oxford University Press, 1988); Jacob Katz, *Out of the Ghetto: The Social Background of Jewish Emancipation, 1770–1870* (New York: Schocken Books, 1978); Jacob Toury, *Die politischen Orientierungen der Juden in Deutschland: Von Jena bis Weimar* (Tübingen: J. C. B. Mohr, 1966); Max Wiener, *Jüdische Religion im Zeitalter der Emanzipation* (Berlin, 1933) (hereafter *JRZE*); David Sorkin, *The Transformation of German Jewry, 1780–1840* (Oxford: Oxford University Press, 1987); Steven M. Lowenstein, "The 1840s and the Creation of the German-Jewish Religious Reform Movement," in *Revolution and Evolution: 1848 in German-Jewish History,* ed. Werner E. Mosse, Arnold Paucker, and Reinhard Rürup (Tübingen: J.C.B. Mohr, 1981), 255–297.

2. My use of the term "political theology" in this essay requires explanation. The concept of "political theology" gains clarification by being defined in opposition to "political *philosophy.*" While political philosophy may be understood as a rational, systematic discourse on political matters, from the vantage point of unassisted human reason, political *theology* is a discourse derived from divine *revelation.* For the political theologian, revelation has significant implications for the way human life is to be ordered in temporal society. Theology understands how God is related to the world and to the human being, the nature of the human being, and the nature of rightful political authority. However, this is not to say that the political theologian would not make use of the tools of rational

and systematic reflection that are the hallmarks of philosophy; the key point of distinction is the reference to a truth inaccessible to unassisted human reason (in Judaism and Islam, the giving of the law, or, in Christianity, the redemptive advent of Christ). Political theology may employ political philosophy but is distinguished from the latter by virtue of its suprarational claims. See Ralph Lerner and Muhsin Madhi, eds., *Medieval Political Philosophy* (Ithaca, NY: Cornell University Press, 1972), 7ff.; Leo Strauss, "What Is Political Philosophy," in *What Is Political Philosophy and Other Studies* (Chicago: University of Chicago Press, 1988), 12ff.; Heinrich Meier, "What Is Political Theology?" in *Interpretation: A Journal of Political Theory* 20, no. 1 (Fall 2002): 79–90. Meier especially stresses the nexus of "authority, revelation, and obedience" in political theology. In the case of premodern Jewish thought, an implied political theology—revelation as the giving of the law—served as the basis of the juridical, and therefore political, order.

In the modern period, the boundaries between "reason" and "revelation," that medieval thought had held in a certain tension, collapse, and the distinction between political theology and philosophy becomes problematic. Theological concepts such as revelation and messianism are transposed into modern categories, losing their supernatural foundation. In the case of the thinkers considered here, "political theology" will be understood simply as a political teaching or stance held to be *derived from religion or religious ideas*. But I suspect that such *modern* political theology is finally a political teaching read into or imposed upon religious sources. Its strategy is to adjoin particular political options with religion, in order to endow the political orientation with religious dignity and power.

3. "Debate on the Eligibility of Jews for Citizenship," Achille-Edmond Halphen, *Recueil des Lois, Décrets, ordonnances, avis du conseil d'état, Arrêtés et Règlements concernant les Israélites depuis la Révolution de 1989* (Paris, 1851), quoted in *The Jew in the Modern World* (Oxford: Oxford University Press, 1995), 115 (hereafter cited as *JMW*). The debate in the National Assembly was closed on December 24, without a decision having been reached. France's Sephardi Jews were granted full citizenship on January 28, 1790; the Askenazim of eastern France on September 27, 1791. See the discussion of the attitude toward the Jews during the Revolution in Arthur Hertzberg, *The French Enlightenment and the Jews* (New York: Columbia University Press, 1968), 314–368.

4. "Debate," in *JMW*, 114ff.

5. "Debate," in *JMW*, 115. The Ashkenazi leadership in eastern France originally wanted to retain legal autonomy. This position was later abandoned. See Hertzberg, 344–347.

6. The complex political, legal, and social process that has become known as "emancipation" was set in motion before the term was employed. See Jacob Katz, "The Term 'Jewish Emancipation': Its Origin and Historical Impact," in *Studies in Nineteenth-Century Jewish Intellectual History*, ed. Alexander Altmann (Cambridge: Harvard University Press, 1964), 1–25; and H. D. Schmitt, "The

Terms of Emancipation 1781–1812," *Leo Baeck Institute Yearbook*, 1 (1956): 28–47.

7. See, for example, Voltaire's famous attacks upon the Jews in his *Philosophical Dictionary*. Advocates of the improvement of the civil status of the Jews, such as Christian Wilhelm von Dohm, regarded the debased condition of the Jewish community as stemming from external causes, i.e., the historical mistreatment of the Jews. Those opposed to a policy of toleration argued that the Jewish religion and law promoted separatism and mutual hatred, or the condition of the Jews was the result of the innate character of the Jewish nation.

8. "Debate," in *JMW*, 115. La Fare was referring to the Jewish Sabbath and festival days during which work was prohibited. The bishop added that "a decree which would give the Jews the rights of citizenship could spark an enormous fire," and "recommend[ed] the revision of all of the legislation concerning the Jews." In his view, the Jews were a foreign body who hoped to form their own state, but whose laws rendered them unproductive; he thought granting them citizenship would only further antagonize their Christian neighbors. He stressed the relation between Judaism and the moral character and economic activities of the Jews, while playing down the effect of previous limitations the government had placed on their vocational opportunities.

9. Many of the early arguments about desirability of Jewish emancipation were bound up with questions regarding the economic utility and the possibility of the moral "improvement" of the Jews. This often obscured the political issue that equal rights ought to be granted all in a given territory, regardless of class, nationality, or religious commitment.

10. Johann Gottlieb Fichte, "Beitrag zur Berichtung der Urteile des Publicums ueber die Franzoesische Revolution" (1793). Speaking as a German nationalist, Fichte stood in greater opposition to the possibility of Jewish integration than the cosmopolitan Kant. Fichte regarded "das Judentum" as a foreign and hostile nation, a people which could be granted civil rights in Germany only if they were decapitated (their Jewish heads to be replaced with new ones without any Jewish ideas)! He did, however, suggest that the best way for Germans to protect themselves from the Jewish menace would be "to conquer their promised land for them and send them all there." Trans. and quoted in *JMW*, 309.

11. Immanuel Kant, *Religion within the Boundaries of Mere Reason*, in *The Cambridge Edition of the Works of Immanuel Kant. Religion and Rational Theology*, trans. and ed. Allen W. Wood and George di Giovanni (Cambridge: Cambridge University Press, 1996) 154.

12. Kant, "The Conflict of the Faculties," in *The Cambridge Edition of the Works of Immanuel Kant, Religion and Rational Theology*, 154.

13. What follows is a brief sketch of the political theology that developed within rabbinic Judaism. I am fully aware of the limitations of such a presentation. Rabbinic Judaism was the result of several centuries of development over a wide

geographical space. Rabbinic teachings were presented in a variety of forms: dicta, commentary on canonical texts (the Hebrew scriptures, the Mishnah), legal argument, and sermons; they were not collected in political treatises.

14. Participation in and support by a number of rabbis in the Bar Kokhba rebellion (132–135 C.E.) demonstrates that the rabbinic leadership was not of one mind regarding the issue of political independence and accommodation to a ruling power. With the defeat of this revolt in 135 C.E., hopes of an imminent reestablishment of Jewish rule were dashed.

15. On Jewish self-rule in medieval Europe and its decline in the early modern age, see Alan L. Mittleman, "Paradigm Lost: The Decline of the Jews as a Polity," in *The Scepter Shall Not Depart from Judah: Perspectives on the Persistence of the Political in Judaism* (Lanham, MD: Lexington Books, 2000), 19–45.

16. Saadia Gaon, *The Book of Beliefs and Opinions* (3:7), trans. Samuel Rosenblatt (New Haven: Yale University Press, 1948), 158.

17. This point needs to be qualified. Some commentators have allowed for a distinction between the realm of Torah ("ultimately not concerned with the political order" but with ability "to induce the appearance of the divine effluence within our nation and [to make it] cleave unto us") and the realm of political association. The task of the king to supplement the Torah with a law aimed at political order, and the appointment of a king is a divine command. But we are not left with a conception of a secular political realm independent of religion. The king is commanded to observe the Torah law and to act to further its observance. The king has some autonomy to act, but he is not independent of the religious order, which is his origin and end. See, for example, the arguments of Nissim Gerondi, in *The Jewish Political Tradition, Volume One: Authority,* ed. Michael Walzer, et al. (New Haven: Yale University Press, 2000), 156ff.

18. On this literature, see Louis Finkelstein, *Jewish Self-Government in the Middle Ages* (New York: Jewish Theological Seminary, 1924). Michael Walzer, Menachem Lorberbaum, and Noam J. Zohar have begun a multivolume project to collect materials demonstrating a "Jewish political tradition." Walzer writes, "Embodied in the Talmud, in midrashic collections of legends and parables, retellings and expansions of the biblical narrative, in commentaries on the Bible and the Talmud, in legal response, and only occasionally and incompletely in philosophical treatises, this interpretative tradition never took on the firm shape of a doctrine or theory" (vol. 1, xxii). The volumes produced thus far provide excerpts from variety of sources, from the Bible, rabbinic literature (midrash, Mishnah and Talmud), and well as selections from commentaries, codes, responsa literature, and philosophical treatises; the volume also features contemporary commentaries by a number of authors. *The Jewish Political Tradition,* vol. 1: *Authority* (New Haven: Yale University Press, 2000); vol. 2: *Membership* (2003).

19. On the political thought of Maimonides, see Amos Funkenstein, "Maimonides: Political Theory and Realistic Messianism," in *Perceptions of Jewish History*

(Berkeley: University of California Press, 1993), 131–155; Joel L. Kraemer, "On Maimonides' Messianic Posture," in *Studies in Medieval Jewish History and Literature*, vol. 2, ed. 1. Twersky (Cambridge: Harvard University Press, 1984), 109–142; Ralph Lerner, "Maimonides' Governance of the Solitary," in *Perspectives on Maimonides: Philosophical and Historical Studies*, ed. Joel Kraemer (Oxford: Oxford University Press, 1991), 33–46.

20. Mittleman, "Paradigm Lost: The Decline of the Jews as a Polity," 20.

21. Consider, for example, the "ultra-orthodox" attempts to shore up the status quo through increased communal and ideological separatism. To oppose the reform movement and to compensate for the diminishing sphere of *halakhic* life, these groups placed great emphasis on maintaining traditional forms of dress as well as the use of Jewish languages and names. In this sense, we might say that what was asserted as traditional was in fact an "invented" response. See Michael K. Silber, "The Emergence of Ultra-Orthodoxy: The Invention of a Tradition," in *The Uses of Tradition: Jewish Continuity in the Modern Era*, ed. Jack Wertheimer (Cambridge: Harvard University Press, 1992), 23–83. On the development of a Jewish "book culture," which displaced the traditional model of learning by imitation, see Haym Soloveitchik, "Rupture and Reconstruction: The Transformation of Contemporary Orthodoxy," *Tradition* 28, no. 4 (1994): 64–130. In contrast to ultra-orthodoxy, the so-called "neo-orthodox" movement wanted to enjoy the benefits of liberalism within the structure of traditional Jewish practice. (This movement also advocated a "mission theory" similar to the reformers.) Both types of "orthodoxy," it should be stressed, were *responses* to modern conditions.

22. Conversion to Christianity was, in some ways, made easier, but in others, more difficult. It was easier due to the greater degree of social mobility and the availability of softer, Protestant options; more difficult, because new converts were looked upon with greater suspicion as opportunists, and on account of the emergence of nationalism as the primary category of identity. One could convert to Christianity but not to "Germanness," for example.

23. Benedictus de Spinoza, *Theological-Political Treatise* (1670), ch. 3.

24. Spinoza has been celebrated as the first "modern" or "secular" Jew, that is, the first who was able to leave the (orthodox) Jewish community without converting to another faith, and therefore presenting the option of a secular Jewish identity. But such an analysis avoids the fact that Spinoza himself demonstrated no interest in a Jewish "identity." Neither did he try to maintain an ongoing affiliation with the Jewish people. Detractors of Spinoza such as Hermann Cohen were perhaps closer to the mark when they perceived him as lacking any true Jewish solidarity.

25. Here I rely on a distinction between integration and assimilation. The latter would entail complete abandonment of Jewish identity (religious, cultural, or ethnic). Nineteenth-century discourse often used the term assimilation to

denote integration. See Gideon Shimoni, *The Zionist Ideology* (Hanover, NH: Brandeis University Press, 1995), 405 n. 85.

26. Mention ought also to be made here of the "positivist-historical," "Breslau" school of Judaism, founded by Zacharias Frankel, which maintained allegiance to a historically mutable *halakhah*.

27. Moses Mendelssohn, *Jerusalem oder über religiöse Macht und Judentum* (Berlin: 1783).

28. Mendelssohn, "Letter to Elkan Herz" (July 23, 1771), quoted in *Jerusalem and Other Jewish Writings*, trans. and ed. Alfred Jospe (New York: Schocken Books, 1969), 137.

29. Saul Ascher, *Leviathan, oder über Religion in Rücksicht des Judenthums* [*Leviathan, or on Religion with Respect to Judaism*] (Berlin, 1792). On Ascher, see Wiener, *JRZE*, 46–48; Ellen Littmann, "Saul Ascher: First Theorist of Progressive Judaism," *Leo Baeck Institute Year Book* 5 (1960): 107–121 (cited hereafter as *LBIYB*); Christoph Schulte, "Saul Ascher's *Leviathan*, or the Invention of Jewish Orthodoxy in 1792," *LBIYB* 45 (2000): 25–34; and Jonathan M. Hess, *Germans, Jews and the Claims of Modernity* (New Haven: Yale University Press, 2002), 137–167. Hess notes that *Leviathan* was published a year before Kant's *Religion*, yet insofar as Kant's arguments against Judaism developed from his critical philosophy and general anti-Jewish currents, "these were clearly in Ascher's mind as he set forth the terms of his Kantian vision of religious reform" (158).

30. Ascher, *Leviathan*, 156.

31. Ascher, *Leviathan*, 157; *JMW*, 100.

32. *Leviathan*, 230.

33. *Leviathan*, 227; *JMW*, 101.

34. *Leviathan*, 231 ff. *JMW*, 101.

35. *Leviathan*, 227 ff. *JMW*, 101.

36. *Leviathan*, 321.

37. *Leviathan*, 322.

38. On the development of the modern Jewish sermon and its growing importance, see Alexander Altmann, "The New Style of Preaching in Nineteenth-Century German Jewry," in *Essays in Jewish Intellectual History* (Hanover, NH: Brandeis University Press, 1981), 190–245. Altmann demonstrates the incorporation by Jewish reformers of Protestant examples of preaching (with its emphasis on edification, moral improvement, and devotion), as well as their use of homiletic manuals and personal instruction by Protestant preachers.

39. Amos Funkenstein, "Reform and History: The Modernization of Western European Jews," in *Perceptions of Jewish History* (Berkeley: University of California Press, 1993), 254ff.

40. On the development of the reform movement in Judaism, see Michael A. Meyer, *Response to Modernity: A History of the Reform Movement in Judaism* (Oxford: Oxford University Press, 1988.); David Philipson, *The Reform Movement in Judaism*, new

and revised ed. (New York: Macmillan, 1931); and Steven M. Lowenstein, "The 1840s and the Creation of the German-Jewish Religious Reform Movement," in *Revolution and Evolution: 1848 in German-Jewish History,* ed. Werner E. Mosse, Arnold Paucker, and Reinhard Rürup (Tübingen: J.C.B. Mohr, 1981), 255–297.

41. On the emergence of the modern rabbi as a teacher, preacher, and university-trained scholar, not a legal scholar or halakhicist, see Ismar Schorsch, "Emancipation and the Crisis of Religious Authority: The Emergence of the Modern Rabbinate," "Scholarship in the Service of Reform," in *From Text to Context: The Turn to History in Modern Judaism* (Hanover, NH: Brandeis University Press, 1994), 9–50, 303–333. See also Yosef Hayim Yerushalmi, *Zakhor: Jewish History and Jewish Memory,* 2nd ed. (Seattle: University of Washington Press, 1996), 77–103.

42. Wiener, *JRZE,* 28–113.

43. Uriel Tal, "German-Jewish Social Thought in the Mid-Nineteenth Century," in *Revolution and Evolution,* 306ff.

44. Schorsch, *From Text to Context,* 268ff.

45. Wiener, *JRZE,* 28–113.

46. Abraham Geiger, "Letter to Dernberg" (September 30, 1833), quoted in Max Wiener, *Abraham Geiger & Liberal Judaism: The Challenge of the Nineteenth Century,* trans. Ernst J. Schlochauer (Cincinnati, OH: Hebrew Union College Press, 1996), 83ff.

47. Katz, *Out of the Ghetto,* 208.

48. According to Paul Mendes-Flohr, the term "ethical monotheism" was coined by A. Kuenen in his *Volksreligion und Weltreligion* (Berlin, 1883), though it existed as the principle of liberal Judaism *avant la lettre.* Mendes-Flohr, "Law and Sacrament: Ritual Observance in Twentieth-Century Jewish Thought," in *Divided Passions* (Detroit: Wayne State University Press, 1991), 362.

49. Katz, *Out of the Ghetto,* 208.

50. Solomon Formstecher, *Die Religion des Geistes, eine wissenschaftliche Darstellung des Judentums nach seinem Character, Entwicklungsgange und Berufe in der Menschheit* (Frankfurt a/M, 1841); Samuel Hirsch, *Das System der religiösen Anschauung der Juden und sein Verhältnis zum Heidentum, Christentum und zur absoluten Philosophie,* vol. 1: *Die Religionsphilosophie der Juden* (Leipzig, 1842). On these thinkers, see Bernard J. Bamberger, "Formstecher's History of Judaism," *Hebrew Union College Annual,* 23, pt. 2 (1950–51): 1–35; Emil L. Fackenheim, "Samuel Hirsch and Hegel," in *Jewish Philosophers and Jewish Philosophy,* ed. Michael L. Morgan (Bloomington: Indiana University Press, 1996), 21–40; Julius Guttmann, *Philosophies of Judaism,* trans. D. W. Silverman (New York: Holt, Rinehart and Winston, 1964), 349–365; and Nathan Rotenstreich, *Jewish Philosophy in Modern Times: From Mendelssohn to Rosenzweig* (New York: Holt, Rinehart and Winston, 1968), 106–136.

51. Hegel's views on Judaism were notoriously ambivalent. Unlike Kant, who was concerned with the relation of religion to ethics, Hegel regarded religion as

comprehending truth in representational form. He was therefore more judicious in his understanding of Judaism, considering it a moment in the dialectical historical development of the religious consciousness, though he had difficulty deciding exactly where in the history of consciousness Judaism fit in. In his view, Judaism posits an absolute separation between spirit and world, God and man; it is one-sided religion of sublimity, a necessary but incomplete stage in the development toward the absolute religion, Christianity, which apprehends the unity of God and man in Christ. Judaism had exhausted itself; its world-historical mission had run its course and was sublated by Christianity, the absolute religion. Judaism was now an anachronism, Jewish belief an attachment to an outmoded form of consciousness. Despite his view that Judaism had been overcome in history, Hegel insisted that the Jews—as human beings—ought to be granted civil rights in the modern constitutional state. We should note here that the argument for the political exclusion of the Jews was made not only on religious grounds, but also on the grounds that the Jews belong, not to the German nation, but to a foreign *Volk*. Accordingly, Hegel understood that the political status of the Jews represented a different sort of problem than that of nonconforming religious groups, such as Quakers and Anabaptists. Nevertheless, reason required their emancipation. G. W. F. Hegel, *Elements of a Philosophy of Right*, trans. H. B. Nisbet, ed. Allen W. Wood (Cambridge: Cambridge University Press, 1991), § 270, n. 295. On Hegel's attitude toward Judaism, see Emil L. Fackenheim, *The Religious Dimension in Hegel's Thought* (Boston: Beacon Press, 1967); Nathan Rotenstreich, *The Recurring Pattern: Studies in Anti-Judaism in Modern Thought* (London: Weidenfeld and Nicolson, 1963); and Yirmiyahu Yovel, *Dark Riddle: Hegel, Nietzsche, and the Jews* (University Park: Pennsylvania State University Press, 1998).

52. Meyer, *Response to Modernity*, 108.

53. Ludwig Philippson, *Die Entwickelung der religiösen Idee im Judenthume, Christenthume und Islam. In zwölf Vorlesungen über Geschichte und Inhalt des Judenthums* (cited hereafter as *Entwickelung*), (Leipzig, 1847); *The Development of the Religious Idea in Judaism, Christianity and Mahomedanism, considered in Twelve Lectures on the History and Purport of Judaism, Delivered in Magdeburg, 1847* (cited hereafter as *Religious Idea*), trans. Anna Maria Goldsmid (London, 1855).

54. Philippson, *Religious Idea*, 37; *Entwickelung*, 26ff.

55. *Religious Idea*, 41.

56. *Religious Idea*, 61; *Entwickelung*, 44.

57. *Religious Idea*, 67; *Entwickelung*, 47.

58. *Religious Idea*, 67; *Entwickelung*, 47ff.

59. *Religious Idea*, 67; *Entwickelung*, 47ff.

60. *Religious Idea*, 231ff., 250.

61. *Religious Idea*, 246.

62. *Religious Idea*, 257.

63. *Religious Idea*, 259.

64. Abraham Geiger, *Das Judentum und seine Geschichte* (hereafter cited as *Das Judentum*) (Breslau, 1910); *Judaism and its History* (translation of vols. 1 and 2, hereafter cited as *Judaism*), trans. Charles Newburgh (New York: Block, 1911). The first volume was published in 1864, the second in 1865, and the third in 1871. On *Das Judentum* as a "summation" of the Reform theory of history, see Schorsch, *From Text to Context*, 268.

65. *Judaism*, 34ff.; *Das Judentum*, 23 (I have modified the translation somewhat).

66. *Judaism*, 37.

67. *Judaism*, 228ff.

68. *Judaism*, 39.

69. *Judaism*, 46.

70. *Judaism*, 46; *Das Judentum*, 34.

71. *Judaism*, 402.

72. *Judaism*, 50.

73. *Judaism*, 50f.

74. *Judaism*, 49.

75. *Judaism*, 80.

76. *Judaism*, 84.

77. *Judaism*, 84ff.; *Das Judentum*, 73.

78. As Susannah Heschel has argued in her important study of Geiger, this conception of "Pharisaism as the liberal, democratic, progressive force within rabbinic Judaism became the basis for his justification of modern-day Reform Judaism: it is recapturing the Judaism of the Pharisees." Susanna Heschel, *Abraham Geiger and the Jewish Jesus* (Chicago: University of Chicago Press, 1998), 160.

79. There was also a debate within the camp of the Jewish reformers regarding the valuation of the Pharisees and Sadducees. More radical reformers, such as Samuel Holdheim, were sympathetic to the Sadducee party. The estimation of the parties of the Second Temple therefore represents an intra-Jewish conflict as well as one between Jews and Protestants.

80. *Judaism*, 117.

81. *Judaism*, 122.

82. *Judaism*, 219; *Das Judentum*, 177.

83. *Judaism*, 167.

84. The so-called "ultra-orthodox" drew the opposite conclusion: such a situation necessitated an even more rigorous faithfulness to the traditional law and customs.

85. *Judaism*, 175ff.

86. *Judaism*, 211.

87. Katz, *Out of the Ghetto*, 213ff.

4

Christianity and the Rise of the Democratic State

Eric Gregory

"TOO CONCRETE, BE MORE ABSTRACT." So reads the sticker in my colleague's office. It is ironic advice that can be dangerous, and not just for enthusiastic undergraduates. In fact, this same colleague's recent work has sought to counter the excessively abstract character of contemporary scholarship on religion and democratic theory.[1] But this idiom also resonates with much of the resurgent interest in political theologies. Indeed, this brief essay will follow that injunction even as it raises questions about the nature of these political theologies. My ambitious task then is to examine the development of political theology within Christianity as it relates to the rise of the democratic state.

Words like equality, rights, freedom, and democracy—and the political and theological stories we tell about them—have an essentially contested history. Some today want to unmask and junk them; others want to give them new meaning. Still others want to tell their old, old stories again, often as chapters in a broader story about Christianity, Enlightenment, and secular modernity. Before turning to some of those stories, I risk a methodological intervention in surveying the landscape of political theologies. I see four ways of doing political theology in contemporary discussions. They are ideal types, often trading on ideal presentations of religious traditions and their politics. There are, no doubt, other possibilities and combinations.

Political Theologies

First, political theology sometimes means anything to do with "religion and politics." This approach usually focuses on questions of power, legitimacy, and church-state issues regarding liberty and accommodation. Such an understanding dominates the social sciences, philosophy, jurisprudence, and even the field of religious studies (which typically is ambivalent about the category of "religion" as a scholarly invention with a decidedly Augustinian-Lutheran heritage). Its popularity stems from the influence of liberal theories of democracy that seek to constrain religious privilege or offer norms to regulate comprehensive visions of the good. For example, consider the massive industry on John Rawls and his critics, debates about civil religion, or the treatment of religion in textbook histories of political philosophy. These discussions often assume the category "religion and politics" as a neutral framing for basic questions of authority. More often than not, they treat religion as a generic feature of human culture. Let's call this the liberal approach to "religion and politics." While it typically evaluates religion from the perspective of secular politics, the liberal approach can also be seen as relying on a Christian background that practically invented ideas of "religion" and "secular" as separate spheres of human activity.[2] For many, it reflects a post-Hobbesian view of how Westerners think about and practice politics without appeal to divine revelation. I take this to be what Mark Lilla calls "the Great Separation."[3]

A second approach shows the influential legacy of Carl Schmitt and Leo Strauss even where their ideas or histories are rejected.[4] It also enjoys a renaissance today given renewed interest in comparative genealogies with increased sensitivity to religious thought. Categories like reason and revelation, *imperium* and *sacerdotium*, theism and atheism, Athens and Jerusalem, are again a part of political theorizing. These efforts identify shared concepts between political philosophy and theology, and then make inferences about both by tracing how theological beliefs, practices, and innovations have illuminated changes in political ideals and arrangements (or the other way around). Images of community, notions of moral obligation, law, and virtue, or statements about human nature are compared and contrasted. This approach might also examine ways in which theological discourse about sovereignty and authority, or legality and morality, finds concrete expression in politics or establishes the problematics of political theory.[5] Among twentieth-century Christian defenders of democracy—notably Reinhold Niebuhr and John Courtney Murray—we find invocations of the "image of God" or "original sin" in positive relation to democratic language about the dignity of the individual and limited government.[6] Most recently, cosmopolitan readings of Paul and critical theory energize radical political thought via thinkers like Žižek, Agamben, and Badiou.

Third, there is a more theologically ambitious approach to political theology, perhaps truer to an original sense of the term. Some of it also appeals to readings of Paul as a political theologian.[7] However, this approach resists the reduction of religion to morality and the general suspicion of God-talk. It is unapologetically *theological* political theology. Unlike other approaches, its focus is neither on the role of religion in politics nor the political implications of religious doctrine (whether democratic or not). Rather, the political is interpreted theologically. As one leading practitioner puts it, political theology seeks a "unifying conceptual structure" that connects "political themes with the history of salvation as a whole."[8] For Oliver O'Donovan, this exegetical task furnishes a charitable interpretation of early modern liberalism (including constitutional democracy) as a response to Christian witness and mission. For heuristic purposes, we might distinguish this approach from the second by stating that Reinhold Niebuhr did Christian political thought but not political theology.

The first type is primarily analytic. The second and third typically pursue historical and analytic approaches. A fourth, emerging model, focuses on concrete social practices. Like Jeffrey Stout's recent work or much of qualitative sociology, it looks more like ethnography, social history, or cultural anthropology. Intellectual history or formal theory need not compete for attention with social practices—indeed, the best of each learn from the other—but this approach tells the story of religion and democracy less in terms of "big ideas" and more in terms of the micro-history of democratic habits, dispositions, and movements. For those with theological convictions, tapping into a tradition inspired by Ernst Troeltsch, H. Richard Niebuhr, and W. E. B. Dubois, democratic practices are taken to be part of God's work of redemption through dense webs of institutions and movements. Recent examples that focus on Christianity and democracy, often tacking between the third and fourth types, include Ted A. Smith's *The New Measures* and Charles Marsh's *The Beloved Community*.[9]

Christianity and the Rise of the Democratic State

Each of these approaches can invoke different stories of origins as a route into normative claims about democracy and its justifications. A standard narrative about the rise of Western democracy focuses on early modern exhaustion from religious violence and the vexed questions it raised.[10] For some, while not incompatible with a principled differentiation of spiritual and political authority, democracy is seen as a pragmatic and contingent response to this grim situation. Here, the origins of the modern democratic state are thought to lie not so much in grand hopes of progress or fundamental respect for conscience, but in fear—the fear of other human beings and the cruelty they inflict upon each other in the name of religion. Can we live together without killing each other over religion? Can there be politics without an established, confessional religion expressed coercively in law? Can there be stability in a pluralist community where free and equal citizens do not share the same or any religious beliefs and practices? Given human passions and pride, the idea of democracy and democratic procedures are thought to best respond to such questions and offer the fairest terms of social cooperation.

In defending this idea and its arrangements, some usual suspects from late scholastic, Reformation, and post-Reformation periods—mostly Christian, with varying degrees of orthodoxy and often engaged in heated ecclesiological struggles—are thought to have begun theorizing about collective self-government, principles of (limited) toleration, and eventually pluralism in the name of peace, justice, and order. Hitched to these theories would come consent-based theories of legitimacy, arguing that certain liberties are forfeited in exchange for the benefits of political society. Various metaphysical and anthropological positions might fund this claim. For example, some theorists, like Kant, whose social contract was transcendental and not historical, held a substantive conception of a political society as part of the kingdom of ends with a strong accent on the ethical personality of individuals. Kant argued there is a duty to support a juridical condition in which human rights are respected, and not merely as a matter of self-interest. Such a political society is "not, as Locke thought, a mere remedy for inconvenience, but a duty of justice."[11] However, a more low-flying justification also emerges from an Augustinian sensibility about the limits of political community and its proper functions. On this reconstructed view, since the state cannot be an agent of salvation, religious liberty becomes a cornerstone of the tradition. After a long, halting history, Christians came to think that there are certain goods for which the state cannot and should not be responsible. Christians should beware of any effort to absorb the Body of Christ into the State—especially since the state often needs religion more than religion needs the state. Augustinian democrats analogized Augustine's own influential story about "two cities" to modern notions of separation of church and state. This separation promotes the responsible rule of law for citizens, not the domination of subjects by arbitrary emperors.

Protestants of different stripes have liked this vision, but they often invoke the Catholic Augustine. Now, Augustine himself was neither liberal nor a democrat. He did not offer a systematic account of church and state, much less a proposal for the best form of government or legal design. He supported religious coercion and often used "domination" and sometimes "servitude" to describe the relation of those who govern and those who are governed. Indeed, he is not the first name on a list of those known for democratic virtues of self-restraint, respect for diversity, and openness to deliberation. Augustine might bristle against claims that authority lies in the will of the people as idolatrous—despite having practically invented the concept of the will. Of course, there is no direct line from Augustine to Kant, Madison, Niebuhr, and Rawls. Jonathan Edwards, America's Augustine, was a defender of monarchy as a proxy for his loyalty to Protestantism. The British Crown, he thought, was the best hope for Protestantism in a New World surrounded by Catholics. Yet the modern debate over democracy has, to a large extent, consisted in variations on received Augustinian themes and responses to them.

For much of the twentieth century, his writings, especially the eschatology and anthropology of Book 19 of the *City of God*, were mined for democratic purposes by Catholics and Protestants facing the threat of totalitarianism and fascism.[12] This strand of thought found political expression in one of Niebuhr's most quoted aphorisms: "Man's capacity for justice makes democracy possible, but man's inclination to injustice makes democracy necessary."[13] For Augustinian defenders of democracy, politics cannot, and should not, embody the whole truth. Christians might be attracted to grander politics and certainly have supported alternative forms of government in the past. Yet they might also be said to reluctantly tolerate democracy, using it to the best extent possible in a fallen world. Politics should not be cut off from the aspirations of virtue, but it lowers our pretensions and so tempers the laments we have about democracy. Democracy is better than pitchforks and spooky metaphysics about collective identity that prematurely imagine a reconciled humanity. Democracy secures penultimate, historical, moral identities responsive to the goods the state can secure. Democracy is an instrument of justice. Justice is prior to democracy as an ideal, but we will never have true justice. So democracy is not an end in itself, but it is not morally bankrupt. There is no ideal normative political arrangement in a non-ideal world. Political culture, and its institutions, shape and create virtues. Some arrangements and the loves they embody and express are morally better than others. Some encourage what is noble, others what is base. Democratic justice, equality, and solidarity are virtues, albeit imperfect ones. This is a path between skepticism and dogmatism about democracy.

To this story, we should add the Catholic Church's endorsement of democracy as the form of government that, as John Paul II, put it, "best coheres with the Church's vision of 'integral human development.'"[14] According to George Weigel, in the nineteenth and early twentieth centuries, the Church saw democracy as the celebration of an individual's independence from God and God's law. Events like the French Revolution, the anti-Church attitude of many liberal thinkers, and the links between liberalism and Darwinism led to the Church's deep skepticism about democracy. As the twentieth century developed, however, the Church came to see its primary opponent no longer as democracy but as totalitarianism. The American experiment was also significant for the development of Catholic understanding of democracy. John Paul II became a critical friend of democratic societies, warning them that a democracy without values easily turns into a kind of totalitarianism of its own.

There are stronger challenges to this narrative, the most critical by writers who see the rise of democracy as a consolidation of the nation-state and its economic and military power.[15] In their view, democracy is not a triumph of Christian or post-Christian humanism. It is instead symptomatic of a decline into moral fragments where a distorted view of freedom replaced classical virtues, aided by missteps made within Christendom itself that prepared the way for a tragic politics drained of real relation to God. Many of today's Augustinians, far from supporting democracy, take their cue from Augustine's critique of bad theologies of empire and expose democracy as a repressed work of violence and lust for domination. John Milbank and Stanley Hauerwas, for example, argue that Augustinian democrats sacrifice orthodoxy in order to make Christianity safe for democracy, a subtle totalitarianism that can only be a parody of the ecclesia. The democratic creed replaces the Christian Gospel; it is taken to be a perversion of justice, not only an imperfection.

But many Christians remain wary, yet willing, defenders of democracy. Indeed, Christian activists promote democratic commitments on the ground in many areas around the globe. At the same time, Christian intellectuals who defend democracy have challenged both self-congratulatory Enlightenment stories of democracy's exclusively secular origins and recent antidemocratic Christian theologies. Nicholas Wolterstorff, for example, has argued that rights—the idiom of democracy—are not the supposed invention of early modern liberals or simply entitlements conferred by the modern state. On his view, their conceptual logic can be found throughout Hebrew and Christian scriptures and early Christian authors.[16]

Judith Shklar famously suggested that "liberalism is monogamously, faithfully, and permanently married to democracy—but it is a marriage of convenience."[17] Christian political theology, given concerns for idolatry, does not seek permanent coalitions with particular political arrangements or theories. By my lights, however, most prophetic challenges to democracy, if an alternative is proposed, bear the marks of central features of a democratic tradition. Fights about democracy are often proxies for other debates, like relativism, value pluralism, or views of morality as mere social agreement. The mainstream focus has shifted to the more narrow debate regarding the role of religious reasons with regard to particular acts of state coercion, or the debate about cultural criticism, but no real challenges to democratic institutions and a registry of rights and correlate civic obligations have emerged from these alternatives.

It is an empirical question whether a democratic society can sustain itself, let alone flourish, without theoretical consensus about the ends of politics or a shared theory of sovereignty. I hope it does not require it. This is not to say that theorizing is bad. Ideas have consequences. Concepts matter. But there is a difference between what satisfies the philosophical Christian and what is necessary for the actual practice of conflict-ridden politics. In my view, most Christian political theology today finds itself in ambivalent relation to the modern ethos of rights, equality, and the power of the democratic state. It worries about the effects of democratic culture, but it supports a democratic politics. This suggests a concessive, ambivalent, and provisional gratitude for democracy as an earthly instrument of justice.

Notes

1. Jeffrey Stout, *Blessed Are the Organized: Grassroots Democracy in America* (Princeton: Princeton University Press, 2010). Stout's work is philosophically minded but aims to "bring the ideal of good citizenship down to earth" (xvi). His analysis looks more from the "bottom up" by way of example and story than from the "top down" by way of formal theorizing. For Stout, however,

"democratic practices, insofar as they involve mutual accountability, themselves give rise to concepts and claims" (314 n. 85).

2. Robert A. Markus, *Christianity and the Secular* (Notre Dame: University of Notre Dame Press, 2006).

3. Mark Lilla, *The Stillborn God: Religion, Politics, and the Modern West* (New York: Alfred A. Knopf, 2007).

4. See, for example, Heinrich Meier, "What is Political Theology?" *Interpretation* 30, no. 1 (Fall 2002): 79–91.

5. Bonnie Honig, *Emergency Politics: Paradox, Law, Democracy* (Princeton: Princeton University Press, 2009), and John Milbank, *Theology and Social Theory: Beyond Secular Reason* (Oxford: Blackwell, 1990).

6. Reinhold Niebuhr, "Democracy, Secularism, and Christianity," in *Christian Realism and Political Problems* (New York: Charles Scribner's Sons, 1953), 95–103, and John Courtney Murray, *We Hold These Truths: Catholic Reflections on the American Proposition* (New York: Rowman and Littlefield, 2005).

7. Note, for example, renewed attention to Jacob Taubes, *The Political Theology of Paul*, trans. Dana Hollander (Stanford: Stanford University Press, 2003).

8. Oliver O'Donovan, *The Desire of the Nations: Rediscovering the Roots of Political Theology* (Cambridge: Cambridge University Press, 1996), 22. According to O'Donovan, political theology "postulates an analogy—not a rhetorical meta-phor only, or a poetic image, but an analogy grounded in reality—between the acts of God and human acts, both of them taking place within the one public his-tory which is the theatre of God's saving purposes and mankind's social under-takings" (2).

9. Ted A. Smith, *The New Measures: A Theological History of Democratic Practice* (Cambridge: Cambridge University Press, 2007), and Charles Marsh, *The Beloved Community: How Faith Shapes Social Justice from the Civil Rights Movement to Today* (New York: Basic Books, 2006).

10. John Rawls, *Political Liberalism* (New York: Columbia University Press, 1996).

11. Christine M. Korsgaard, "Taking the Law into Our Own Hands: Kant on the Right to Revolution," in *Reclaiming the History of Ethics: Essays for John Rawls*, ed. Andrews Reath, Barbara Herman, and Christine M. Korsgaard (Cambridge: Cambridge University Press, 1997), 312.

12. See Eric Gregory, *Politics & The Order of Love: An Augustinian Ethic of Democratic Citizenship* (Chicago: University of Chicago Press, 2008). In particular, various authors promoted "secular" and "liberal" readings of *City of God* 19:24, where Augustine redefines Cicero's *res publica* in terms of "common objects of love."

13. Reinhold Niebuhr, *The Children of Light and the Children of Darkness: A Vindication of Democracy and a Critique of Its Traditional Defense* (New York: Charles Scribner's Sons, 1944), xi.

14. George Weigel, *The Soul of the World: Notes on the Future of Public Catholicism* (Grand Rapids, MI: Eerdmans, 1996), 99.

15. William T. Cavanaugh, *The Myth of Religious Violence: Secular Ideology and the Rise of Modern Conflict* (Oxford: Oxford University Press, 2009).

16. Nicholas Wolterstroff, *Justice: Rights and Wrongs* (Princeton, NJ: Princeton University Press, 2007). On Protestant appropriations of Jewish sources for democratic purposes, see Eric Nelson, *The Hebrew Republic: Jewish Sources and the Transformation of European Political Thought* (Cambridge, MA: Harvard University Press, 2010), and Eric Gregory, "The Jewish Roots of the Modern Republic," *Harvard Theological Review* 105, no. 3 (2012): 372–380.

17. Judith N. Shklar, "Liberalism of Fear," in *Liberalism and the Moral Life*, ed. Nancy L. Rosenblum (Cambridge, MA: Harvard University Press, 1989), 37. See also, Judith Skhlar, "Giving Injustice Its Due," *The Yale Law Journal* 98, no. 6 (April 1989): 1135–1151.

5

Is the King a Democrat? The Politics of Islam in Morocco

Paul Heck

MOROCCO OFFERS A rich study for the emergent discipline of political theology. The reason for this is simple. Religion, even more so than the concept of citizenship, defines the nature of politics in Morocco, including its democratic side. This makes it necessary to think theologically and not simply philosophically in positing a theory of politics for Morocco. The idea that religion defines the nature of politics in Morocco does not mean that the concept of citizenship is absent. Still, it is religious belonging more so than political convention that informs national identity. Islam, more so than the idea of a social contract, is understood to hold the nation together. Islam is the exclusive reference point for the nation's politics even if other concepts are at play. Do people in Morocco think of themselves as fellow believers or fellow citizens in the way they interact in public life? It is probably a bit of both, but we can definitely say that the values shaping the social imagination as well as the expectations of public behavior in Morocco are those of Islam.

All this is not to suggest that the politics of Morocco is like that of Muslim societies elsewhere. Things are manifestly different from one Muslim society to another, depending on the form of rule as well as the particular histories and cultural specificities of the country in question, making it necessary to consider each on its own terms. In this essay, I explore the democratic side of politics in Morocco by examining the religious principles that shape understandings of the polity. I concentrate on two factors that contribute to a democratic outlook: (1) The recognition on the part of the rulers that rule exists for the sake of society's interests as a whole and not only those of the elite, and (2) the assumption on the part of the people that they are capable of self-governance. Does Islam say that the purpose of government rule is service of the common good and also that people at large have the inherent capacity to govern themselves—and how are such things at play in the politics of Morocco? To answer this question, I will proceed in two parts. First, I look at the form of governance in Morocco, which is a constitutional monarchy, and the ways in which power is understood to be limited in principle if not always in practice, implying, in theory, that individuals enjoy a measure of personal inviolability vis-à-vis power. Second, I examine the understanding of freedom in Islam and the way in which it has been invoked for the sake of self-determination in Morocco, again in principle if not always in practice.

To be sure, democracy is one thing and liberalism another. In the second section of this chapter, I consider whether Morocco falls under the rubric of "the open Muslim society," where Islam is promoted and patronized by the state but with tolerance for other beliefs and convictions. In many societies, including Morocco, the meaning of democracy is effectively limited to a process of transferring power (i.e., via elections) and does not include the freedom to determine one's religious and moral destiny. The religious and moral life of the nation is the affair not of individuals but of society as a whole. As a result, a country such as Morocco, a signatory to the International Convention on Civil and Political Rights, may affirm, for example, religious freedom without equating it with a right to choose one's religion, especially when that means opting out of Islam. Whatever democratic principles may be at play in the politics of Morocco, there is currently no viable option for a Moroccan to be anything but a Muslim.

At the same time, even if national identity in Morocco is defined in terms of Islam, neither piety nor politics in Morocco is homogeneous. There are highly pious Moroccans, but many others are more interested in going to the beach than to the mosque on a regular basis. For the bulk of Moroccans, attachment to Islam is often mediated through the bonds of family, especially on feast days that combine fidelity to family and loyalty to religion. There are red lines, as we will see, but Islam in Morocco is generally a flexible affair.

Even if the symbols of Islam are manifest in society, religion is not always the first thing on people's minds. Moroccans, like people everywhere, are more likely thinking about their jobs and their families or conversing with friends in a café. Watching soccer is second to none as a national pastime. There is no uniform dress code in Morocco. Some men are bearded and some are not. Some women cover their heads or veil their faces and some do not. Many are interested in keeping up with the fashion standards of Paris and not Islam's standards of modest dress, and Morocco has its own rich heritage of couture. As for youth, they are much like youth everywhere. They hope to be popular among their peers. They hope to earn a good deal of money one day. They hope eventually to have a family and prosper. Such hopes are not always realized in a country with high levels of poverty and illiteracy. Some turn to petty crime, drugs, begging, and prostitution. Others try to make it to Europe. Finally, Morocco, which is widely considered to be Arab, is actually quite diverse culturally: A sizeable Berber population has, only in recent years, received official recognition of their language, and there are many Moroccans who use French as their primary language. All this feeds into sometimes fierce controversy over the cultural identity of the country.

Additionally, despite the religious basis of the polity, politics in Morocco is by no means a simple matter. Islam can serve as a reference point for multiple trends, all which accept the truth of Islam but, nevertheless, disagree on its implications for the shape of the polity and the nature of rule. Politics in Morocco includes royalists, socialists, Islamists, environmentalists, and feminists, to name just a handful of participants. As well, there is a vast network of what could be called nonelected democracy where traditional religious associations, rural notables, and tribal groups intersect with systems of political patronage on behalf of their "constituencies."

This variety of political actors and views, even if more pronounced today, is hardly new. Morocco, like all societies, embraced a measure of political diversity long before democracy became the world's normative political paradigm. The concept was simple: The ruler is the holder but not the arbiter of power. Other voices in society, especially but not only religious authorities, acted as interpreters of the limits and legitimate use of power. One case helpfully illustrates the point: Sultan Sulayman (ruled 1792–1822) sought to style himself not only as holder of power but also its arbiter.[1] He tried to assert a religious authority of his own over the scholarly class, the traditional interpreters of power, by advancing a more literalist piety that dispensed with the jurisprudential expertise of the scholarly class. In the end, he was unsuccessful. He was simply unable to marginalize the authority that the scholarly class enjoyed, not only within their own ranks but also among the people at large, who looked to them, not the sultan, as the source of the moral teachings that give society its coherence and stability. The idea of the ruler as arbiter of his own power stood at odds with the long-standing expectation in Islam that God holds the ruler accountable on judgment day, not only for his own failings but also for those of his subjects. Ironically, Salafists in Morocco today look to the reign of Sulayman as a model of religious rule that puts aside the fine points of traditional jurisprudence in favor of a literal reading of texts that all believers are expected to accept.[2] In their support of his literal reading of religion, Salafists overlook the fact that he actually sought to do away with the divine limits that Islam has long placed on human power.

The point is that power is never simply a given, even when all have agreed on the truth of Islam. Power in Muslim society is always being negotiated, sometimes by force but usually through a broad discourse in society where a variety of voices advance competing notions of good governance. The question today, of course, is whether the people as a whole, and not simply their religious leaders, enjoy the authority to decide when power in Morocco conforms to the truths of Islam and when it does not. Here lies a conundrum. Democracy means that people are to be trusted to know what is best for the polity, but it does not necessarily turn individuals into religious and moral authorities. How exactly do assumptions of popular authority—and the political freedom that goes with it—square with assumptions of religious and moral truth? Do Moroccans in general consider themselves authorities in any sense at all?

In Islam historically, the legitimacy of rule has long been linked to the common good. When it comes to the affairs of the polity, in contrast to the rituals and morals of Islam, the will of God is not revealed in advance but is discerned in light of a number of principles that are both recognized by the human mind and confirmed by the religious tradition—for example, justice and equity. In this sense, while we cannot speak of what today are known as individual rights, there was—and is—a very strong sense in Islam that every member of society is to get his or her due, namely, the basic necessities of existence, including rights of property ownership and expectations of family life. Also, authors of political treatises, such as Abu l-Hasan al-Mawardi (d. 1058) and Ibn Khaldun (d. 1406), and even Ibn Taymiyya (d. 1328), among many others, all recognized that unjust rule, even if ostensibly Muslim, does not last. It is simply God's way with his creation. Unjust rule exploits and oppresses people, discouraging them from taking economic initiative and even encouraging the more capable to leave the realm and ply their trade elsewhere where they can hope to enjoy the fruits of their labor. Indeed, unjust governance eventually threatens the prosperity of society as a whole and will sooner or later leave the ruler with no subjects to govern.

Because of this divine manner of ordering the world, a ruler who is not responsive to the welfare of his subjects risks his throne. It is, of course, one thing to say that Islam recognizes the common good as the purpose of rule and another thing to say that the people are the authority determining the legitimacy of power. The democratic project is based on the notion of popular authority, but this does not mean that all popular authority is conceived in the same way. In the eyes of some, investing people at large with authority is contrary to the truths of Islam. Also, the comment is occasionally heard in Morocco that the masses, given the high percentage of illiteracy, are simply incapable of self-governance. Can human freedom coexist with a heritage of religious and moral truths such that the affirmation of one does not require the denial of the other? Does one need to be literate to know what is best for one's local society? Such questions will be examined in the second section of the chapter. Here, I first consider the nature of rule in Morocco today.

Constitutional Monarchy in Morocco: Rule With or Without Limits?

Morocco is a monarchy, a constitutional monarchy, where final power exists with the court. Thus, the government that is supposed to represent the people is subordinate to a court that forms the institutional embodiment of the monarchy. But it should be remembered that when Morocco gained its independence from France in 1956, the sultan, at the time Muhammad V (1909–1961), was very much the centerpiece of the movement for national independence. The figure of the sultan coexisted symbiotically, if not always in perfect harmony, with popular aspirations for self-determination. This represented a significant development from the constitutional movement that emerged just before the establishment of the French Protectorate in 1912. That movement, initiated in 1907 with the specter of colonial rule on the horizon, succeeded not only in dethroning one sultan, 'Abd al-Aziz (ruled 1894–1908), for his complicity with French authorities but also in imposing conditions on the pledge of allegiance given to the new sultan, 'Abd al-Hafiz (ruled 1912–1927). Although these conditions meant nothing to French control of Morocco, "the conditional pledge of allegiance" is remembered today as the beginnings of Moroccan constitutionalism. However, it must be stressed, the conditions placed on the pledge of allegiance to the sultan cannot be taken as a call for popular sovereignty. The pledge was not democratic in nature but sought only to bind the sultan's privileges to the oversight of the elite in general and the religious class in particular.[3] It is therefore fair to conclude that the location of Muhammad V at the head of the nationalist movement for independence from France raised expectations about the role of the nation as a whole in the process of rule that were not operative in the so-called constitutional movement of 1907.

These expectations were not realized with independence. Hasan II (ruled 1961–1999), in many ways the real founder of Morocco as a nation-state, ruled with a strong hand—some would say brutal.[4] He nonetheless gave the monarchy a shape that continues today under his son and successor Muhammad VI (ruled 1999–). Final power, including the military, is ultimately in the hands of the court. The ruling dynasty, which first came to the throne in the seventeenth century, based its prestige on its claim of descent from the Prophet Muhammad. Royalty in Morocco, as in Islam in general, is not about a divine right to rule. Rather, it is geared to the ability of a dynasty to represent the body of the prophet as leader of the Muslim polity. The blood of the prophet may run in the veins of the leaders of a particular dynasty, but the dynasty still has to prove itself worthy of representing its prophetic lineage. In Morocco, Hasan II drew on this heritage to give greater sanctity to his throne. He was not only ruler but also "the commander of the faithful," which has now become the most significant title of the Moroccan monarchy. Still, the monarch has to prove himself. Prophetic lineage, while a clear advantage in advancing claims to royalty, does not guarantee rule in Morocco. There are other families in Morocco that also enjoy prophetic lineage and that in the past have posed a rivalry to the current dynasty. This danger, however, no longer exists in the postcolonial state with its unprecedented ability to centralize power in the court. The dynasty, of course, remains susceptible to challenges, but such challenges now come not from families of prophetic nobility (*sharaf*) but rather from military officers and popular movements of discontent.

Hasan II was able to survive a number of military coups. Also, the court, known as the *Makhzen*, has proven its skill at marginalizing, diffusing, and co-opting popular-based political opposition, whether secular or religious in character. After independence, the court was able to bring the religious establishment under its direct tutelage through the ministry of religious affairs, which controls mosques, sermons, and religious education in the schools.[5] Through its various channels, it promotes a religious identity that is alleged to be specific to Morocco; the implication being that as head of the nation the king alone ensures its religious character no less than its political well-being. Article 19 of the constitution defines the king as "the commander of the faithful...supreme representative of the nation and symbol of its unity...guarantor of the perpetuation and continuity of the state...protector of the rights and liberties of the citizens, social groups, and organizations." Article 23 states that "the person of the king is sacred and inviolable," making his word final in national policymaking.[6] It is simply illegal to oppose the king.[7] Such constitutional language is reinforced by national rituals whereby the king's body becomes the object of identification for his male subjects who dress in white robes in imitation of him, affirming the bond between the body of the king and the body of the polity as a whole.[8] It would seem, then, that the nature of the modern state has allowed the court to become both holder and arbiter of power, especially with the incorporation of the traditional religious class into the bureaucratic structure via the ministry of religious affairs and its related institutions. A well-known review of local politics, *Point of View* (*Wajhat Nazr*), echoes the idea that the court stands above accountability. Titles of recent issues include the following: "The Death of Political Parties" (no. 36–37, 2008); "The Sacred Monarchy and the Illusion of Change" (no. 42, 2009); and "The Tools of Subjugation and Control" (no. 38, 2008).

The staging of royal prestige, via a plethora of decrees and ceremonies, does much to secure the affinity of the people for their king. The impression on the ground is that many in Morocco, perhaps most, love their king. Whatever the truth of the matter, popular identification for the person of the king does not mean the court can ignore other sources of power, including various piety-minded movements that seek a measure of constitutional reform. In short, the monarchy may be the most formidable institution in Morocco, but it has critics who hold it to account, calling it to responsibility for the society it governs.

Is there a democratic process in Morocco that functions independently from royal oversight? Much of the affairs of government are in the hands of ministries that answer directly to the court, but it is not in the interest of the court to govern all affairs directly. Much is left to the parliament and municipal administrations. A plethora of political parties vie for seats in these bodies through elections that are largely free and fair, even if they do not always attract wide participation. Morocco has had a multiparty political system since independence in 1956 where all parties recognize the authority of the monarchy. The older parties, known for their nationalist and socialist orientations, were at one time inspired by charismatic leaders, notably Mehdi Ben Barka (1920–1965) assassinated in Paris likely at the orders of Moroccan authorities and possibly with the complicity of the French government. But these parties are now largely networks of political patronage without distinct objectives. As of 2011, two govern in coalition: the Party of Independence and the Socialist Union of Popular Forces. In contrast, smaller parties seek not so much to win seats as to advance a particular issue, such as the Party of the Environment and Sustainable Development, led by Dr. Ahmed Alami, which works to draw attention at both national and international levels to the critical importance of a healthy environment for societal well-being.

A final example is the Party of Justice and Development (PJD), which is the Islamist party in Morocco.[9] The PJD has done much to separate its policy platforms from religious rhetoric, demonstrating that a religiously inspired politics can operate without religious authorities. Its spokesmen affirm that the will of God is not revealed in advance when it comes to the political domain. Rituals and morals have been fixed for all time by God, but politics is not. Politics, then, is a good common to all with principles that are knowable by all irrespective of religious training. One need not be a religious authority to know where the interests of society lie. The PJD, along with the Movement for Unity and Reform, the Islamist movement with which it is twinned, has as its goal service of the needs of society and not retrieval of a religious past to impose on contemporary society arbitrarily. Its piety is therefore forward-looking, allowing it to make alliances with other parties for the sake of its political goals, even if such alliances do not always please all its members.

However, it is not clear how the PJD differs from other political parties. It repeatedly claims the moral high ground in the way it presents itself to the nation, but its own members, once elected to office, have not always demonstrated a commitment to the interests of the people over their own interests in political patronage. Moreover, the PJD has certainly not won the hearts of the lowest classes in Morocco. Its chief constituency lies within the urban middle class. Still, even if hampered by its own members' shortcomings, to say nothing of the attacks of its opponents, the PJD will continue to act as a voice of discontent for the foreseeable future. Its rhetoric bespeaks a confidence that the people are capable of self-governance. For example, it calls for a sharing of religious authority between official and nonofficial channels. Since religious authority goes hand-in-hand with political authority in Morocco, the PJD, without directly accusing the state of failing the values of the nation, is suggesting that the only way the needs of the nation can be met is through greater empowerment of nonstate actors.

The institutions of governance in Morocco are therefore not without a measure of democratic life. Elections for parliament and municipal governance garner a good deal of attention in the press, and there are no restrictions on voting eligibility such as literacy. Candidates often dole out commodities during campaigns, including foodstuffs, partly because the electorate is not always confident that their promises will be kept. Still, elections in Morocco are a means for the peaceful transfer of power below that of the monarchy. People leave office when elected out. However, the court does have a hand in the nation's democratic processes. The prime minister, who is chosen from the governing coalition, is not elected by his peers in parliament but is appointed directly by the king. (The constitutional changes—proposed by the king in response to the Arab Spring and affirmed by the nation via plebiscite on July 1, 2011—now stipulate that the prime minister will be elected. See the postscript to this essay.) Moreover, the court has its friends in the party system. The Party of Authenticity and Modernity, founded in 2008 under the leadership of Fu'ad 'Ali Himma, former minister of the interior, cannot be entirely reduced to a court plot as some allege, but it has had the effect of drawing votes away from other parties, including the PJD, thereby acting to frustrate as much as invigorate democratic processes in Morocco.

All this should seen as part of a still unfolding shift away from authoritarian rule that reached its height during "the years of lead" under Hasan II. In general, it can be said that a turn to a more open society is the result of intolerable levels of oppression that finally reach a breaking point. The contemporary conception of human rights did not emerge as abstract ideas but concrete means to protect individuals and societies from tyrannical rule. This is no less true of Muslim societies that have suffered various forms of arbitrary rule in recent decades. More than anything else, the experience of undemocratic power has made human rights a vibrant part of the political discourse in Muslim society today. In the face of such circumstances, religion can be invoked as a source of liberation. Here, then, freedom is defined not as the end and very purpose of human existence but as a necessary means for preserving the welfare of society. One sees this today in Iran, where the call for freedom, even if directed against a state that governs in the name of Islam, takes its inspiration in part from the religious tradition. This is also true in Turkey, where piety-minded circles that had long castigated democracy and human rights as non-Muslim innovations came to embrace them in the face of a state hostile to civil society in general and piety-minded forms of civil association in particular. As a result, many, but by no means all, religious circles in Turkey today affirm civil liberties as something good for Islam. The movement of Fethullah Gülen is a leading example of that. They certainly do not view freedom as a license for individuals to do whatever they want, but they do see freedom as a religious value since its absence demonstrably hinders the ability of Islam to flourish in society.

In Morocco, there are far-reaching discussions on the relation of individual liberties to the moral life of the nation. Even those who are not highly pious might not object to what other societies would view as a violation of human rights, such as prohibitions against openly violating the fast during Ramadan, choosing a religion other than Islam, or pursuing a homosexual lifestyle. Such prohibitions, which many circles, especially in the West, would see as a violation of civil liberties, are seen as necessary measures to protect a way of life that is dear to society as a whole. This does not mean that human rights are not valued or that authoritarian rule is tolerated without protest. Again, freedom is understood to be applicable not so much to religious and moral issues but more so to the political order. In Morocco, it has not been due to a sense that society's religious and moral sentiments are under attack that people have called for greater liberties. As noted previously, in the case of Iran and Turkey, also in Morocco, it is excessive forms of political oppression that have forced the state to grant greater freedoms in society. A horrific case involved the police chief of Casablanca, Mohamed Mostafa Tabet, executed in 1993 for using the power of his office to rape more than five hundred women and recording his criminal acts on video with the help of his officers. Did the state and its police forces exist to protect or terrorize society? The case shocked the nation, including its royal ruler. A greater measure of freedom would have to be granted, especially to the press (see below). However, it remains unclear what shape such freedom is to take in a country where rule is traditionally the privilege of a particular family. Is the king to become a democrat?

The press in Morocco today enjoys unprecedented if still limited freedom, although this freedom is sometimes viewed as much as a license to titillate the populace with sex scandals as a responsibility to provide critical analysis of national and international events. Still, a free press, even if limited in what it can say about the monarchy, does monitor abuse of power by police forces and government officials in a way previously impossible. Also, torture, while not completely absent from the prison system, is by no means as widespread as it once was. All this demonstrates that authoritarian rule, even if persistent, is no longer the accepted norm, but it is not clear how this shift is embodied at the institutional level. Unions in Morocco are not independent but function as extension of political parties. Many so-called nongovernmental organizations, while providing valuable services to the needy, are indirectly sponsored by the court or members of the elite whose prestige over the masses is bolstered by its ability to access EU sources of support.[10] Finally, the judicial system, known for its lack of independence, remains a major obstacle to the rule of law in Morocco.

The legitimacy of the king, it should be remembered, is not only a function of his prophetic descent. The modern nation of Morocco came into existence through the combined forces of the sultan and the nationalist movement. While this alliance between dynastic ruler and people did not continue after independence as expected, it offers a reference point for the king's legitimacy, and the king can draw on this populist side of his rule, especially in moments of crises. Hasan II, needing to reassert his legitimacy after a number of attempted coups, called for the Green March in 1975, leading over a quarter-million of his subjects in a peaceful walk into the Spanish Sahara to claim it as part of Morocco's territorial integrity. (This "democratic" side of the monarchy has been confirmed by recent developments in Morocco in the wake of the Arab Spring. See postscript.)

The king can also draw upon this democratic side of his rule as a way to garner popular affirmation of his royal mandate, reinforcing expectations that his rule exists to serve the common good. Muhammad VI, on assuming power in 1999, granted amnesty to political prisoners, including monetary compensation; established a council for truth and reconciliation to examine the use of torture during his father's reign; and generally styled himself as the people's king. This has not ended authoritarian patterns of political administration, but it has suggested that rule, no matter how royal, has a responsibility to popular expectations. The pledge of allegiance to the king, renewed every year, does not specify limits to his rule, making it unimaginable that he could ever be deposed. Indeed, the widely held assumption of the religious character of rule can encourage the idea that hierarchy, rather than democracy, is the proper form of governance for the nation. No matter how difficult socioeconomic conditions might be, there is a sense that the monarch is political heir to the prophet and will somehow ensure the blessings of the nation. Of course, this raises the stakes for the king; he has to show in concrete ways that he is indeed the source of the nation's blessings, especially in the face of calls for constitutional reform that would limit his political privileges.

In this sense, the king cannot jeopardize the favor of the people. Ironically, then, the monarchy has been partly integrated into the emergent democratic imagination of the nation. For example, the idea of development—from internationally financed construction projects to the creation of health clinics and computer centers in poorer areas—is one way the monarchy demonstrates its political effectiveness and responsiveness to the needs of the people. Since the king, with his extraordinary wealth, can deliver the goods in a way that other groups cannot, including political parties, he will retain a pull on the people who want a leader to take care of the nation. In this sense, he is the final standard of the common good of the nation. The people around him might be corrupt and conniving, failing to give him the best counsel, but he remains the final "court of appeal" by which all dispute in society is at least potentially resolvable.

All these examples suggest that monarchy in Morocco is by no means understood as arbitrary rule. To some extent, the people, either directly or through popular movements and political parties, have some impact on the way power is interpreted. To be sure, the emphasis placed on the religious identity of the nation by the organs of the state is one way for the elite to harness the pious sentiments of the people to the preservation of the regime and its favored clientele. This, in turn, can deflect demands for greater power sharing and wealth distribution. The political elite is adept at using Islam to mobilize popular sympathy for the regime without, however, abiding by the limits that Islam would place on their own privileges. In short, unless the elite are willing to view the masses not as their servants but as their co-citizens, it will be difficult for the democratic journey of the nation to bear fruit in the end. However, the fact that the monarchy, despite its hierarchical nature, is very much implicated in the common good of the nation can encourage kingly recognition of the voice of the people, keeping alive the hope that the ruler and people do not exist at cross purposes. This, it should be added, is not simply a pragmatic arrangement. In part, it reflects the theology of rule in Islam that sees the ruler as responsible custodian of his people's interests even if not necessarily their elected representative.

Freedom in Islam: Political Self-Determination
as a Religious Demand?

A well-known hadith relates one of the teachings of Muhammad as follows: "God gives the example of a straight path: On each side are two walls that have open doors with curtains lowered over them. At the gate of the path is a caller who says, 'O people, enter the path, all of you, and do not turn off it.' Above the path is a caller who calls out whenever a person wants to open one of those doors, saying, 'Woe to you, do not open it, for if you open it, you will enter it.' The path is Islam, the two walls are the limits that God has set, the caller at the head of the path is the book of God, and the caller above the path is the admonisher of God in the heart of every Muslim." (The hadith is narrated in the canonical collections of al-Tirmidhi, no. 2859.)

This teaching can be seen as a summary of Muslim life: The Qur'an is your guide at the start, but it is up to you to avoid the temptations that keep you from reaching the goal. Noteworthy in this hadith is the existence of "the admonisher of God in the heart of every Muslim," implying a religious source for conscience. Conscience here is not understood as a license for the believer to do whatever he wants, and it does not make the individual believer a religious and moral authority in his own right. The source of truth is the Qur'an. However, the hadith does suggest that the Muslim has a resource of divine origin within himself, instructing him to do what is good and avoid what is evil. This, again, does not make individual believers arbiters of their own religious and moral destiny. The teaching assumes some kind of prior formation in the faith and the principles of right and wrong. Still, it does imply that the individual believer has a divinely endowed capacity for self-governance. This idea is complemented by the long-standing recognition in Islam that the mind is able to distinguish between good and evil. How else could humans be held accountable on judgment day? This does not mean that humans determine standards of good and evil—that is the exclusive right of God—but they are able to comprehend them and act in accordance with them. There are satanic tendencies within the human condition that explain why people do not choose to act in accordance with the good, but humans have what it takes to be responsible and can therefore be trusted to know at some level where the greater interests of society lie.

The heritage of Islam thus can support the notion that humans are free to govern themselves in accordance with principles of right and wrong.

The concept of freedom in Islam does not quite coincide with modern and postmodern notions of freedom, where freedom is sometimes seen as the end and very purpose of human existence. Freedom always has limits, even in a liberal society where space is given to a range of life-styles in the public arena, and freedom is certainly not something that belongs to one culture as opposed to another. All societies recognize the idea of freedom, but the way it is formulated depends in part on the theological history of the society in question. For example, in the United States, a very specific deployment was made of the biblical teaching that humans are made in the image and likeness of God, making individuals religious and moral—and therefore also political—authorities capable of self-governance and by nature free from all external authorities.[11] This theological history, particular to the American context, has encouraged individuals to see themselves as the makers of their own religious and moral destinies no less than their political fortunes. In that context, freedom tends to be seen as the end and very purpose of human existence, a notion that many Americans assume to be universally valid. However, in other societies, freedom is understood not as the end but the means to realize truths that exist apart from the human subject. These truths may be revealed by God or embodied in a natural order governing society, but the point is that humans are free to pursue the truths set before them. Freedom, then, is about individual responsibility to truth more so than it is about individual authority to determine truth. When it comes to the life of the polity, the idea is that individuals, capable of knowing the common good, set aside individual preferences for the sake of the shared virtues that guide society as a whole.

This reflects something of the situation in Morocco. Individuals do not see themselves as religious and moral authorities, but they do very much see themselves as free. Americans might see a contradiction in this, but a different conception of freedom is operative here, one that does not exalt individual lifestyle choice but rather individual responsibility to protect and promote a shared set of virtues understood to be in harmony with Islam. In this sense, obedience—to father, to king, to God—is very much part and parcel of freedom. The annual expression of fidelity to the king during the Feast of the Throne is a cause for personal pride. It is a visible expression of national independence from foreign forces that would deny the nation the freedom it requires to be obedient to its particular heritage. This is the kind of argument advanced by the nationalist leader, 'Allal al-Fasi (1910–1974), who wrote significantly on the concept of freedom, defining it as a necessary requirement for responsible living as a nation.[12] For the nation to be responsible to its own truths, it must be free from colonial oversight. Freedom here does not turn individuals into authorities in their own right but rather calls them to take responsibility for the common good of the nation.

Things in Morocco today are a bit different from the days of the nationalist struggle for independence. Obedience easily becomes a source of resentment, especially among youth, when its purpose is no longer clear and when it no longer brings concrete benefits but instead only frustration. Still, it remains a key mark of the social imagination in Morocco. Sons may resent the obedience they owe their fathers, but no son wants to be known as disobedient. The press tests the red lines set by the court but grudgingly obeys when admonished for crossing them, only to test them again. Very few Moroccans, perhaps none, would publicly declare that they happily disobey the will of God. To be sure, a few here and there will admit that they do not conduct their daily prayers, and many transgress the teachings of Islam without remorse, but there are limits, protected by law, which affirm the shared virtues that embody the identity of the nation.

Three areas in particular are off limits: eating publicly in Ramadan during daylight hours (Article 222 of the penal code), conversion out of Islam (Article 220), and homosexual activity (Article 489). Such things do exist in private: there are those who do not keep the fast within the walls of their own home; there are those who do not consider themselves Muslims, and some privately opt for other religions; and there are those who are homosexually active for personal or professional reasons.[13] Such things must be kept out of the public eye lest society's very reason for existence be questioned, namely, the preservation of the virtues of Islam. Indeed, those who challenge these limits will face a harsh response from society at large, including politicians and the press. In September 2009, a group of Moroccans were arrested for plans to break the fast in public during Ramadan. In March 2010, a number of Christian missionaries were suddenly thrown out of Morocco after years of discrete work with unwanted orphans. In 2007, several youth in a town south of Tangiers were arrested for allegedly conducting a gay marriage at a private party. None of these security measures was seen as a violation of human rights. On the contrary, society in general applauded them. Mustafa Benhamza, a well-known figure in the religious establishment, referred to the 2009 Ramadan incident as a threat to the stability and security of the nation, describing it as "the first signs of social agitation, a truly wretched under-standing of the purpose of liberties, and a manifest challenge to the collec-tive conscience of Moroccans."

Still, the future will not be one of uniformity. The reality on the ground is a highly pluralistic society—not a multireligious society, but a society where people identify with Islam in diverse ways. There is a low-intensity cultural war within Morocco and even within the ministry of religious affairs. The unspoken question is whether Morocco can be classified under the rubric of "the open Muslim society," similar in some respects to Turkey, where Islam is promoted and patronized by the state in its cer-emonies and in the national curriculum, and where the symbols of Islam remain prominent in society, but where individual citizens have the right to choose whether to conform to the religious tradition of the nation. This would imply a decoupling of citizenship and religion, but it need not mean that Morocco would no longer be first and foremost a Muslim society.

Taha 'Abd al-Rahman, one of the more prominent intellectuals in Morocco today, promotes what he calls "the right of difference" (*haqq al-ikhtilāf*), a concept that is based in Islam and that he distinguishes from freedom of expression.[14] The Islamic concept, he says, is more conducive to a truly global ethics. This is because the modern concept of freedom of expression is often used to insult others in the name of freedom, whereas the Islamic concept, while permitting the right of individuals to dissent, in no way licenses attack on others. Freedom here is not a license but a means to protect individuals. For the most part, 'Abd al-Rahman directs his rhetoric at the European context where in his view Muslim communi-ties should have, first of all, the right to be different in a society that does not always acknowledge differences in the name of religion and, secondly, the right not to have their differences insulted and mocked in the name of freedom of expression. However, one could ask 'Abd al-Rahman whether the argument he advances to empower Muslims in Europe also applies in Morocco. Are Moroccans free to be different so long as they do not use this freedom to insult and mock others? Many would say that in Morocco, the right to be different poses a threat to the fabric of the Muslim society, and yet the reality on the ground suggests the existence of the open Muslim society. Within limits, there is broad tolerance in Morocco for different kinds of behavior even if the norm remains Islam.

Two points need to be made before concluding. The first is the burden of history: The concept of individual rights and liberties cannot be dis-cussed without reference to the historical imagination of Morocco that,

for example, views the Christian as enemy. The existence of Christian missionaries, then, is not a simple question of individual freedom to identify
in public with a religion other than Islam. Why does the Christian continue to be viewed as the enemy? The second point is the universal quality
of both freedom and truth: All groups in Morocco, from secularists to
Salafists, want greater freedom from the court to promote their principles,
while assuming that the truths they espouse should guide society as a
whole. If I want freedom for my truth claims, I should, in all fairness,
be ready to grant it to others whose truth claims I do not accept. This,
however, would potentially put truth at risk, subjecting it to the whims
of personal preference. Is there a way for freedom to be affirmed within
a framework of truth? Is there a way for truth to be preserved without
prejudice to the freedom of all? Do people have the freedom to be wrong?
Or does freedom invariably lead to the abandonment of right and wrong?
Morocco has only recently arrived at a moment in its postcolonial history when it can seriously consider these questions. Self-determination is
no longer a question of independence from the colonial overlord. It now
involves a whole set of issues related to the way society currently exists.
To be sure, the truths that will guide the nation in its postauthoritarian
moment are not reducible to rules of political procedure aside from the
virtues of Islam. However, what is still unfolding is the way those virtues
will be held up alongside the realities of nonconformity in contemporary
Morocco—"the right of difference" as 'Abd al-Rahman puts it. This is not
the place to ponder how things will turn out but to point to two theologically relevant concerns that will have place in the process.

The first concern involves the burden of history. In the historical imagination of the nation, Morocco is understood not simply as a member of
the international community. It is also at the edge of the so-called abode
of Islam, putting it at the front of the battle with the infidel other.[15] The
memory of former colonial empires to the north—Portugal, Spain, and
France—sometimes encourages Moroccans to conceive of themselves
as a nation under attack. Today, in an age of internationally recognized
boundaries, military attack is no longer a significant concern. (Morocco
has expended much energy and resources in recent decades fighting a
movement for political autonomy in the Western Sahara, but that is
another matter.) However, people in Morocco continue to hold onto their
self-understanding as a people under threat. Thus, with the encouragement of Al Jazeera TV, which has to a large degree become the conscience
of the nation, many in Morocco see themselves under intellectual attack

from a West that they continue to identify wholly with Christian tyranny. It therefore makes sense to the nation to expel Christian missionaries who are seen as the latest phase of a colonial project aiming to undermine the cultural mores of society and sap the spirit of the nation.

This is not to explain away the 2010 expulsion of the so-called Christian missionaries and the abuse suffered by the orphans in their care. Rather, it is simply to say that the anxiety over a multireligious society in Morocco is not simply about freedom of conscience, a principle that many in Morocco would likely affirm. This anxiety is as much a byproduct of a past that has yet to be redeemed. As a result, freedom becomes collateral damage in a battle that actually no longer exists but is still being fought. Self-determination as national independence has been achieved, but the past continues to dictate the terms of self-determination in Morocco today, a past where the Christian is enemy par excellence, and this at a time when national independence is hardly in question. How is self-determination to be enacted today? Islam is the religion of Morocco, but national attitudes toward the "other" work to define the scope of freedom at home. The ongoing realization of self-determination in Morocco therefore depends in part on the readiness of Muslims and Christians to redeem the past through cooperative projects that establish the trust necessary for the two communities to view each other as partners and not as adversaries. The same thing could be said, *mutatis mutandis*, about Moroccan attitudes toward other religious communities such as the Shi'a. The theology of civil liberties in Morocco cannot be entirely framed in terms of individual conscience. There is a history that cannot be ignored.

The second concern involves the universality of both freedom and truth: In Morocco today, people look beyond the nation for sources of truth to guide their daily lives. This is a result of the globalizing moment but is also in part a byproduct of discontent with the state, especially among youth, and its attempt to set the parameters of personal identity. Some look to hip-hop, sometimes lacing their lyrics with religious sentiment. Others look to Salafism as broadcast via satellite from Saudi Arabia. There is also a plethora of local groups that exist as parallel societies. One is the Group of Justice and Charity, led by 'Abd al-Salam Yasin, which has opted out of the political system. It rejects the monarchy but does not call for democracy, operating as a network of brotherly solidarity under the authority of Yasin, their spiritual guide. The group condemns the nation's persistently high levels of social injustice and class inequality more so than it criticizes any deficiencies in the nation's religious character. If the group decides to join the political game, its participation is likely to be marked by openness to a diversity of belief, so long as such openness does not prejudice the demands of human solidarity on the national stage. Another group, the Butshishiyya, although enjoying the favor of the court, exists independently as a religious brotherhood under its own authority, personified in Hamza Ibn 'Abbas, a holy figure residing in permanent retreat outside the city of Oujda near the eastern border with Algeria. The Butshishiyya mix tradition with a modern conscious-ness, seeking harmony with all through the lens of a global spirituality they cultivate within their own ranks. The PJD, discussed earlier as the political wing of Morocco's Islamist movement, is committed to Islam as the ultimate reference point for national legislation, but it has learned to interact with secularist groups on a range of issues. These examples underscore the significant diversity in the way groups in Morocco identify with Islam and interact with society as a whole, coexisting peacefully, by and large, and this is to say nothing of the significant secularist presence in Morocco and its impact on the nation.[16] Such plurality, a reality on the ground, seems not to pose a threat to the nation's character. A measure of individual freedom in public is in point of fact tacitly acknowledged in today's Morocco.

Salafists are a bit more complex than other groups. They tend to be condemnatory of society on account of what they see as a pervasive licen-tiousness that violates the teachings of Islam, from the production and consumption of alcohol, to the existence of prostitution, immodest dress, sex tourism, usury, gambling, and homosexuality, to the alleged state encouragement of Christian and Shi'i proselytism. Interestingly, Salafists attribute the moral degeneracy of the nation to a lack of freedom on the part of religious scholars to play their traditional role of guiding youth in the values of Islam. Having been incorporated into the institutions of the state, the religious establishment now exists, Salafists argue, merely to cloak state interests in religious veneer. They are no longer free to guide the nation, especially its youth, a situation that Salafists cite as one of the main causes contributing to terrorism today.

Salafists claim that a state under the guidance of Islam would exist in Morocco had it not been for the machinations of the French protec-torate and its postcolonial successors. However, the social reality on the ground has not, for the most part, led to the radicalization of Salafists in Morocco. Indeed, they are largely apolitical, a result of rhetoric coming from religious authorities in Saudi Arabia who justify political quietism with the adage that "abandoning politics is a political position." In other words, while Salafists in Morroco are activists in promoting a brand of piety believed to be the sole route to salvation, they have essentially written off the politics of the nation as godless. In this sense, the freedom that Salafists want is one that would permit them to live apart from society as the saved sect according to the Qur'an and Sunna. This, ironically, is where Salafists and secularists converge, because both demand to be able to live in accordance with personally chosen beliefs, free from state control and social recrimination. At the same time, Salafists and secularists alike do not seem to realize the implications of their common demand that personal piety be free of state control. They all want greater freedom from state oversight while still assuming that their respective vision should prevail over the nation. In reality, those who identify with either Salafism or secularism are largely free to pursue their own lifestyles within certain limits. In this sense, one sees a number of truth claims existing on the ground in Morocco, largely in harmony, but what is lacking is a national formula that acknowledges this pluralistic reality without prejudice to the preeminence of Islam.

We may conclude that there is currently a crisis of political confidence in Morocco that fosters resentment, if not overt antagonism, between the society at large and the ruling elite. There are no effective unions and no rising industry, as in Turkey, that could bridge the gap between state and society. More significantly, most Moroccans do not have the luxury to think about democracy. They are too busy simply surviving. Still, there are important signs of transition away from authoritarian rule. In contrast to "the years of lead," there are now sharper expectations of the way society should operate. This does not mean that power is in the hands of the people or that the people see themselves as authorities over the nation, but there are certain theological concepts within the tradition of Islam about the purpose of rule and the responsibility of individuals that increasingly interact with emergent realities in Morocco. It is not clear where it is all going, but there is democratic sentiment in the mix. Such democratic sentiment faces significant challenges, including widespread frustration with political parties themselves. Still, however great the frustration, people look to the virtues of Islam to guide the nation, virtues that are seen as sources of stability and coherence apart from the form of rule and that include values which, as discussed in this chapter, coincide with the democratic aspirations of a people who have suffered and continue to suffer and yet have not been deprived of hope.

Postscript

This paper was first drafted well before the events known as the Arab Spring. It is therefore necessary to tie this essay to this dramatic turn of events in the Arab world. The situation varies from country to country. The specific developments in Morocco seem to support this essay's arguments, especially the idea that the king has a democratic side. On July 1, 2011, the Moroccan electorate approved the constitutional changes proposed by the king. Shortly thereafter, the king called for early elections (nearly a year early in October 2011) to bring the country into line with the new constitutional situation. The major change is that the prime minister will no longer be appointed by the king but will be elected in the fashion of the British system. The king will retain control over the military and police and also over the country's foreign relations, but it would seem that governance of domestic affairs will be much more squarely in the hands of the people and their elected representatives. It remains to be seen what will transpire on the ground as a result of these changes. Also, even if this apparently democratic initiative does take hold, it will not likely change the place of Islam in the national consciousness. Since the constitutional changes were approved, there has been much discussion about their effects on the relation of religious institutions to the state, but no one has suggested that Islam will not form the basis of the nation's identity. It will be interesting, then, to see how concepts of citizenship crystallize over the years ahead in Morocco with its national vision that is rooted in Islam and also increasingly democratic in sentiment. Will "the Muslim open society" become not only a reality on the ground but also the formula by which the Moroccan nation defines itself?

Notes

1. See, in general, Mohamed El Mansour, *Morocco in the Reign of Mulay Sulayman* (Wisbech: MENAS Press, 1988); and ʿAbd al-Jalīl Bādū, *al-Salafiyya wa-l-Islāh* (Tangiers: Salīkī Ikhwān, 2007).
2. See, for example, the series of articles by Hammād al-Qibāj in *al-Sabīl*, a bi-monthly journal in Morocco. I have had access to two articles in the series titled "al-Salafiyya wa-l-Dawla: Ayy ʿIlaqa?": *al-Sabīl*, no. 54, May 16, 2009, 14 and no. 55, June 1, 2009, 14.
3. For a view that connects this event with broader currents of Arab nationalism, see Stefan Reichmuth, "The Arabo-Islamic Constitutional Thought of 1907: ʿAbd al-Karim Murad (d. 1926) and His Draft Constitution for Morocco," in *Intellectuals*

in the Modern Islamic Work: Transmission, Transformation, Communication, ed. Stéphane A. Dudoignon et al. (Abingdon, OXON: Routledge 2006).

4. For insights into the mind of Hasan II, see Hassan II, *Le Génie de la moderation: Réflexions sur les vérités de l'Islam—Entretiens avec Eric Laurent* (Paris: Plon, 2000).

5. Malika Zeghal, "S'éloigner, se rapprocher: la gestion et le contrôle de l'islam dans la république de Bourguiba et la monarchie de Hassan II," in *Monarchie arabes: Transitions et dérives dynastiques,* ed. Rémy Leveau and Abdellah Hammoudi (Paris: La Documentation française, 2002), 50–79.

6. Joseph A. Kéchichian, *Power and Succession in Arab Monarchies* (Boulder, CO: Lynne Rienner, 2008), 383–407.

7. Ann Elizabeth Mayer, "Conundrums in Constitutionalism: Islamic Monarchies in an Era of Transition," *UCLA Journal of Islam and Near Eastern Law,* 1 (2002): 183–228.

8. M. Elaine Combs-Schilling, "Performing Monarchy, Staging Nation," in *In the Shadow of the Sultan: Culture, Power, and Politics in Morocco,* ed. Rahma Bourqia and Susan Gilson Miller (Cambridge, MA: Harvard University Press, 1999), 176–214.

9. For Islamist organization under kingship, see Gudrun Krämer, "Good Counsel to the King: The Islamist Opposition in Saudi Arabia, Jordan, and Morocco," in *Middle East Monarchies: The Challenge of Modernity,* ed. Joseph Kostiner (Boulder, CO: Lynne Rienner, 2000), 257–287.

10. Bohdana Dimitrovova, "Reshaping Civil Society in Morocco: Boundary Setting, Integration and Consolidation," CEPS Working Document No. 323, December 2009.

11. Mark A. Noll, *America's God: From Jonathan Edwards to Abraham Lincoln* (Oxford: Oxford University Press, 2002).

12. 'Allal al-Fasi, *al-Huriyya,* with introduction by 'Abd al-Karim Ghulab (Rabat: Matba'at al-Risala, 1977).

13. It is worth noting the attempts to support the legitimacy of homosexuality by rooting it within the particular religious heritage of Morocco. The Hamdushiyya is a traditional form of Sufism but it has become patronized by the gay community. This is done through reference to Lalla 'Aisha, a patron saint of the Hamdushiyya, who miraculously turned into a powerful man when her sexual integrity was threatened. This story is used to suggest that ambiguous sexuality has its place in the national heritage. The Hamdushiyya leadership, of course, has to walk a fine line between accusations of providing religious cover for "lewd" acts that violate the penal code and the financial patronage of the gay community.

14. See, for example, Taha 'Abd al-Rahman, *al-Ḥaqq al-Islāmī fī al-Ikhtilāf al-Fikrī* (Casablanca: al-Markaz al-Thaqāfī al-'Arabī, 2005).

15. 'Abd al-Qādir al-'Āfiyya, *al-Maghrib wa-l-Jihād al-Ta'rīkhī,* 2nd ed. (Sale: al-Ma'had al-Mutakhassis lil-Tiknūlūjiyyā al-Tatbīqiyya, 1999).

16. For one example of the impact of secularist mobilization in Morocco, see Janine A. Clark and Amy E. Young, "Islamism and Family Law Reform in Morocco and Jordan," *Mediterranean Politics* 13, no. 3 (2008): 333–352.

PART THREE

Confronting Pluralism

Main Trends in Political Theologies Today

6

Difference, Resemblance, Dialogue

SOME GOALS FOR COMPARATIVE POLITICAL
THEOLOGY IN A PLURAL AGE

Michael Jon Kessler

I.

PLURALISM POSES A challenge for political theology.[1] Reflection about a range of issues, including the legitimation of political participation, institutional power arrangements, and sovereignty; the role of religio-ethical ideas in will formation and political justification; and the diffuse processes of social integration in increasingly diverse societies, forces a scholar of political theology to confront an array of beliefs, practices, and worldviews, many of which are laden with conflicting ontological elements.[2] When casting an eye to the political ideas of fellow citizens, one confronts justifications for political participation and legitimacy often very different from one's own. This pluralism is magnified for any reflection—descriptive or normative—which looks beyond one's own polity to examine how citizens of other polities undertake processes of political legitimation and policy formation in light of their deepest principles. The political theories and political theologies that serve as conceptual and moral resources for political agents in our diverse and interconnected world are increasingly in need of careful description and comparative analysis.

While there are many definitions of "political theology," I use the term to denote reflection about the religio-ethical bases of the justifications for political principles, norms, practices, and institutions.[3] Political theology, on my account, takes a broader view of these justifications than does political philosophy; it incorporates reflection about these justifications beyond exclusively rational concepts and anthropological features to include the religio-ethical languages, cultures, and concepts comprising the full spectrum of the ways various humans describe the meaning, value, and legitimacy of political ideas, practices, motivations, and institutions. Political theology is both a descriptive enterprise that apprehends, catalogs, and analyzes empirical political phenomena (including institutional and power arrangements, concepts, justifications, and policies) and a constructive enterprise in which theory is developed and critically applied in normative and prescriptive statements about the way politics ought to be configured.

To cast political theology in this way is already to position it as a comparative enterprise. Reflection about political practices and norms will lead beyond one's own views to those of others which need to be clarified, translated, and critiqued. Likewise, political engagement will inevitably lead both to encounters with those of different normative viewpoints and with those who are citizens of other political orders. Such encounters will require communicative clarity—often difficult to forge—across divergent background assumptions, worldviews, and legitimating norms.

Yet comparison as a *method* is more than simply broadening the range of theories that one incorporates into one's own political justifications and reflections. Merely expanding our repertoire of texts and thinkers is certainly a noble endeavor, but it is not comparison *per se*. Rather, comparison in political theology would seem to aim at a greater purpose: identifying particular similarities and differences in normative ideas and practices across plural political traditions in order to advance understanding of existing political realities and possibilities, to sharpen and expand our own positions vis-à-vis other positions, and to thereby deepen understanding in a way that improves upon the outcomes of political interactions between diverse individuals and groups.

As a discipline, political theology is increasingly showing signs of confronting these comparative issues, particularly in light of recent work to assess the political ideals and prospects of Islamic societies.[4] There is also some guidance for this move from the political science subfield of political theory. Fred Dallmayr has usefully urged political theorists to incorporate a comparative approach.[5] Dallmayr proposes to "supplement the rehearsal of routinized canons with a turn to global, cross-cultural or 'comparative' political theorizing."[6] Dallmayr takes seriously the ongoing dynamics of globalization and urges that theorists understand the contexts of their political theorizing alongside other configurations in the "global village."[7] A recognition of this fact coupled with an imperative of interpretive responsibility requires the theorist to understand they cannot maintain an imperialistic position of the supremacy of their own political ideas but must move to dialogical interaction and engagement with those beyond one's own theoretical tradition. Dallmayr cites Raimundo Panikkar approvingly, to insist that "striving toward a global picture of the world" by bringing the "other theory" into one's own canon is a mode of hegemonic control. Instead, he implores the need for "diatopical hermeneutics" that is "a mode of interpretation required when the difference to be negotiated is 'the distance between two (or more) cultures which have independently developed in different spaces (*topoi*) their own forms of philosophizing and ways of reaching intelligibility.'"[8]

While those pursuing the study of political theology across traditions and political boundaries must endeavor to maintain clarity about the goals and purposes for comparison, *defining* those goals and purposes is an exceedingly difficult task. What is the goal for comparison, besides curiosity and engaging in classification of similarity and difference? As a discipline, political theology is only beginning to take a comparative turn, and there is little theoretical reflection about the purpose of comparison in political theology. An insight of this chapter is that the methods and purposes of other comparative enterprises in religious studies, namely comparative religious ethics, can help any future comparative political theology in developing a coherent answer to this "purpose question."

2.

Comparative religious ethics (CRE) is a relatively established subdiscipline in religious ethics.[9] There has been no shortage of methodological discussion in CRE—in fact, a significant amount of writing in the CRE genre seems to be *about* the process of doing CRE. Yet, for all the concern about *how* to undertake CRE, there has been little success in articulating *what* CRE accomplishes. What is the goal of setting this tradition of moral reflection next to that tradition? What does the reader of comparative religious ethics learn? What effect does this inquiry have on the reader's own normative reflection? This is a deceptively simple set of questions. Yet the difficulties CRE theorists have faced in this task, I contend, is a cautionary tale for scholars hoping to engage in comparisons across traditions of political theology.

Perhaps the most prescient critique was offered by Jeffrey Stout not long after the first attempts at CRE appeared:

> Comparative ethics is less a discipline than a sort of floating seminar in which scholars from various fields trade information and discuss methodology. Because most people around the seminar table know only one or two traditions intimately and are rightly anxious to resist hasty generalization, most of the information being exchanged is introductory and fragmentary in nature.[10]

Stout identifies a number of problems that have come to plague the field. First, articulating a *goal* for comparison beyond trading interesting moments of difference and similarity is a significant hurdle. This methodological impotence reflects the larger problems of whether moral categories and concepts are translatable across traditions, thus invoking caution about generalizing from particular cases to universals.[11] Further, at the practical level, it is hard enough for the scholar to gain adequate knowledge about a single tradition of moral reflection; knowing enough about two traditions to offer any useful insights is a significant hurdle. As Stout put it:

> If we could somehow produce a generation of scholars who knew much more than any of us knows about the history and variety of ethical traditions, then the conversation would surely be worthwhile. But it seems doubtful that the hope for a generation of renaissance comparativists will ever be realized. Life is short, and human minds are finite. So there is some danger that the next generation's comparativists will know less than we do about anything in particular and that they will have even more trouble than we have had explaining why anyone outside the guild ought to take their pronouncements seriously...Comparativists may someday have a more secure niche within the academic bureaucracy than we have had...but what of moral and historical substance will they have to offer their students and readers?[12]

What Stout seems to be begging for, besides humility about how much a single individual can accomplish with expertise, is for the comparative enterprise to state well-articulated goals for the comparison. Even if we assume that CRE scholars engage in scholarship adequate to the demands of the respective traditions, to what end are these comparisons directed?

3.

A brief review of the development of CRE over the past thirty-five years reveals that while there has been no shortage of methodological theorizing, a full accounting of the goals of CRE has not been well-established.[13] At least since Durkheim attempted to lay out the "permanent elements which constitute that which is permanent and human in religion" across all particular, diverse manifestations, there has been a comparative task within the study of religions in general.[14] For Durkheim, this comparative task extended to the science of morality, and how diverse societies bonded once religious bases of collectivity began to dissolve in the modern period. Comparison in ethics, however, has even earlier origins. As Max Stackhouse put it:

> The comparative evaluation of the religious ethics of many traditions is, in fact, quite old. It is deeply embedded in the apologetic, dialogical, and even polemical theologies of the early church, in the encounters of Judaic, Islamic, and Christian scholars in the Middle Ages, and in the formation of anthropology, comparative religion, philology and linguistics, and area studies (often at the hands of missionaries and the children of missionaries) in the nineteenth century, and in a host of contemporary dialogues and debates where traditions are encountering each other as living options.[15]

The basic methodological options for CRE were articulated in the late 1970s, during what could be dubbed a "classical" age of CRE. Ronald Green's *Religious Reason: The Rational and Moral Basis of Religious Belief* marked out a method of universalizing moral categories (in this case, based on Green's interpretation of Kant) which then served to guide an exploration of particular religious ethical reasoning across traditions (in this case, Christianity, Judaism, and Indian religions).[16] Particular local ethical beliefs and practices are analyzed as manifestations of a general conceptual framework of universal morality. Such an account of moral categories, which at their general level are common across the particularities of history, cultures, and geographies, led many to question the efficacy and even the possibility of such a "grand-theory" approach.[17] Can moral categories be developed from the study of one tradition which apply to moral phenomena in other traditions? Can one develop an objective and universal structure of moral concepts that applies to all particular phenomena?

By contrast, David Little and Sumner Twiss identified "common attributes of the concepts of morality, religion, and law" which bear family resemblances to each other and guided them through case studies across traditions.[18] More modest in their approach than Green, they attempted a "reconstruction," from the available textual and historical evidence, of the way "a group understood its behavior."[19] In this way, they hoped to "illuminate a significant field of concepts" which bear resemblance to each other across moral traditions regarding the mode of practical justification of actions.[20] Some theorists critiqued their work for failing to offer adequate conceptual clarity:

> They have at least given some reasons for their definitions and these definitions "have a strong ring of plausibility to them." But we are left in the dark about the purposes of inquiry. The appropriate question is not whether we ought to allow normative and explanatory aims into our descriptive work, but rather which aims we ought to have and how we can avoid having such aims unduly prejudice our findings. Without such aims in view, we shall lack criteria for assessing whatever descriptions and definitions we produce. If Little and Twiss hear a "strong ring of plausibility" in their own definitions, but have trouble saying why, it is probably because they have normative and explanatory aims after all—aims sufficiently close to consciousness to make the definitions ring but too successfully repressed to make the reasons evident.[21]

At the other end of the spectrum from Green, Robin Lovin and Frank Reynolds worked from the starting point of the radical diversity of moral communities, the specific linguistic and cultural horizons of moral rationality and beliefs, and the difficulties with the universalizing tendencies of scholarly observation across different, even incommensurable, ethical worlds. They seemed to have taken the central insight of Donald Swearer to heart: "Comparisons must not only be appropriate to the method of analysis but, more importantly, faithful to the traditions under scrutiny."[22] They assembled a comparative study of cosmogony that was nonsystematic, a rather loose collection that was "seldom comparative in a direct way," since the authors "focus their work within the context of a single tradition."[23] In spite of this seemingly disconnected particularity, the "broad meaning of cosmogony and ethics which the authors employ allows them to delineate significant patterns of cosmogonic thinking and significant modes of relating cosmogonic motifs to ethical norms and issues. This...permits comparisons that still respect the authors' grasp of the unity and integrity of the cultures they have studied."[24] This method, which they dub "ethical naturalism" and others have called "pragmatic holism," "seeks to describe the relationships between worldviews and norms in ways that accurately reflect the tensions and controversies in a community's experience, in ways that reproduce the complexity of a tradition and allow the identification and meaningful comparison of the most crucial elements within it."[25]

The recognition of the pluralism inherent in diverse moral and religious worldviews has led to a rejection of most attempts like Green's to catalog and rank particular moral positions under a universal structure.[26] As Lee Yearley put this, pluralism forces moral theorists to recognize that "many legitimate goods exist and that whatever [moral] goods you pursue, they are but one among possible sets of goods."[27] In spite of the continuing insistence on recognizing the reality of pluralism, it is an interesting fact that most contemporary CRE theorists also reject moral relativism and complete incommensurability. Aaron Stalnaker representatively argues that while "social context does matter to moral evaluation," the idea that "any culture or community can and should only be judged by that culture or community's own norms" is held to be a "failure on multiple levels."[28]

4.

More recent work by a new generation of theorists takes up the issues of this classical era of CRE yet, unfortunately, this work does not articulate a fully comprehensive answer to the purpose of comparison. Speaking in broad categories, Sumner Twiss describes recent CRE as having a number of aims "ranging across enriched moral self-understanding, appreciation of other traditions, enhancement of cross-cultural communication, addressing shared social problems, and systematic theorizing about religion and ethics."[29] The "more robust" versions "explicitly compare two different traditions, thinkers, texts, or genres in order to elicit significant similarities and differences between the objects of comparison."[30]

David Decosimo's "Comparison and the Ubiquity of Resemblance" helpfully frames the basic methodological issues taken up in this recent work. He begins with an insight from Nelson Goodman, "Similarity is relative, variable, and context-dependent...anything is in some way like anything else...every two things have some property in common."[31] This basic fact of the world—certain features are shared by different things and can bear resemblance to each other—implies that resemblance is ubiquitous and therefore, at one level, trivial. Merely pointing out similarity, as such, of two beliefs or practices does not necessarily bear any scholarly fruit in advancing ethical thought.

Decosimo points to the necessary judgments which we import into comparison as an additional layer: "genuine" resemblance is more than "sharedness" because the features we point to in comparison are deemed "significant." The attribution of significance necessarily involves "judgments that necessarily reflect our values, commitments, interests, and purposes."³² As such, these judgments "vary according to a range of factors from our cultural location and personal commitments, to, especially, our purposes in undertaking the comparison."³³ At the same time, CRE theorists can overdetermine the significance of resemblance. We might think that since similarities exist, they must mean something important. In this way, CRE theorists are prone to "overabundant or reckless ascriptions of significance" of the resemblances between features of different traditions.

Taken together, Decosimo thinks these problems can lead CRE theorists to be blind to the values and purposes that underlie the comparative task and the judgments of resemblance.³⁴ To counter this tendency, he urges that "it is essential that comparativists clearly and explicitly identify the particular goals of their comparisons." By clearly stating their goals, CRE theorists thereby establish "norms for judging whether the chosen objects of comparison are *appropriate*, whether, in a basic way, the comparison is *coherent* or *makes sense*." Thus Decosimo implores CRE theorists to aim for a "minimum coherence in comparison" which involves a "connection between the purpose of the comparison and the objects being compared."³⁵

Setting clear goals is a challenge taken up by a recent collection of essays in the *Journal of Religious Ethics*. The essays find a common enterprise in "probing the connection between 'anthropos' and 'ethics' in a comparative context."³⁶ While noting the general dichotomy between generality and particularity at the core of the CRE enterprise (do we start with categories which frame our descriptive work, or do we engage in the empirical description that helps generate more general categories?), the authors push for more inclusive and varied models, all of which can fit under the task of CRE: "a diversity of concerns and differences in the demands of the materials legitimate numerous styles of comparison." While this wide net approach may sound optimistic, it forces the question of what outcome CRE hopes to accomplish. The authors suggest that CRE can bring about an alternative to choosing between universal norms or "a large collection of incommensurable views." "Patterns across traditions" can be discerned in the process of describing "conceptions of and relations between self and other." This inquiry can then ground the development of "typologies" which "highlight significant similarities and differences among the various perspectives."[37]

Description that extends beyond any particular tradition to generate typologies and general patterns of similarity does not, however, sufficiently answer the underlying question concerning *why* an author would attempt CRE in the first place. Beyond fascination with resemblances, what is the purpose for the *ethical theorist* to engage in this comparison? The authors, for their part, point to a few benefits that they think emerge from such a typological purpose. First, in "an increasingly multicultural world," marked by the now everyday phenomenon of cross-cultural communication, "the dialogue of comparison" is now "not merely a theoretical goal but a practical necessity."[38] Thus, the authors assert that CRE somehow is *useful* to cross-cultural communication. The benefits and scope of this utility remain unexplored in the introductory essay or in the essays that follow, other than to raise an implicit assertion that cross-cultural clarity is useful for an as-yet unspecified outcome.

Second, the authors contend that CRE expands our view of tools, issues, and methods that we may have overlooked in a particular tradition or text. "The process of comparison places distinctive features of a given tradition in relief." Thus comparison, it is claimed, does not diminish detailed context-specific study of a particular tradition, but contributes to it since we may understand better our own tradition of practice or study through our investigations into other ethical traditions. Third, comparative studies can help shake up our own categories and concepts derived from "European-focused" scholarship in religious ethics. "By making the basic categories of analysis explicit as well as modifying and refining them in the process of comparison, the authors seek both to be attentive to historical particularity and to engage in a kind of rational reconstruction" of concepts, the very process of which connects historical and constructive work and exemplifies the transformation of the scholar's own concepts through the comparative project.[39]

Of the recent theorists, Aaron Stalnaker provides the best example of a scholar attempting to work through the issues of methodology, specifically how to justify the features of the ethical tradition one seeks to compare. On a reading of two recent methodological essays in the *Journal of Religious Ethics*, Stalnaker begins by recalling the widespread insistence (typified by the naturalist approach) on "interpreting texts and social practices strictly in terms of their local cultural and intellectual contexts."[40] This poses an a priori challenge for the comparativist—how to compare responsibly across the diverse cultural contexts, especially when the comparison is between ideas abstracted from their embedded context. For Stalnaker, CRE should aim to accurately describe religious phenomena and therefore expertise is required in linguistic and historical skills. The CRE observer then seeks to use these skills to "gain insight" through comparison of different phenomena across traditions which "are similar enough in certain respects to be mutually illuminating, and thought-provoking *for the observer*." The observations ultimately allow better "normative reflection in our own pluralistic, conflicted, and possibility-strewn contemporary context." This broad reach across traditions problematically conflicts with the demand of the expert to be context-specific (and the demand of the ethical naturalist to maintain fidelity to the tradition on its own terms)—"historical accuracy and insight are compromised by comparative interests."[41]

Stalnaker attempts to overcome this problem by developing the idea of a "bridge concept" which he calls a "conceptual apparatus...[a] more-or-less systematic construction a thinker has made of a given culture and era's contested repertoire of concepts and images." The observer "makes" and "represents" the tradition under review, presenting "them as theoretical interlocutors," to "attend to the complex and sophisticated ways *they themselves* theorize questions of human nature and ethical formation." This mode of representing thinkers supposedly can "bring distant religious statements into conversation and simultaneously...preserve their distinctiveness within this interrelation." Citing Charles Taylor, Stalnaker posits that CRE can construct "languages of perspicuous contrast" through "carefully chosen bridge concepts [that] can help the comparativist to mediate between different visions in such a way that aspects of them, at least, can be carefully and productively contrasted." In this way, Stalnaker claims that the CRE observer sets up a dialogue between traditions, but "in this case, the dialogue is an imaginary one provoked by various contemporary concerns, and carried through an interpreter's own imaginative matchmaking and midwifery."[42] Comparison can thereby generate better ethical analysis by provoking questions that might not be otherwise developed when the observer's perspective is constrained by being "within" a tradition.

Implicit in this approach is an awareness that all reflective engagement with other traditions—as well as one's own—includes a normative face.[43] As Stalnaker puts this: "Comparative ethicists can only evaluate from wherever we already are, as engaged scholars of religion who live in a particular place and time within a complex, globalized world, drawing on those moral traditions, models, and principles that seem most compelling to each of us." This leads to a "sharing of interpretations and reasons for judgment" that can spur "practical reform of human communities and individual lives."[44]

Stalnaker calls this observational standpoint a mode of "contemporary bricolage," in which the CRE observer who is working on their own normative project "should not feel bashful about taking ideas out of context." Stalnaker doubles down on this idea in a later essay: when constructing our comparative projects, we not only extract ideas from their context (although with careful attention to their linguistic and historical contexts), but we inevitably will subject them to ethical evaluation.[45] We judge comparatively all of the time, but to do it well, we must recognize that the frames of comparison are not given in reality. Citing J. Z. Smith's insight that there is nothing given or natural about the elements we select to compare, Stalnaker merges this with a rejection of relativism (in which all concepts are so embedded and contextual such that we can never judge them unless we are "in" the context ourselves). Thus, a CRE observer can, while being "cautious and wary" of hasty judgment, evaluate others from "wherever we already are, as engaged scholars of religion who live in a particular place and time, within a complex, globalized world, drawing on those moral traditions, models, and principles that seem most compelling and insightful to each of us." The limits to comparison are keyed only to the promise of the comparativist's imagination: "The creativity and insight of the interpreter in drawing the conceptions between some distant debate, practice, or theory and contemporary ethical debate provide the only de facto limits on when it might be worth explicitly evaluating the practices of distant others." This "sharing of interpretations and reasons for judgment offer the best hope for refinement of these 'moral sources' over time, as well as practical reform of human communities and individual lives."[46]

An immediate challenge to this mode of comparison can be made based on concerns about cultural and moral imperialism.[47] This is a standard and well-trodden problem of moral theory: When we critically evaluate another's moral practices and beliefs, some moral theorists would claim that we are inevitably imposing our own moral frame onto the other tradition.

Yet, an equally fundamental challenge that can be raised against Stalnaker's account regards his insistence that we engage in encounter through *construction* of the nonnative tradition. This is a variant of the moral relativism problem, yet is about our way of categorizing the phenomena under review, not specifically about how we judge them normatively. In one's choice of objects to compare, and the manner in which we represent them, how are we to be assured that we are not imposing our own frame of reference on the phenomena under examination? How are we assured the bridge concepts bear any resemblance to the concepts as the native practitioner and believer might hold them (if, indeed, such an internal view is to have any validity)?[48] It remains striking to me that Stalnaker's hope for practical reform through dialogical interaction among religious ethical traditions is presented as possible, not through *actual* dialogue, nor in light of a developed argument about maintaining some mode of accurate interpretation, but through our own creativity in framing and appropriating the concepts and practices of others. Notice there is nothing intrinsic to the process Stalnaker lays out that requires actual encounter with the other—only a (virtuoso-like) perusal of the conceptual and practical artifacts of their lives. Pluralism requires that the ethical thinker only expand one's thoughts, not one's interactions. On Stalnaker's reading, it seems that we ultimately engage in comparison with these imagined others for our own purposes. The outcome is that our "reconstruction and interpretation of some distant normative debate forces us to question our own conceptions of the good and or the right...we generate problems for ourselves that should be resolved through comparative ethical reflection," which allows *us* to "learn and become wiser." Stalnaker claims this process is Gadamerian, yet *constructing* what another holds to be the case ethically seems not at all to be dialogical.[49] Lee Yearley recognizes this danger for all comparison when he proposes that "to do justice" to the texts read across traditions, "we must bring them into a kind of reasoned conversation with our own ideas and do so in a way that gives absolute pride of place to neither."[50]

Decosimo also challenges Stalnaker for a related reason. He finds it "disappointing and surprising" that Stalnaker, in his *Overcoming Evil*, does not provide an adequate articulation for "why" he chose the particular figures to compare.[51] Indeed, the choice of objects of comparison is intimately related to the purpose for comparison. What does the reader learn from the comparison? Why is the author setting up this particular mode of practical ethical action or that particular concept as significantly related across two traditions of moral inquiry? Stalnaker offers the following: "Both [Augustine and Xunzi] develop subtle and insightful accounts of personal formation that include detailed analysis and advocacy of particular practices" and "build their accounts of personal formation on the basis of clear-eyed but distinctive assessments of humanity's propensities to do evil."[52] On top of this basic "similarity in the general morphology of their views" across the linguistic, cultural, and temporal distance, Stalnaker articulates the payoff: "Grappling with Augustine's and Xunzi's accounts of these matters can help us to reflect both on substantive questions of anthropology and ethical formation, and on possible vocabularies for such reflection."[53] In spite of this hope, it seems difficult to see how this general morphological similarity between such vastly different figures yields anything but *separate* vocabularies for ethical reflection.

Even with this criticism, Decosimo follows Stalnaker down the path in which the goals and objects of comparison are "ours to choose." A CRE theorist will not (cannot?) have "one overarching goal" but should instead seek to "let a thousand flowers bloom" in the field of CRE. Our judgments about the appropriateness of comparing different elements of traditions and practices are thus to be made on a case-by-case basis and toward the observer's own goals. By these accountings, does CRE offer no other reason than utility and personal interest as the outcomes of comparison? Surely one can hope for a more substantial purpose and contribution to the wider work of ethical reflection.

5.

Critical interpretation of another tradition is neither submission in the face of the other nor completely a product of our own scholarly and personal interests. Likewise, encounters with representatives of other traditions open the possibility for broadened moral understanding in spite of linguistic, cultural, and conceptual differences. Theological ethicist William Schweiker developed a hermeneutical structure for CRE that proposed how understanding between moral representatives can transpire even though moral practices and traditions differ substantially. Hermeneutical theory, in my judgment, provides a clear and substantive goal for comparative work and specifies, more precisely than other alternatives, the scope of responsibility one bears when encountering another tradition.

On Schweiker's account (which is indebted to Tillich, Ricouer, and Gadamer, among others), moral understanding arises through reciprocal action within a shared temporal and spatial order mediated by linguistic, symbolic forms.[54] Through their dynamic process of living, every human leaves traces, artifacts, and impressions in cultural and linguistic forms. The common structure of this process of living (a form of mimesis for Schweiker, in which we picture, make, and form a lifeworld), is evident throughout human existence (insofar as we are linguistic and conceptual creatures) even while the content and particularities are vastly diverse. The task of comparative ethics "is concerned with moral worlds but...the question of a 'world' must take seriously the discursive, symbolic forms enacted in communities that give rise to a sense of reality and possible ways of life." All attempts at understanding, and especially understanding others removed from proximity to our traditions, requires "translating or carrying over beliefs, practices, texts, and symbols into a language the interpreter can comprehend."[55]

Notice that at the level of discursive, symbolic, and cultural interpretation, the comparative theorist encounters other *actual* human lives, in all of their complexity. Therefore the comparativist does not generate the object of study. Rather, we *encounter* the other moral phenomena in the practices, texts, and symbols of the other, as well as in face-to-face encounters. Translation and interpretation is not creation all the way down. Any encounter in this linguistic horizon is neither fabrication nor imposition, but reciprocation:

> Just because cultures and religions enact different "worlds" that define and shape character and conduct does not negate the fact that to be human is to have a world presented *through patterns of reciprocal action*. It is this shared fact that makes complete moral relativism spurious. The differences between religions are not incommensurable ones. This is because...comparative interpretation is itself the enactment of a common world of meaning...Through interpretation a shared world of meaning allows us to understand what remains different from us and requires respect for that difference.[56]

In this mode of interpretation, the comparativist is not in the mode of bricoleur. Rather, the comparativist is always a moral human being

encountering and engaging in a common enterprise of understanding with someone inhabiting a world filled with different possibilities
and particularities. As a self-consciously hermeneutical investigator, the
scholar is not driven exclusively and primarily by one's own "subjective
purposes" but, *pace* Habermas, is responsible to the demands of the interpreted: "A correct interpretation fits, suits, or explicates the meaning of the
interpretandum."[57] The comparativist explores "the complex practices communities use to symbolize their own lives," a process that "transpires in
language, not simply as a system of signs but as discourse, as the medium
of reciprocal, dialogic action *between* agents. The scholar enters this dialogical space through the unique effort of interpretation. By engaging the
symbols, texts, and actions of other communities the comparativist presents a new shared world of meaning."[58]

Schweiker thus imposes a regulative ideal of interpretive goodwill
upon the comparative theorist: "The practice of comparative ethics contributes to the enactment of a shared moral universe in which the diverse
ways of being human are preserved amid the claims of responsibility... to
see interpretation as a form of responsibility means that the comparativist must respond to the claim of the other and be accountable for his or
her actions." Our representations and interpretations of another's moral
world are bound up with responsiveness to the integrity of the other and
our responsibility to interact with this moral representative in a way that
respects their integrity. Responsible comparison traces "a common structure to mimetic action while insisting that one must think comparatively
by engaging not only that structure but the figurations, symbols, beliefs,
and practices that mark a community's moral world."[59]

As Schweiker frames it, comparative interpretation entails "analogical
insight in translation."[60] Such interpretation enacts a common world of
understanding that is

> a metaphorized world that we invent in order to discover some-
> thing about others and ourselves. This shared world is enacted in
> a practice (interpretation) characterized by a movement between
> worlds (translation) with its own good (insight) and under the
> moral demand (responsibility) to adhere to the formal criterion of
> comparison.[61]

Schweiker's role for the "metaphorized world that we invent" is not reproduction of the other in our own minds for our own purposes, but a *shared*

moral space, where we encounter others and responsibly seek wisdom, mutual insight, and conceptual sharing, even as we critically interact with others' positions and our own. Translation entails interpretive encounter with *actual others* who are themselves moral beings presenting and enacting a world that can be glimpsed, shared, and interpreted through our own moral judgment. We thereby escape the tyranny of *imposed* interpretation insofar as we hold to the demand of responsible interpretation and fidelity to the honest and accurate reception and representations of the others' beliefs and practices: "The event of understanding is not a transcendence of the world; it is a participation through interaction in the emergence of a common world of meaning." And here, the dialogical view of comparative interpretation reveals a clear purpose: "encountering others in the performative act of interpretation [where] there is some apprehension of the shape, texture, and direction of their lives and our own within a shared space of meaning and responsibility."[62] What dialogue and encounter in a comparative moral enterprise can achieve is the fulfillment of a type of human flourishing—authentic encounter between persons who hold each other to be moral agents and treat each other as worthy of respect. Unlike universalist positions such as that of Green, this dialogical view of encounter accommodates a diverse range of different moral approaches, distinct moral vocabularies, and many worldviews, each offered in encounter with different persons. The goal is not unification but openness to probing and discussing the other human's ideas, principles, beliefs, and policies with attention to all the differences— moral, cultural, cognitive, linguistic, and religious, among many others— which distinguish us from our fellow humans.

6.

A few CRE theorists have envisioned such a path of *actual* dialogue. Bruce Grelle, for instance, pushed for CRE to engage with practical problems shared across religious, moral, and cultural differences; this movement was in part an outgrowth of shifts in the field of ethics in general earlier in the twentieth century.[63] The aim of comparative ethics on Grelle's account is a kind of interreligious moral dialogue where participants "seek to address the question of how we are to think about and respond to the moral problems...in a religiously and culturally pluralistic world."[64]

In this way, the empirical differences across religious ethical traditions can provide fruitful grounds for theorists representing those traditions to enter into *actual* dialogue around some specific set of problems mutually

confronting the distinct ethical communities: "Those who take an empirical approach are able to focus instead on the hopeful fact that when moral
systems do come into conflict, the parties involved are able to establish
communication on the issues that are at stake, and may eventually arrive
at an agreement that incorporates some of the elements present in each of
their ways of looking at reality and evaluating action."[65] Grelle recognizes
the reality of moral and cultural pluralism but insists that "all people and
groups share similar sorts of practical moral problems."[66] The comparativist's point of departure is a common moral challenge around which she
seeks "to construct a common moral world (a fusion of horizons) between
one's own moral tradition...and the moral tradition(s) being studied."
Whether the problem is as large in scale as global environmental disruptions or as local as corruption in a local governmental office, the comparativist seeks to uncover and bridge divides in the moral worldviews of those
different fellows who are mutually confronted by the common challenge.
This comparative "moral praxis" involves a "dialectic of translation from
one moral world to another...of receptivity to the other (insight into the
other's moral world)" and a "constructive effort to answer how we and
the other should live."[67] Working within a tradition, the comparativist can
thus "collaborate on seeking answers to shared moral dilemmas cutting
across traditional and cultural boundaries."[68] Such work can range across
biomedical and ethical challenges as well as more political issues of state
legitimacy, war-making, and human rights and usefully challenge and
expand Western paradigms for handling the dilemmas.

7.

It is here that scholars of political theology can learn from the challenges
CRE has faced. In this essay I sketch only a preliminary contribution to
comparative political theology. As a step in that direction, I offer here a few
theses to draw together the insights and lessons from the preceding study
of CRE as a way to begin to develop some basic principles, purposes, and
methods that may guide future projects in comparative political theology.[69]

Thesis 1: *Comparison is basic to all understanding, a method we use to
elucidate similarities and resemblances between phenomena and translate the
foreign into the more familiar.* As part of any theoretical analyses and judgment, we seek resemblances between disparate ideas and phenomena,
in order to understand the alien through its similarity to the familiar
(whether the alien is near or far, old or new, that which is close to us

or quite foreign). Comparativists utilize classification in order to create a taxonomy that helps to describe, organize, and understand the disparate phenomena under investigation.

Thesis 2: *A basic purpose of comparison across traditions of political theology is to elucidate the different ways in which other political actors (within and across political communities) draw meaning from political action, how they legitimate political authority, what they envision as moral and political challenges, and why they structure political institutions and policy in the way they do toward achieving their ideas of human goods.* As a method of inquiry in political theory, comparison investigates and catalogs diverse political concepts and ideas and describes how political systems are configured and legitimated by various agents acting within and through the different resources available to political agents and their communities: languages, concepts, beliefs, traditions, cultural systems, and worldviews. Comparative political theology plumbs the depths of these various ideas about the nature, scope, meaning, and legitimacy of politics, with attention to our ultimate concerns, values, and substantive conceptions of reality and human flourishing. Comparative political theology seeks to clarify the ideas, meaning structures, practices, institutional policies, and prophetic-critical stances of diverse political agents and polities and seeks to make sense of why different political actors and institutions respond differently to similar material and political phenomena. Why is there diversity in perceiving the scope and severity of particular problems and challenges (e.g., famine or infant mortality), differences in motivating responses, or even differences in what diverse traditions and agents perceive to be problems in the first place?

Thesis 3: *Comparative political theology may be an abstract, ideal-type analysis in which the comparativist reconstructs a view of the other tradition by using the standard scholarly tools of theoretical, historical, and linguistic-cultural analysis to probe the content and meaning of a traditions texts, ideas, and representations.* Such scholarship requires fidelity to the interpretdatum, that is, the accurate interpretation of the phenomena of the other tradition available to the scholarly observer. Yet the comparative scholar does not create the other's views and should not pick and choose selective aspects apart from their enrooted contexts. The comparative scholar aims to responsibly translate and interpret the religio-ethical phenomena in the practices, texts, and symbols of the other's moral and political tradition, practices, and institutions, in order to gain insight into the other's moral and political worldview.

Thesis 4: *Comparative political theology may describe and analyze the actual representations of diverse agents' beliefs and ideas underlying their policies and practices in order to inform and guide dialogue about better solutions to shared problems and crises.* Political theology—even in its purely theoretical moments—is reflection engaged from within the realities of mutually shared political histories and situations. Natural and intersubjective realities press upon us *together*, within shared and across different moral and political traditions and institutions. Religiously motivated actors who are open to and seek encounters with fellow humans find themselves pressed upon by common, shared challenges that require coordinated action in policy, political, and legal spheres by persons from different religious and moral traditions.

Scholars of political theology insist that any policy or political action emerges from a horizon of beliefs, ideologies, and concepts which must be carefully analyzed in order to clarify their full import and meaning.[70] Actors within and across traditions will ground and construct these beliefs, policies, and practices differently. These differences inform how moral agents acting in shared political spaces orient themselves individually and collectively to identify solutions to problems, what resources they utilize, and what they perceive to be problems in the first place. Much comparison results from actual encounters with political agents whose religio-ethical views must be interpreted and clarified in order to make sense of their policy and political stances.

Thesis 5: *Another goal of dialogical comparison in political theology is to gain further clarity about the possibilities and limits of coordination among diverse actors and groups to develop solutions to these challenges/problems.* Comparative study of other perspectives may triangulate around a specific problem and reveal a path forward for consensus, in spite of fundamental disagreements and/or differing backgrounds that at first appeared to stifle dialogue. When the religio-ethical values of our political ideas conflict, we can dialogue over these issues and probe our deepest convictions (with clarity for our dialogue partners) while aiming to build mutual understanding (even as we recognize points of mutual disagreement). Comparison across political theologies can helpfully illuminate the various ways different political configurations, actors, and traditions identify and solve these problems. Clarifying different viewpoints will reveal the sometimes intractable differences in resources and conceptual foundations that may keep dialogue bounded within a limited horizon of outcomes. Yet the clarity made possible by responsible comparison is a substantial advance in the dialogical horizon of a global community of religio-ethical political thinking.

Thesis 6: *The comparative scholar of political theology is doubly respon-*
sible, both to develop the clearest understanding of another's position and to
critically interpret this position in light of his or her own reasoned judgment and
principles. Individuals, representing their own perspectives in their moral
and political traditions, encounter each other by choice and, at times,
necessity (as when our communities collide under the impact of some
common, shared problem). These encounters become actual conversations about moral problems and are shaped by enrootedness in linguistic
and conceptual worlds that can become partially shared through dialogical
action. As much as our texts, traditions, principles, and inclinations may
be shaped in vastly different cultures, languages, histories, and with different principles and concepts, our mutual confrontation with some vital
challenge can fruitfully create a shared moral horizon with other moral
agents. Following the canon of responsibility intrinsic to hermeneutical
methods and principles, we are neither cheerleaders nor apologists for
the other's positions, nor are we uncritical advocates of our own positions.
Moral encounter in a dialogical horizon requires responsible interpretation (both respect for the "other" encountered and respect for critical
inquiry) and risks decentering our own ideas.

Yet comparative political theology is a critical enterprise. As Bruce
Lincoln put it, "Reverence is a religious, and not a scholarly virtue. When
good manners and good conscience cannot be reconciled, the demands
of the latter ought to prevail."[71] One critical task for comparative political theologies is to determine how we can responsibly confront political
theologies that have destructive consequences, without simply dismissing
the religio-ethical background of vicious acts. Do we condemn the acts
but recognize some coherence and legitimacy in the religio-ethical nexus
motivating the actions? Do we—can we—encourage liberalization using
resources from within the tradition? Can our own perspective judge adequately what resources may be revolutionary and promote a more "just"
vision of the wider world?

Comparative methods contribute descriptive analysis of similarities of
features in common between these different moral traditions and practices.
This sort of comparison is an important but small part of a larger goal.
Comparison also clarifies the similarities and differences between moral
agents' traditions and beliefs allowing those engaged in *real* dialogue over
crucial challenges to come to fruitful understanding about a shared moral
horizon and points at which intractable differences remain. This purpose
transcends any individual comparative theorist's fascinations and personal

interests and suggests, instead, that comparative theorists are, in part, responsive to the conditions imposed by the circumstances which gave rise to the comparison in the first place. The comparative theorist doesn't create the horizon of inquiry *ex nihilo* but *responsively*. As the hermeneutical comparativist must insist, this condition obtains whether one encounters a representative of another tradition or the accumulated texts, concepts, and practices of the other tradition. Comparison requires dialogical translation and the comparativist's responsibility to interpret well.

Thesis 7: *Dialogical comparison also aims to bolster the common enterprise of seeking human goods and flourishing by engaging in dialogue across differing modes of political legitimacy and structures.* Encounter and dialogue leads to engaging in a broader vision of normative debate and justification, with partners drawn from a wider array of fellows than if we stayed within our own political theoretical tradition. This common dialogue about the comparative *religio-ethical* dimension of political phenomena inscribes each communicant into a common moral horizon, as developed in the discussion of Schweiker's hermeneutical theory.

John Cobb, likewise, argued that complete incommensurability among religious traditions is not the only result from the linguistic turn and coherentist assumptions about meaning.[72] On Cobb's account, languages are not the "final contexts of life and meaning." The dynamic process of life involves experiences that transcend our linguistic vocabulary and concepts. "We can grope for ways to express aspects of our experience that are obscured by the language we know."[73] Thus for Cobb, our encounter with other moral and religious languages can help us express aspects of experience that are otherwise obscured by our own tradition's limited vocabulary. Comparison can focus on concepts, ideas, and practices with similarities across traditions, but it also involves the shared task of dynamically and reflexively engaging the world and ordering our common life. In this encounter and dialogue with others, what is disclosed is both that the worlds we inhabit are less different that the incommensurability thesis would have us imagine and at the same time dialogue confirms "the extent to which language shapes our apprehension of [the] larger world and how difficult it is to communicate effectively between the great traditions."[74]

Cobb insists that a range of global crises with ethical dimensions will "affect all peoples in much the same way" and "offer valuable opportunities to the student of comparative religion" to evaluate and coordinate different religious and moral responses to global challenges.[75] Importantly, this dynamic encounter shapes and changes each moral and religious tradition by expanding the stock of conceptual, linguistic, and experiential resources of each person and group. Indeed, the problem of incommensurability is muted in this regard as a problem for static stystems—"what is incommensurable before interaction becomes in some measure commensurable through action" in a dynamic interaction between communicants.[76]

Thesis 8: *Our comparative interaction with other perspectives may uncover new ways of reflecting upon our own ideas and beliefs and working out problems within our own tradition.*[77] Our epistemic and conceptual horizon may be strengthened, particularly in the way that we modify or adapt our justifications for our political ideas. Comparison may also reveal new problems we have not previously perceived or new ways of approaching old problems. This comparative method opens our own positions to critique, expansion, further justification, and validation.[78] Comparative political theology can thereby lead to the destabilization and decentering of our own positions. Instead of picturing the world through our accustomed framework, conversation with others about a shared moral dilemma forces recognition that we may be wrong, that we may have an incomplete picture of the world, or that we have misperceived the problem facing us and misdiagnosed the solution. As Robin Lovin put this, comparison is far more than "identification and classification"; at the heart of the comparative project is a "moral" question.[79] The result of comparative encounter, on Lovin's realist account, is unsettling: comparison "challenges our 'moral poise' and…changes our lives so that naïve moral certainty is no longer an option."[80] This realist view does not reduce traditions to relativist visions of isolated language games, but at the same time, we cannot merely reconstruct another's moral framework in our own head. Lovin helpfully challenges this idea: "The order in our minds only partly maps the order that is there in reality."[81] Actual dialogue in a comparative encounter builds up a coherentist structure that is constantly adapting to, improving upon, and expanding our picture of our world. Sometimes, we unsettle ourselves by encountering another's view of the world. Sometimes, the other's view is critically rejected—their view of an issue is too contrary or disruptive of principles we cherish. Yet this model of truly dialogical comparison situates us in a real moral horizon that is shared by our fellows with whom we must interact to address our common challenges.

8.

The global problems humans face in our fragile, fraught, and interconnected world will continue to grow in complexity and urgency. Pluralism is a basic fact of this chaotic world. Even with the best of intentions and responsible actions, we will suffer from resource scarcity; coordination challenges; and pathologies of will, greed, and power. Scholars of political theology will need the clarity of comparative reflection and responsible interpretation in order to help our many, diverse fellows to confront these challenges and achieve some measure of human flourishing. Ethicists and scholars of political theology could be well positioned to address those challenges, if they work responsibly to incorporate carefully crafted comparative methods into their work within and between traditions. The fruits of responsible dialogue between traditions of moral and theological reflection about our common political lives may turn out to be the methodological nourishment needed to resist forces of destruction and division and build up decent, humane, and just political institutions.

Notes

1. I have been greatly aided in thinking about this problem through many conversations with Thomas Banchoff, Elizabeth Bucar, David Clairmont, Jerome Copulsky, Paul Heck, Daniel Madigan, Charles Mathewes, William Schweiker, and Kara Ward. For a helpful account of the basic challenges of pluralism to moral thinking, see William Schweiker, *Theological Ethics and Global Dynamics: In the Time of Many Worlds* (Malden, MA: Blackwell, 2004).

2. See, for instance, Jürgen Habermas, *Between Facts and Norms: Contributions to a Discourse Theory of Law and Democracy*, trans. William Rehg (Cambridge, MA: MIT Press, 1996), ch. 1.

3. The editors of a recent collection of essays on political theology define the term as "the analysis and criticism of political arrangements (including cultural-psychological, social and economic aspects) from the perspective of differing interpretations of God's ways with the world," William Cavanaugh and Peter Scott, introduction to *The Blackwell Companion to Political Theology*, ed. Peter Scott and William Cavanaugh (Malden, MA: Blackwell, 2007), 2. See also the definition by Carl Schmitt: "All significant concepts of the modern theory of the state are secularized theological concepts not only because of their historical development—in which they are transferred from theology to the theory of the state...—but also because of their systematic structure" in *Political Theology: Four Chapters on the Concept of Sovereignty*, trans. George Schwab (Chicago: University of Chicago Press, 2005), 36. Mark Lilla contrasts political theology from political philosophy. The former is a "primordial form of human thought" in which "the basic political structures of society are imagined and criticized by referring to divine authority," while in the latter, humans developed "habits of thinking and talking about politics exclusively in human terms, without appeal to divine revelation or cosmological speculation." Mark

Lilla, *The Stillborn God: Religion, Politics, and the Modern West* (New York: Alfred A. Knopf, 2007), 2–5. Paul Kahn has argued that political theology is a descriptive phenomenological method used to "identify and describe the presence of the sacred, wherever it appears." Paul Kahn, *Political Theology: Four New Chapters on the Concept of Sovereignty* (New York: Columbia University Press, 2011), 25. Following Schmitt, such a method can "pierce the [modern liberal] state's self-presentation as an efficient means of justly advancing individual welfare and look to the *experience* of the political," which at its core is imbued with the "*mysterium tremendum* of the sacred, with its tremendous power for both destruction and construction," a reality that political theory in general misses in its analysis (26–7).

4. See for instance, Seyla Benhabib, "The Return of Political Theology: The Scarf Affair in Comparative Constitutional Perspective in France, Germany and Turkey," *Philosophy & Social Criticism* 36, no. 3–4 (2010): 451–471.

5. While outside the realm of "political theology" proper, Fred Dallmayr has pushed for a new subfield of comparative political theory, much of which attempts to compare Western political concepts with non-Western, often religiously based, thinkers. See Fred Dallmayr, ed., *Border Crossings: Toward a Comparative Political Theory* (New York: Lexington Books, 1999), a volume in a series edited by Dallmayr called *Global Encounters: Studies in Comparative Political Theory*. See also Fred Dallmayr, ed., *Comparative Political Theory: An Introduction* (New York: Palgrave MacMillan, 2010). For an excellent and sustained critique of Dallmayr's comparative project, see Andrew March, "What Is Comparative Political Theory," *The Review of Politics*, 71 (2009): 531–565.

6. Fred Dallmayr, "Beyond Monologue: For a Comparative Political Theory," *Perspectives on Politics* 2, no. 2 (June 2004): 249.

7. Ibid., 249. For further elaboration of the concept of "global village," see Fred Dallmayr, "Introduction: Toward a Comparative Political Theory," *The Review of Politics* 59, no. 3 (Summer 1997): 421ff.

8. Dallmayr, "Beyond Monologue" at 251–252 quoting Raimundo Pannaker, "What Is Comparative Philosophy Comparing?" in *Interpreting Across Boundaries: New Essays in Comparative Philosophy*, ed. Gerald Larson and Eliot Deutsch (Princeton: Princeton University Press, 1988), 132–134.

9. Comparison in religious studies is a long-standing inquiry. For the best, recent example, see Jonathan Z. Smith, *Relating Religion: Essays in the Study of Religion* (Chicago: University of Chicago Press, 2004), esp. chs. 2, 3, and 7–14.

10. Jeffrey Stout, "The Rhetoric of Revolution: Comparative Ethics after Kuhn and Gunnemann," in *Religion and Practical Reason: New Essays in the Comparative Philosophy of Religions*, ed. Frank Reynolds and David Tracy (New York: SUNY Press, 1994), 356.

11. For Stout's views on pluralism and moral discourse, see *Ethics After Babel: The Languages of Morals and Their Discontents* (Boston: Beacon Press, 1988).

12. Ibid., 356–357.

13. For an excellent genealogy of the field of CRE, see Sumner Twiss, "Comparison in Religious Ethics," in *The Blackwell Companion to Religious Ethics*, ed. William Schweiker (Malden, MA: Blackwell USA, 2008), 146ff. For other categorizations of different types of methods in CRE, see, for instance, Elizabeth Bucar, "Methodological Invention as a Constructive Project: Exploring the Production of Ethical Knowledge Through the Interaction of Discursive Logics," *Journal of Religious Ethics* 36, no. 3 (2008): 356–361; see also the introduction to a focus on Theravāda Buddhist Ethics "Methodological Issues in Comparative Religious Ethics," *Journal of Religious Ethics* 7, no. 1 (1979):1–10.

14. Emile Durkheim, *The Elementary Forms of the Religious Life*, trans. Joseph Swain (New York: Free Press, 1965), 17.

15. Max L. Stackhouse, "Assessing an Assessment," *Journal of Religious Ethics* 25, no. 3 (1997): 276–277.

16. Ronald Green, *Religious Reason: The Rational and Moral Basis of Religious Belief* (New York: Oxford, 1978).

17. See, for instance, David Little, "The Present State of the Comparative Study of Religious Ethics," *Journal of Religious Ethics* 9, no. 2 (1981): 210–227; Francisca Cho, "Leaping into the Boundless: A Daoist Reading of Comparative Religious Ethics," *Journal of Religious Ethics* 26, no. 1 (1998): 139–165.

18. David Little and Sumner Twiss, *Comparative Religious Ethics: A New Method* (New York: Harper and Row, 1978), 10.

19. Ibid., 12.

20. Ibid., 17, and see 96ff.

21. Jeffrey Stout, "Weber's Progeny, Once Removed," *Religious Studies Review*, 6 (1980): 291.

22. Donald K. Swearer, "Bhikku Boddhadasa on Ethics and Society," *Journal of Religious Ethics* 7, no. 1 (1979): 64. Cf. Donald Swearer, "History of Religions," in *The Blackwell Companion to Religious Ethics*, 138–146.

23. Robin Lovin and Frank Reynolds, *Cosmogony and Ethical Order: New Studies in Comparative Ethics* (Chicago: University of Chicago Press, 1985), 8.

24. Ibid., 8.

25. Ibid., 30.

26. For an excellent overview of this, see Bruce Grelle, "Culture and Moral Pluralism," in *The Blackwell Companion to Religious Ethics*, 129–137.

27. Lee H. Yearley, "New Religious Virtues and the Study of Religion" (Fifteenth Annual University Lecture in Religion, Arizona State University, February 10, 1994), http://web.archive.org/web/20030107173308/http://www.asu.edu/clas/religious_studies/home/1994lec.html.

28. Aaron Stalnaker, "Judging Others: History, Ethics, and the Purposes of Comparison," *Journal of Religious Ethics* 36, no. 3 (2008): 434–435. Stalnaker states: "The norms to which anyone might appeal as belonging to some culture [and therefore immune from external moral criticism] do not exist in a vacuum, but are contested and contestable, both from within and without."

29. Twiss, "Comparison," 150.

30. Ibid., 151.

31. David Decosimo, "Comparison and the Ubiquity of Resemblance," *Journal of the American Academy of Religion* 78, no. 1 (2010): 227.

32. Ibid., 232.

33. Ibid.

34. Ibid., 232–36.

35. Ibid., 236; ibid., 239; ibid., 241.

36. Thomas A. Lewis, Jonathan Wyn Schofer, Aaron Stalnaker and Mark A. Berkson, "Anthropos and Ethics: Categories of Inquiry and Procedures of Comparison," *Journal of Religious Ethics* 33, no. 2 (2005): 178.

37. Ibid., 180.

38. Ibid., 181.

39. Ibid., 181; ibid., 182.

40. Aaron Stalnaker, "Comparative Religious Ethics and the Problem of 'Human Nature,'" *Journal of Religious Ethics* 33, no. 2 (2005): 187.

41. Ibid., 189; ibid., emphasis mine; ibid., 189; ibid., 214.

42. Ibid., 190. ibid., 194; ibid., 193–194; ibid., 191.

43. See David Clairmont's excellent discussion of the normative framework of comparison in "Persons as Religious Classics: Comparative Ethics and the Theology of Bridge Concepts," *Journal of the American Academy of Religion* 78, no. 3 (2010): 687–716.

44. Stalnaker, "Judging," 435.

45. Ibid., 429–31.

46. Ibid., 435; ibid., 437; ibid., 435.

47. See the invited response to Stalnaker's essay, which lays out the basic case for navigating between relativism and imperialism in Jonathan Wyn Schofer, "Virtues and Vices of Relativism," *Journal of Religious Ethics* 36, no. 4 (Dec. 2008): 709–715.

48. Bruce Lincoln's thirteen theses challenge this view: "13. When one permits those whom one studies to define the terms in which they will be understood, suspends one's interest in the temporal and contingent, or fails to distinguish between 'truths,' 'truth-claims,' and 'regimes of truth,' one has ceased to function as historian or scholar. In that moment, a variety of roles are available: some perfectly respectable (amanuensis, collector, friend and advocate), and some less appealing (cheerleader, voyeur, retailer of import goods). None, however, should be confused with scholarship." Bruce Lincoln, "Theses on Method," *Method and Theory in the Study of Religion*, 8 (1996): 225–227.

49. Stalnaker, "Judging," 437; ibid., 438. "The Gadamerian hermeneutical imperative to use and rely on our own judgments when striving to understand others." Except, Gadamer was concerned with the self-reflexive nature of dialogical encounter with *real* interlocutors (even in text and interpreter), not those constructed in our own armchair imaginings.

50. Lee Yearley, "Selves, Virtues, Odd Genres, and Alien Guides: An Approach to Religious Ethics," *Journal of Religious Ethics* 25, no. 3 (1997): 128.

51. Decosimo, "Comparison," 242.

52. Aaron Stalnaker, *Overcoming Our Evil: Human Nature and Spiritual Exercises in Xunzi and Augustine* (Washington, D.C.: Georgetown University Press, 2006), 19.

53. Ibid., 21, 20.

54. William Schweiker, "The Drama of Interpretation and the Philosophy of Religions: An Essay on Understanding in Comparative Religious Ethics," in *Discourse and Practice*, ed. Frank Reynolds and David Tracy (Albany: SUNY Press, 1992), 283.

55. Ibid., 284; ibid., 271.

56. Ibid., 283.

57. Jürgen Habermas, *Moral Consciousness and Communicative Action*, trans. Christian Lenhardt and Shierry Weber Nicholsen (Cambridge, MA: MIT Press, 1990), 27. Quoted by Schweiker, "Drama," 282.

58. Schweiker, "Drama," 277.

59. Ibid., 285; ibid., 283.

60. Ibid., 285.

61. Ibid., 285. For Schweiker's full account of the moral demand of responsibility, see his *Responsibility & Christian Ethics* (New York: Cambridge University Press, 1999).

62. Schweiker, "Drama," 276; ibid., 285.

63. See Bruce Grelle, "Scholarship and Citizenship: Comparative Religious Ethicists as Public Intellectuals," in *Explorations in Global Ethics: Comparative Religious Ethics and Interreligious Dialogue*, ed. Sumner B. Twiss and Bruce Grelle (Boulder, CO: Westview Press, 2000). As James Gustafson described, the general trajectory arising from movements such as the Protestant Social Gospel gave rise to a gradual shift in the task of moral philosophers and theologians to devote further attention to the social and policy sciences and apply ethical theory within specific practical areas, such as medicine, the environment, and business, among others. See James Gustafson, "A Retrospective Interpretation of American Religious Ethics, 1948–1998," *Journal of Religious Ethics* 25, no. 3 (1997): 15–18.

64. Grelle, "Scholarship," 35.

65. Lovin and Reynolds, *Cosmogony and Ethical Order*, 28–29.

66. Grelle, "Scholarship," 42.

67. Ibid.

68. Twiss, "Comparison," 153.

69. The idea for using theses to sketch this preliminary analysis came from Lincoln, "Theses," 225–227.

70. For one classic account, see Quentin Skinner, "Some Problems in the Analysis of Political Thought and Action," *Political Theory*, 2 (1974): 277–303. For more recent discussions of the implications of Skinner's understanding of the relation

between ideas and political action, see James Tully, ed. *Meaning and Context: Quentin Skinner and His Critics* (Princeton: Princeton University Press, 1989).

71. Lincoln, "Theses," 226.

72. John Cobb, "Incommensurability: Can Comparative Religious Ethics Help?" *Buddhist-Christian Studies*, 16 (1996): 39–45.

73. Ibid., 40.

74. Ibid., 41.

75. Ibid.

76. Ibid., 45.

77. One can see this trend in the developing field of comparative theology. Francis Clooney, for instance, defines comparative theology as "acts of faith seeking understanding which are rooted in a particular faith tradition but which, from that foundation, venture into learning from one or more other faith traditions. This learning is sought for the sake of fresh theological insights that are indebted to the newly encountered tradition/s as well as the home tradition." For Clooney, this comparison "starts with the intuition of an intriguing resemblance that prompts us to place two realities—texts, images, practices, doctrines, persons—near one another, so that they may be seen over and again, side by side. In this necessarily arbitrary and intuitive practice we understand each differently because the other is near, and by cumulative insight also begin to comprehend related matters differently too. Finally we see ourselves differently, intuitively uncovering dimensions of ourselves that would not otherwise—come to the fore."

78. Mill's general vision in *On Liberty* is instructive here. John Stuart Mill, "On Liberty," in *The Basic Writings of John Stuart Mill* (New York: Modern Library, 2002).

79. Robin Lovin, "Cue the Chorus," *Journal of the American Academy of Religion* 78, no. 1 (2010): 260.

80. Ibid., 261.

81. Ibid.

7

Gauging the Status of Political Theologies

RHETORICAL ANALYSIS OF THE MEDIA
CONSTRUCTION OF POLITICAL ISLAM

Elizabeth Bucar

READING MAINSTREAM MEDIA coverage on Muslim politics can be difficult
for scholars of Islamic studies. From emotionally charged rhetoric about
proposed Islamic cultural centers, to one-dimensional portraits of veiled
Muslim women as oppressed, to the flattening of Islamic terms like jihad
and piety, I spend much time encouraging others to read media accounts
of political Islam with a suspicious eye. Often the media, despite its best
intentions, perpetuates misunderstanding about Muslims or their faith. Of
course, scholars of Islamic studies are not alone in judging that media covers
politics and religion in a biased way. Both the political Left and Right commonly make this charge, as do apologists for and critics of specific religious
traditions. These judgments, even as they differ in religious or political motivation, posit journalistic rhetoric as the *creator* of political norms. Readers are
naturally influenced by what they read, but journalists do not necessarily set
out to form public opinion about religion or politics. They are primarily in
the business of selling newspapers, so part of their job is to tap into what the
public already thinks and believes. In this essay, rather than judging media
institutions and journalists, my goal is to read journalistic rhetoric in order
to gauge its audience's prevalent assumptions about political Islam.[1]

   If media rhetoric is to be fruitful as the primary data for the study of
local political theologies, one challenge is analyzing how media reports

envision an audience. A rhetorical lens helps refocus our eye. As Michel de Certeau suggests, rhetoric "describes the 'turns' or tropes of which language can be both the site and the object...In the space of a language (as in that of games), a society makes more explicit the formal rules of action and the operations that differentiate them."[2] Since rhetoric is the space where "formal rules of actions" are justified, it is also the space where proper political roles of specific theologies are expressed. This process of expression, in turn, reveals inconsistencies, logical gaps, and strongly held assumptions that must be understood, and perhaps changed, before Islam can meaningfully contribute to political theory and practice.

In order to gauge the logics that media rhetoric entails, I propose a method of analysis that focuses on four rhetorical categories of assumptions (facts, presumptions, values, and hierarchies). I then apply this method to a case study of the media construction of political Islam in the United States, through a close reading of two 2007 news stories: (1) rumors that then-Senator and presidential candidate Barack Obama was a Muslim, and (2) Iranian President Mahmoud Ahmadinejad's 2007 address at Columbia University during which he purportedly claimed there were no homosexuals in Iran. Coverage of "Obama's Muslim problem" illuminates presumptions that make positive contributions from Islam to U.S. politics difficult, such as the idea that having a connection to Islam makes a president simultaneously sympathetic to Islamic extremists and a target of them (as an apostate).[3] Ahmadinejad's representation in mainstream media as a delusional tyrant, with no conception of political freedom or identity politics, demonstrates how ontological and epistemological judgments about Islam have become so commonsensical that the media no longer feels it is necessary to explain or defend them.[4] Exposing journalistic rhetoric about political figures, in comparative focus, can usefully serve as a window into the public status and perception of political theologies. This methodology has broad applicability in pluralistic contexts and in comparative perspectives.

1. Classical Rhetoric and Its Audience

The earliest occurrence in text of the term "rhetoric" is attributed to Plato's dialogue *Gorgias*,[5] although rhetoric appeared in earlier writings from Mesopotamia and the Hebrew scriptures.[6] As Aristotle did for many philosophical categories, he provided this subject with a detailed schematization. In chapter 2 of *On Rhetoric,* he defines the term as follows: "Let rhetoric be an ability, in each [particular] case, to see the available means of persuasion" (I.2.1).⁷ This definition has three components. First, by "ability to see" Aristotle categorizes rhetoric not only as a practical art but also as an art that operates on the theoretical level, a level that is able to survey a particular case and identify its rhetorical implications. In other words, rhetoric is not just the method of delivery but also the "seeing" which precedes that delivery and entails analysis and identification of methods of persuasion. In the case of journalistic rhetoric, this "seeing" involves knowing your target audience well, such as understanding what the audience knows, what it thinks its knows, as well as what the audience values, all of which effects what they want to read about. Second, good rhetoric for Aristotle is not only that which successfully persuades (which depends on the audience's response). Good rhetoric reflects a proper deduction of the "available means of persuasion" (which depends on the skill of the speaker). This is important because it allows for the analysis of rhetoric from the perspective of both logical validity and its effects on a specific audience. In this essay's case study, the focus will be on what logical tactics of persuasion the journalists use. Third, "in each case" signifies the specificity of a rhetorical argument. Rhetoric is context-sensitive and this is why the study of rhetoric allows gauging the status of specific theologies in specific political contexts.

In the third chapter of *On Rhetoric*, Aristotle argues that there are three, and only three, modes of rhetoric. These modes are classified, based on their intended audiences, as either deliberative, judicial, or epideictic:

> The species [*eide*] of rhetoric are three in number; for such is the number [of classes] to which the hearers of speeches belong. A speech [situation] consists of three things: a speaker and a subject on which he speaks and someone addressed, and the objective [*telos*] of the speech relates to the last (I mean the hearer). Now it is necessary for the hearer to be either a spectator [*theoros*] or a judge [*krites*], and [in the latter case] a judge of either the past or future happenings...Thus, there would necessarily be three genera of rhetorics; *symbouleutikon* [deliberative], *dikanikon* [judicial], *epideiktikon* [demonstrative] (I.3.1–3).

Considering journalistic rhetoric as epideictic rhetoric helps to conceptualize it within a specific political or national context. Epideictic rhetoric is characterized by the fact that the audience does not judge it in the same way as the other two forms because it is built on shared understandings. For Aristotle, the nonjudgmental characteristic stems from the existence of a community of adherence, not from the passive role of the audience.[8] Within such a community, a speaker engaged in epideictic rhetoric works to convince the hearer that the specific position being put forward is something she already believed. In other words, epideictic rhetoric "is not judged" insofar as it does not aim to convince the audience of a new abstract truth; it assumes the truth of the community and concerns itself with previously unexamined implications of this truth.

According to Aristotle, all modes of rhetoric rationally persuade through logical form and affectivity, which leverages the emotional and intuitive commitments of the audience. These two modes of persuasion can be seen in Aristotle's discussion of *enthymeme*, the rhetorical syllogism. An enthymeme persuades in part through a logical form conveyed through deductivity, probability, and brevity (I.1). Journalistic rhetoric will have some place for deduction because it aims to persuade an audience, and, according to Aristotle, we are most likely to be persuaded by arguments we think have been logically proven. However, since the goal of rhetoric is persuasion and not logical validity per se, it is less important that this enthymeme be a true deduction.

In addition to its logical form, enthymeme's use of affectivity allows it not only to convince but also to motivate. The verb enthymeme has a range of meanings, including "consider well" or "form a plan."[9] The root of enthymeme, *thymos*, literally means heart, and two hearts are implicated in media rhetoric: the heart of the audience and of the journalist. The heart of the journalistic endeavor must consider the heart of the particular audience in order to persuasively reach them. The heart of the audience will in turn think deeply about, infer, and conclude in relation to the journalist's article. The successful journalist is able to empathize with the audience by not only understanding their factual knowledge base but also by being aware of and sensitive to the value-charged ideas that a community adheres to. Moreover, like rhetoric's goal to persuade, a newspaper's goal to increase its circulation is helped when the audience is able to identify themselves with a particular stance of the orator. Therefore the heart of the journalist strategically attends to the heart of the audience.

In summary, in order to persuade, journalistic rhetoric will entail some logical structure and will access emotional and intuitive commitments of the audience. A technique of rhetorical analysis could work on both these levels, attempting to isolate both logical form and affective logos.[10] In this

essay, I focus on how even reporting "just the facts" requires some understanding of audience assumptions (its heart) related to political Islam. I do
not offer a close reading of the internal rationality of media reports, such
as identifying the grounds, warrants, and backings on which the logical
structure of the reports depend. Instead my goal is to stand back in order
to see the web of agreement assumed in journalistic rhetoric, which will
identify in turn the general views of communal adherence of the U.S. public. This level of analysis not only helps to gauge the status of specific theologies in national politics, but it may also provide insights into potentially
fruitful areas of future interreligious dialogue in pluralistic contexts.

2. A Method of Rhetorical Analysis of Audience Assumptions

The method I propose for identifying the audience assumptions implied in
journalistic rhetoric draws on Chaïm Perelman and L. Olbrechts-Tyteca's
influential work *The New Rhetoric*, in which they focus on connections
between modern discourse and the ancient tradition of Greek rhetoric and
dialectic. They intend to break away from the focus on reason, reasoning,
and "the idea of self-evidence," all of which they attribute to Descartes and
claim has dominated Western philosophy for the last three centuries.[11] For
Perelman and Olbrechts-Tyteca, all arguments address a specific audience
and aim to affect that audience's minds, rather than abstractly deploying
universal rational principles. Their concern in part is conceptualizing
how a speaker "relies on his hearer's adherence to the propositions from
which he will start,"[12] and specifically "what sort of agreements can serve
as premises."[13]

Four elements from Perelman and Olbrechts-Tyteca's work are useful for my purposes to isolate the parameters of agreement upon which
the orator bases his or her argument: facts, presumptions, values, and
hierarchies.[14] Their first category of assumptions is facts and truths, but
since all their categories function as truths insofar as they are assumed to
be true, I use only "facts" here. Facts are agreements held relating to data.
If the facts used in an argument are to be accepted, they must conform
to the audience's understanding of reality, and therefore even facts "will
be connected to a specific viewpoint which is necessarily identified with
some particular audience."[15] Given one fact, another fact may be implied.
Although they are reflections of reality, facts can be challenged, either by
the addition of new facts or a change in the audience by the addition of

new members who interpret reality differently. In the analysis that follows, the question will be, What facts about Muslims as political leaders and the impact of Islam on politics are assumed in the media's coverage of stories about political Islam?

Second, presumptions are opinions of an audience, and they are often based on what the audience considers to be normal or customary. Perelman and Olbrechts-Tyteca point out the most common presumption is the opinion "what has been the case can be expected to continue to be the case."[16] Presumptions can be modified when new information is introduced or when an individual within the group deviates outside conventional standards, thereby modifying the group's conception of normality. But arguments or actions seen as too far outside the normal will be ignored or rejected by the group. In other words, presumptions relevant to a discussion of political Islam are related to the audience's opinions about the proper role of religion in politics in general, as well as opinions of any perceived threats or benefits of an existing or increased role of political Islam.

Third, a special relationship between action and values is conceived by Perelman and Olbrechts-Tyteca. They describe agreement over a value, which can take an abstract or concrete form, as the "admission that an object, a thing, or an ideal must have a specific influence on action and on disposition toward action."[17] Values influence action and are embodied in right action; they provide criteria for judging if a particular practice is morally good. Any value can be disputed, but it is not possible to reject all values. In some fields—including politics—values can be observed at many levels of the argument, and analysis of journalistic rhetoric can uncover different criteria for judging politicians based on their relationship to Islam, either real or imagined.

Finally, hierarchies work to establish "the intensity with which one value is adhered to as compared to another."[18] They can be concrete (e.g., humans are higher/more important than animals) or abstract (e.g., justice is higher/more important than utility). Hierarchies are tricky things. On one hand, we might wish to rid ourselves of all discursive hierarchies, assuming that the use of conceptual hierarchies leads necessarily to the discrimination of specific groups or individuals in practice. But hierarchies are useful in political rhetoric because they work to order values when simultaneous commitment to two of more values is impossible. The ways in which hierarchies differ between different religions as well as different national contexts will be of acute interest here.

Perelman and Olbrechts-Tyteca's theory of rhetoric assists us in a number of ways. First, it makes possible investigation into not only the logical structure of rhetoric but also analysis of how rhetoric uses affective logos through referencing an audience's prior assumptions.

Second, it also offers a way to understand why journalistic rhetoric is so powerful. Rhetoric sets "out to increase the intensity of adherence to certain values, which might not be contested when considered on their own but may nevertheless not prevail against other values that might come into conflict with them."[19] Journalistic rhetoric may or may not appear value laden. However, in order to make, for example, headlines provocative, the rhetoric is often connected to the audience members' stance through ideas the audience understands and emotionally feels to be significant. In other words, even if media rhetoric does not originate misunderstanding of political Islam, by utilizing what I have called affectivity, it can make these misunderstandings more firmly held.

Third, Perelman and Olbrechts-Tyteca's understanding of rhetoric means that specific rhetorical events can serve as sources for gauging specific audience assumptions. Since their categories of assumptions are focused on the audience, it is important not to conclude that just because a journalist uses a given fact, value, or hierarchy, she personally believes it to be true. Rather, these categories tell us what the journalist thinks her audience believes true. For example, a journalist emphasizes some aspects of a story over others, selecting elements that she will give "presence." Although this selection highlights some aspects of reality rather than others, it is done from within a specific audience's existing worldview. The central role of the audience in Perelman and Olbrechts-Tyteca's understanding of rhetoric means that articles pitched for one market would not necessarily work for another and allows us to use journalistic rhetoric as a mirror of its target market's ideas, beliefs, and norms.

Finally, this level of rhetorical analysis also allows understanding of what different arguments have in common. At the level of informal argumentation, we would not expect components to line up: liberal and conservative media outlets reported in different ways on Obama as a Muslim and Ahmadinejad's denial of gays in Iran. But both sets of arguments began with agreements about political Islam. And if we are able to understand what these agreements were, through analysis of specific arguments, we can think about the possibilities and limitations of the future of political Islam.

3. Case Study: The Status of Political Islam in the United States

This section analyzes the journalistic rhetoric of these two events, both of which received much attention in the United States. Both occurred in 2007, both were prominent enough to be satirized on a *New Yorker* cover,[20] and both focused on the relationship of specific politicians—then presidential candidate Barack Obama and Iranian President Mahmoud Ahmadinejad—to Islam. The newsworthiness of each event is based on assumptions about political Islam; an overview of each media story allows the identification of the major premises the journalistic rhetoric relied on.

3a. Obama's Muslim Problem

Given that political Islam is the subject of this essay, it may seem strange to use media coverage of Barack Obama, who is not a Muslim, as a source. However, this is warranted because rumors of Obama's secret Muslim upbringing forced the media to think out loud about the proper role of Islam in U.S. politics. Specifically, the way the media reported on Obama's purported Muslim faith exposed assumptions about Islam and politics in the United States.

The reader might still object to my use of this example, claiming that Obama's Muslim problem cannot tell us about the future of Islam in U.S. politics as a whole, but rather only its future among a small group of conservative, conspiracy-theory minded, Islamophobic citizens who started and perpetuated these rumors. In fact, it is in the coverage by the liberal press that some of the most widespread assumptions about political Islam can be found. And most important, those who spread the rumors attempted to leverage preexisting assumptions about Islam and politics in order to undermine Obama's candidacy. The fact that these rumors became such a major news story suggests they successfully tapped into these assumptions.

The first report that Obama had significant ties to Islam was posted in January 2007 on the online version of *Insight* magazine, owned by Rev. Sun Myung Moon, founder of the Unification Church. Cable news networks brought this report mainstream: the Fox News channel discussed those rumors as fact, and rival CNN made an effort to debunk the report and in the process to question the quality of Fox News' journalism.[21] By now, every major news outlet has covered these rumors multiple times, from dailies like the *New York Times, New York Post,* and *Washington Post,* to weeklies like *Newsweek* and *New Yorker,* making Obama's Muslim problem the first and most long-lasting media controversy of the 2008 presidential campaign. Although, rumors that Obama is a Muslim continue to be covered by journalists,[22] my analysis here focuses on journalistic rhetoric in 2007. The reasons why these rumors were still considered newsworthy even after they were adequately debunked will be explored in order to understand the contours of audience assumptions the journalistic rhetoric entailed.

The initial *Insight* report claimed Obama "spent at least four years in a so-called madrassa, or Muslim seminary, in Indonesia," implying he was educated in radical Islam in the largest Muslim population country in the world. Even after CNN and the Associated Press debunked this madrassa story, Jeffrey Kuhner, *Insight*'s editor, maintained that it had merit because "concealment and deception was to be the issue, not so much his Muslim heritage."[23] The problem, according to Kuhner, was that Obama intentionally withheld facts from the U.S. public about significant cultural and religious ties to Islam. The fact that the debunked story continued to warrant headlines in mainstream journalism demonstrates that a level of unease about the uncertainty of Obama's religious ties remained, especially his possible ties to Islam.

Even coverage that criticized *Insight*'s posting shared one important premise: calling someone a Muslim is a political smear. For example, the *Washington Post* published a strongly worded editorial that claimed calling Obama by his full name, Barack Hussein Obama, was a "sleazy tactic." Although Obama has never "tried to hide his past or his family name," the editorial continued, he "does not use his middle name. Those who take pains to insert it when referring to him are trying, none too subtly, to stir up scary images of menacing terrorists and evil dictators."[24] The *New York Times* called the reports "politically volatile," "scurrilous charges," and "anonymous smears" that "victimized" then-Senator Obama.[25] These papers, even as they argued false reports only make the perpetrators look bad, in fact themselves operated upon a rhetorical premise that being linked to Islam, even just by name, would deal a fatal blow to a presidential candidate's political viability in the United States.[26]

By the end of 2007, some journalists began to question the continued coverage of the rumors. When Perry Bacon wrote a front-page article for the *Washington Post* titled "Foes Use Obama's Muslim Ties to Fuel Rumors About Him," the newspaper also ran a sharply worded editorial by Deborah Howell that questioned the article's merits. The rumors were old, Howell wrote, and "to make the story worth page one, there needed to be new, credible information."[27] That lack of new information in Bacon's piece is glaringly obvious, as the article merely revisited Obama's background, old Pew polls, and various rumors. A less obvious premise was raised by Bill Hamilton, *Washington Post* assistant managing editor for politics and editor of Bacon's controversial story. Hamilton was quoted in Howell's piece as follows: "I thought that in this context saying it was a rumor meant it wasn't true, but clearly some people didn't see it that same way."[28] Howell's reaction was evidence that the rhetorical use of "rumor" instead of, for example, "false report" relied on the premise that there is something powerful about an unsubstantiated story that Obama has ties to Islam: it was an acknowledgment that both supporters of Obama and his critics think this rumor still had political power.[29]

When "new evidence" related to Obama's Muslim problem was offered in that first year of coverage, it often took the form of reports of U.S. citizens who were still confused about whether Obama was Muslim. For example, Michael Saul of the *Daily News*, reporting from the campaign trail in December, used the fact that Iowa voter Becky Michael asked Obama to explain his "Muslim background" as evidence of the political trouble the rumor was still causing the candidate.[30] Michael is quoted as saying, "It's not so important that he is a Christian, although I'm very thankful he is... But it's very important he's not a Muslim."[31] The premise, in Michael's statement and the journalist's rhetoric, was that despite the debunking of claims that Obama is a Muslim, some U.S. voters still needed to be reassured that he is not Muslim before they cast their vote. This desire was assumed to be newsworthy, not simple ignorance, prejudice, or discrimination.

Even more telling was the inclusion of Michael's other statement about why being a Muslim mattered:

> I'm glad I got an answer because the Middle East is being run by the Muslims. And their kind of freedom is not the freedom that America has fought for all our lives, and I want to know that the next President of the United States, if it's Barack Obama, will be fighting for the freedom that America has fought for.[32]

Saul ended his article with this quote, providing no further elaboration or comment. Michael's words and Saul's placement of the quote points to an assumption that Islam is antithetical to Western democracy and that a Muslim president would necessarily establish a theocratic state.

3b. Ahmadinejad's Denial of Gays in Iran

In September of 2007, six months after the rumors that Obama had secret roots in Islam first garnered media attention, Iranian president Mahmoud Ahmadinejad visited the United States. The journalistic rhetoric about this visit offers another vantage point to gauge the status of political Islam in the United States. Ahmadinejad was in New York primarily to attend a meeting at the United Nations; however, his remarks during an address at Columbia University received much more media attention than the UN meeting, in part for Ahmadinejad's now infamous declaration: "In Iran we don't have homosexuals."[33] Two patterns emerge from this coverage: a specific interpretation of his comments that day about homosexuality and an acceptance of the audience's reactions to him.

Although various excerpts from his remarks were reported in a number of mainstream newspapers including the *New York Times*, *Washington Times*, and *Daily News*, all these reports included the quote, "In Iran we don't have homosexuals." Rarely did journalists focus on the qualification Ahmadinejad offered in the rest of the sentence: "In Iran we don't have homosexuals like in your country." This second clause is important because it can change the meaning of his statement from "there are not people in Iran who desire or practice same-sex intercourse" to "we do not have individuals who identify as homosexuals, in the same way that people do in the United States." In other words, there was another way to interpret his remarks, mainly as an assertion that U.S. gay culture does not exist in Iran and that some categories of sexual identity are not cross-cultural.

A number of recent scholarly studies have argued that even when same-sex desire and sexual acts occur, that does not necessarily mean that a "homosexual identity" exists. Joseph Massad and Afsaneh Najmabadi, for example, both argue that "same-sex desire," which undoubtedly does exist in Iran, is not the same thing as homosexual identity, which draws specifically on a Western understanding of human rights and identity politics.[34] This means that in some cases, Iranians who engage in same-sex intercourse do not identify as gay.[35] In this understanding of sexuality, Ahmadinejad's comments may have been accurate: homosexuality and homosexuals do not exist in Iran *in the same way that they do in the United States*. However, every mainstream article on his remark assumed he was lying or delusional.

The tone of the coverage of the treatment of the Iranian president that day is also instructive to the status of political Islam. Most media coverage mentioned that his audience at Columbia University reacted to him with booing and laughter. Some published the opening remarks of University President Lee Bollinger, in which he said to Ahmadinejad, who at the time sat only twenty-five feet from him, "you exhibit all the signs of a petty and cruel dictator," and "you are either brazenly provocative or astonishingly uneducated."[36] That journalists joined in on making fun of Ahmadinejad in editorials is to be expected; slightly less expected was the tone of almost every non-opinion piece that not only did not critique this treatment of a head of state but also participated in name-calling. For example, *New York Times* reporter's Nazila Fathi could not seem to help making the following snide comment: "For a country that is said to have no homosexuality, Iran goes to great lengths to ban it."[37] The *Washington Times* editor and chief Wesley Pruden called Ahmadinejad "the Iranian fruitcake," "piggish" and "Public Enemy No. 1 in America."[38] This journalistic rhetoric shared a premise that Ahmadinejad is an out-of-touch tyrant who willfully denies sexual freedoms to his citizens.

4. Reading Shared Audience Assumptions

With a sketch of some of the details of the journalistic rhetoric of the two news stories in hand, it is now possible to take a step back and read the two cases together. In the following section, the unstated premises in both stories are explored as evidence of facts, values, presumptions, and hierarchies about political Islam assumed by the American public.

4a. Facts

Facts are agreements held relating to data that conform to the audience's understanding of reality. Contention over facts was central to the rumors that led to Obama's Muslim problem, and in order to understand the future of Islam in U.S. politics, one should consider which facts were assumed relevant to a presidential candidacy, such as Obama's enrollment in an Islamic school or his middle name, Hussein. In addition, the journalistic rhetoric on Obama's Muslim problem made it clear that some important facts about Islam are missing from mainstream political discourse. For example, there was little mention that in Muslim-majority nations, like Indonesia, a form of civil Islam exists that makes a secular madrassa possible. Nor was it discussed that a middle name of Hussein does not necessarily make one a Muslim or that being Muslim is not the same thing as sympathizing with Muslim extremists.[39]

In the coverage of Ahmadinejad's remarks about gays in Iran, the following facts grounded the journalistic premises: sexuality is constrained in Iran, shari'a is antithetical to individual freedom, and Islamic theocracy is necessarily despotic. Some of these facts may be true in some cases, but nevertheless they are gross oversimplifications of the current situation in Iran. In the case of LGBT rights, for example, there is a much more nuanced story the journalists could have told. After the Islamic Revolution, same-sex acts did become illegal in Iran through attempts to codify a particular interpretation of shari'a law.[40] However, conviction of this crime requires either four men to give eyewitness testimony or the accused to confess four times.[41] This high threshold of proof means a private, consensual sex between two adults should not find its way to the courts.

4b. Presumptions

Presumptions are the second category of audience assumptions that we can glean from rhetoric. They are opinions often based on what the audience considers to be normal or customary. The media coverage of Obama as a Muslim demonstrated the presumption that, despite the First Amendment protection of the free exercise of religions, the religious beliefs and practices of a presidential candidate matter to the U.S. public. Another presumption is that a Muslim cannot become president of the United States. This presumption is based on yet another one, mainly that a connection to Islam, even a tenuous one, would make a president either more sympathetic to Islamic extremists or as an apostate a target of them. Both these scenarios would have a negative effect on the presidency and U.S. foreign policy.

The journalistic rhetoric on Ahmadinejad relied on opinions about the nature of all Islamic governments as tyrannical. In addition, Iran was presumed to not be the political peer of the United States, making it okay to treat its president with disdain. These presumptions are obstacles to a positive contribution of Islam to political theory and practice in the United States. They indicate the widely held opinions that when Islamic norms and principles are put into practice, the only possible outcome is theocracy, which in turn leads to repression and terror.

4c. Values

Values can be understood as criteria for judging concrete actions. The previous analysis of journalistic rhetoric uncovers different criteria for judging politicians based on their relationship to Islam, either real or imagined. For example, part of the reason the rumors were originally newsworthy, according to *Insight*'s Kuhner, is that if Obama hid his Muslim background, this would be a major violation of the U.S. public's trust, with implications about Obama's character and thus suitability as president.[42] Here the value relied on is the necessity of full disclosure of religious affiliation and ties, all the more important when a connection to Islam is at stake.[43] Even the liberal press assumed that calling Obama a Muslim was a political smear, thus displaying an assumption that Muslim politicians will be harshly judged in the United States. There is also a concern in the journalistic rhetoric with the values of non-Americans, especially Muslims, who might view Obama's denial of his Muslim heritage as an act of apostasy. In this way, actions that might compromise the ability of non-American Muslims to cooperate with the United States are judged harshly in the current geopolitical climate.

In the media coverage of Ahmadinejad, the most prominent value is that Islamic epistemology leads to repressive politics, allowing the harsh judgment of all Muslim leaders and Islamic nations to seem commonsensical. The journalistic rhetoric also mixes LGBT values and Orientalism, which allows the media to assume that despite the fact that homophobia still has real political consequences in the United States, Americans are outraged at the existence of antisodomy laws in Iran. For example, few mainstream media reports noted the fact that Ahmadinejad's comments came the same week U.S. Senator Larry Craig "began legal efforts to show he is not gay even though he appeared to be trolling for sex in an airport men's room."[44] This value is at the same time grounded on a hierarchy: the United States (and presumably European countries) has a better understanding of freedom than Muslim-majority countries.

4d. Hierarchies

A fourth type of audience assumption that can be identified in journalistic rhetoric is hierarchy, which establishes the importance of one value compared to another. In the Ahmadinejad coverage the hierarchy is simple, if all encompassing: the United States is better—understood as more enlightened, freer, and more just—than Iran. A number of hierarchies underlie the rumors about Obama as well as the campaign's responses to them. One is seen in Iowa voter Michael's comments: in terms of the religious affiliation of a presidential candidate, Christian is better than Muslim.

Another, perhaps more subtle, hierarchy is found in the stark contrast between Obama's response to the charges that his pastor, Rev. Jeremiah Wright, is racist and his response to the rumors that he himself is Muslim. The first became an opportunity for what many view as a remarkably honest speech about the status of race in U.S. politics today, an opportunity to deepen the conversation about race.[45] This was not the case with the Muslim rumors. Obama has denied them, but he has not strongly questioned the rumors' premises, such as why would it matter if he was Muslim, or why Islam and American patriotism are assumed to be inconsistent.[46] This implies a hierarchy of sorts, in terms of what issue is most important to Obama (racism versus Islamophobia), and perhaps which issue he thinks is more politically expedient in the U.S. context.

5. Summary

No, Obama is not a Muslim. Yes, homosexual acts do take place in Iran. But beyond these facts, more interesting things can be said by reading these media accounts about commonly held assumptions in the United States related to political Islam. The four categories of audience assumptions discussed—facts, presumptions, values, and hierarchies—provide categories for taking a snapshot of the current status of Islam and U.S. politics. This snapshot, in turn, is useful for forecasting the role of Islam in U.S. politics and the challenges to creating a meaningful Islamic presence in the U.S. political system. By reconsidering media coverage of Obama's Muslim problem and Ahmadinejad's "no gays in Iran" comment, we can see the obstacles preventing Islamic forms of knowledge and practice from being integrated into mainstream U.S. politics. By knowing where we stand today, we know better what has to be done to reeducate the American public about the potential positive contributions of Islamic candidates, theologies, and ways of life.

Notes

1. The method of rhetorical analysis I use here was developed in my earlier publications, "Speaking of Motherhood: The Epideictic Rhetoric of John Paul II and Ayatollah Khomeini," *Journal of the Society of Christian Ethics* 26, no. 2 (2006):

93–123. Georgetown University Press granted permission for portions of that essay to be reproduced here.

2. Michel de Certeau, *The Practice of Everyday Life*, trans. Steven Rendall (Berkeley: University of California Press, 1984), xx.

3. I borrow the phrase "Obama's Muslim problem" from my colleague William D. Hart's article, "Obama's Muslim Problem—And Ours." In that essay Hart riffs on Norman Podhoretz's 1963 essay, "My Negro Problem—And Ours," and convincingly argues that "Obama's repetitive denial that he is not a Muslim has the same effect as a white person who repetitively denies that she is a 'nigger-lover,' a liberal who denies that he is a communist, or a heterosexual who denies that he is gay. Such denials lend aid and comfort to the bigots who make them; repetitive denials serve a bigoted agenda." William D. Hart, "Obama's Muslim Problem— And Ours," *Religion Dispatches*, July 18, 2008, http://www.religiondispatches.org/archive/politics/361/obama%27s_muslim_problem%E2%80%94and_ours.

4. These assumptions about Islam are rooted in Orientalism, Edward Said's term for "an ontological and epistemological distinction made between 'the Orient' and (most of the time) 'the Occident.'" Edward Said, *Orientalism* (New York: Vintage Books, 1979), 2.

5. George Kennedy, *Comparative Rhetoric: An Historical and Cross-Cultural Introduction* (New York: Oxford University Press, 1998), 3.

6. For further reading, see George Kennedy, *A New History of Classical Rhetoric* (Princeton: Princeton University Press, 1994).

7. All citations from Aristotle's *On Rhetoric* come from, unless otherwise noted, Kennedy's translation. Aristotle, *On Rhetoric*, trans. George Kennedy (New York: Oxford University Press, 1991).

8. Insofar as rhetoric in general has fallen into disrepute as trickery and propaganda, epideictic rhetoric has often been demonized as the worst of the worst. This is based on an interpretation of Aristotle's characterization of epideictic audiences as "spectators," which has been understood to mean that the epideictic audience does not judge at all, and that epideictic rhetoric is mere propaganda, a flowery presentation, whose merit is based solely on the skill of presentation. What Aristotle actually says, however, is that epideictic audiences are *theoros*. According to Liddell and Scott's Oxford-published *Intermediate Greek-English Lexicon*, *theoria* means a looking at, a viewing and beholding— when associated with the mind, a contemplation or speculation. More than just passive reception, the term invokes a sense of reasoning, or, as Oravec argues, "a kind of insight or power of generalization, as well as passive viewing." Christine Oravec, "'Observation' in Aristotle's Theory of Epideictic," *Philosophy and Rhetoric*, 9 (1976): 164. Oravec refers to Liddell: Henry George Liddell and Robert Scott, *An Intermediate Greek-English Lexicon*. Founded on the seventh edition of Liddell and Scott's *Greek-English Lexicon* (Oxford: Clarendon Press, 1889). Characterizing the audience as *theoros* in this way has subtle implications: instead of a stance of antagonism, the audience has a generous view of

the speaker/writer. There is still an interpretative moment that must occur, but it begins with an assumption that the speaker shares with the hearer a world-view, horizon, and context.

9. Arthur B. Miller and John D. Bee, "Enthymeme: Body and Soul," *Philosophy and Rhetoric*, 5 (1972): 202.

10. I develop a two-part method elsewhere. See Bucar, "Speaking of Motherhood," and "Methodological Invention as a Constructive Project: Exploring the Production of Ethical Knowledge through the Interaction of Discursive Logics," *Journal of Religious Ethics* 36, no. 3 (2008): 355–373.

11. Chaïm Perelman and L. Olbrechts-Tyteca, *The New Rhetoric: A Treatise on Argumentation* (Notre Dame, IN: University of Notre Dame Press, 1969), 1, 3.

12. Ibid., 65.

13. Ibid., 66.

14. Ibid., 67–95. Perelman and Olbrechts-Tyteca offer a fifth category as well: loci. Perelman defines loci as "premises of a general nature that can serve as the bases for values and hierarchies." Ibid., 84. Loci is a meta-category of general logical assumptions or "rule sets" that connect facts, presumptions, and hierarchies. Locus of quantity, for example, affirms "that this one is better than another for quantitative reasons," such as democracy, which gives a voice to a greater number of citizens than other forms of government. Ibid., 85. Loci can take many forms, but the more specific they become (e.g., "locus of person-hood" or "locus of order") the closer they become to values and hierarchies and the more difficult it is to distinguish loci from these other elements. As analysis of general premises, loci are a way to step back and identify broader assumptions of rhetorical performances. I don't use loci here as a category of rhetorical analysis because I have found it less illuminating than the other categories.

15. Ibid., 66.

16. Ibid., 71.

17. Ibid., 74.

18. Ibid., 81.

19. Ibid., 51.

20. The October 8, 2007, *New Yorker* cover depicted Iranian President Ahmadinejad soliciting sex in a public bathroom, and the July 21, 2008, cover depicted Barack Obama in a turban, fist-bumping his AK-47-carrying wife.

21. President of CNN U.S., Jon Klein, said his network's report was "not a response to Fox per se, though they did seem to relish repeating the Insight-reported rumor without bothering to—or being able to—ascertain the facts." Wolf Blitzer, CCN anchor, also scolded Fox News' journalistic practices. "CNN did what any serious news organization is supposed to do in this kind of situation," Blitzer said. "We actually conducted an exclusive firsthand investigation inside Indonesia to check out the school." As quoted in Bill Carter, "Rivals CNN and Fox News Spar Over Obama Report," *New York Times*, January 24, 2007.

22. See, for example, David Gardiner, "'I Pray My Grandson Barak Turns Muslim,'" *Daily Mail* (London), November 26, 2010, and Christi Parsons and Peter Nicholas, "Obama Talks About Faith," *Los Angeles Times*, September 29, 2010.

23. Perry Bacon, "Foes Use Obama's Muslim Ties to Fuel Rumors About Him," *Washington Post*, November 29, 2007.

24. Editorial, "Sticks, Stones and Mr. Obama: Misleading Aspersions about the Senator's Background Only Make the Perpetrators Look Bad," *Washington Post*, January 28, 2007.

25. See, for example, Bill Carter, "Rivals CNN and Fox News Spar"; David D. Kirkpatrick, "Feeding Frenzy for a Big Story, Even If It's False," *New York Times*, January 29, 2007.

26. *The Washington Post* quotes Ibrahim Hooper, of the Council of American-Islamic Relations, making the same point: "The underlying point is that if you can somehow pin Islam on him, that would be a fatal blow." Bacon, "Foes Use Obama's Muslim Ties."

27. Deborah Howell, "Refuting, or Feeding, the Rumor Mill?" *Washington Post*, December 9, 2007.

28. Ibid.

29. Hart argues convincingly that the status of rumor "owes as much to the Obama campaign's response as to the claim itself. The pernicious power of rumors, especially when they are false, depends heavily on the response. The wrong response suggests that the normative assumptions underlying the false claim are true. Whether true or false, a rumor can 'smear' a candidate, in this case Obama, only if he accepts the normative assumption—that Muslims are bad, and that a Muslim president is unacceptable—that underlies the truthful denial that he is a Muslim." Hart, "Obama's Muslim Problem."

30. Michael Saul, "I'm No Muslim, Says Bam. Christian Barack Lays Rumors on His Religious Ties to Rest," *Daily News*, December, 23, 2007.

31. Ibid.

32. Ibid.

33. See, for example, Betsy Pisik, "Ill Will for Ahmadinejad; Iranian Defends Views at Columbia," *Washington Times*, September 25, 2007; Rueters, "Iran Clarifies Leader's Remarks on Gays," *New York Times*, October 11, 2007; Tamer el-Ghobashy and Bill Hutchinson, "Wipe the Smirk Off Your Evil Face," *Daily News*, September 25, 2007; Wesley Pruden, "Getting Tough in the Ivy League," *Washington Times*, September 25, 2007; Editorial, "Western Exposure in Speech," *DallasNews.com*, September 25, 2007; Nazila Fathi, "Despite President's Denials, Gays Insist They Exist, If Quietly, in Iran," *New York Times*, September 30, 2007; Editorial, "Mr. Ahmadinejad Speaks," *New York Times*, September 25, 2007.

34. Joseph Massad, *Desiring Arabs* (Chicago: University of Chicago Press, 2007); Afsaneh Najmabadi, "Transing and Transpassing Across Sex-Gender Walls in

Iran," *Women's Studies Quarterly* 36, no. 3–4 (2008): 23–42. Afsaneh Najmabadi, *Women with Mustaches and Men without Beards: Gender and Sexual Anxieties of Iranian Modernity* (Berkeley: University of California Press, 2005).

35. William Beeman argues that in Iran sexual behavior is classified into "active" and "passive" roles, so that "active" same-sex partners do not consider themselves to be homosexual. William Beeman, "No Gays in Iran...But Many Same-Sex Couples," *New America Media*, September 26, 2007.

36. It is noteworthy that it was not until the U.S. media covered Iranian responses to the event that the appropriateness of Bollinger's comments was questioned. As reported in the *New York Times*, the Iranian state television coverage depicted Bollinger's introduction as an "ambush of personal insults," and the former head of the Revolutionary Guards, Mohsen Rezai, was quoted as saying, "He is the president of a country...It is shocking that a country that claims to be civilized treats him that way." Nazila Fathi, "Iran's Media Assail President's Treatment," *New York Times*, September 26, 2007.

37. Fathi, "Despite President's Denials."

38. Pruden, "Getting Tough in the Ivy League."

39. The media has a role in making beliefs about political Islam into facts, insofar as they have the aura of reality. According to a Pew Forum poll, nearly one-in-five Americans (18 percent) said that Obama is a Muslim in August 2010, up from 11 percent in March 2009. More telling is that when asked how they learned about Obama's religion, 60 percent cite the media. The same media role can be presumably said of Iran and Islam, as the majority of U.S. citizens have no access to the Persian-language press that is critical of the Western media's characterization of Iran, Ahmadinejad, and Islam's compatibility with modern democracy. The Pew Forum on Religion and Public Life, "Growing Number of Americans Say Obama is a Muslim," August 18, 2010, http://www.pewforum.org/Politics-and-Elections/Growing-Number-of-Americans-Say-Obama-is-a-Muslim.aspx.

40. In the Iranian Penal Code, Articles 108–126 outline the punishment for sodomy [*lavat*] (defined in Art. 108 as penetrative sex between two men). Although punishment is to some extent left up to the discretion of the shari'a judge (Art. 110, 120), for adults, the maximum punishment for consensual sodomy is death (Art. 109–111). Punishment for genital acts between women [*mosahegheh*] differs: 100 lashes for each party involved (Art. 129), although if the act is proven four times, the penalty is death (Art. 131).

41. Iranian Penal Code, Art. 114, 117, 128.

42. Daniel Pipes, a conservative political commentator, makes a very similar claim: "If [Obama] was born and raised a Muslim and is now hiding that fact, this points to a major deceit, a fundamental misrepresentation about himself that has profound implications about his character and his suitability as president." Daniel Pipes, "Barack Obama's Muslim Childhood," *FrontPageMagazine.com*, April 29, 2008, http://www.danielpipes.org/5544/barack-obamas-muslim-childhood.

43. In fact, according to a Pew Forum poll, people who currently think Obama is Muslim are more likely to disapprove of his job performance: "Beliefs about Obama's religion are closely linked to political judgments about him. Those who say he is a Muslim overwhelmingly disapprove of his job performance, while a majority of those who think he is a Christian approve of the job Obama is doing." Pew Forum, "Growing Number of Americans."

44. Exceptions include this quoted *St. Petersburg Times* article and the October 8, 2007, *New Yorker* cover depicting Iranian President Ahmadinejad soliciting sex in a public bathroom. Susan Taylor Martin, "Face of Homosexuality Is Veiled but Real in Iran," *St. Petersburg Times*, September 30, 2007.

45. Barack Obama, "A More Perfect Union," Constitution Center Philadelphia, Pennsylvania, March 18, 2008, http://www.huffingtonpost.com/2008/03/18/ob ama-race-speech-read-th_n_92077.html.

46. One notable exception was Colin Powell's remarks to *Meet the Press* on October 19, 2008, during which he questioned the assumption that "there something wrong with being a Muslim in this country." The full transcript can be read at http://www.msnbc.msn.com/id/27266223/ns/meet_the_press/t/meet-press-transcript-oct/.

8

The Future of Political Theology

FROM CRISIS TO PLURALISM

Robin Lovin

I.

POLITICAL THEOLOGY BEGINS with the relationship between God and political authority, providing an account of God and the human condition that authorizes certain persons to decide political questions and then enjoins obedience to those decisions, "not only because of wrath, but also because of conscience" (Romans 13:5). In modern times, political theology has been concerned especially with the state, and the power to decide has been conferred, with few qualifications, on the person or party holding power in the state. From Thomas Hobbes to Carl Schmitt, modern political thinkers have concluded that the state requires a unity that can only be supplied by a single center of power. Where that unity is lacking, any dispute may end in violence, and a weakened government may leave the state exposed to external threats. Political necessity and a theological assessment of fallen humanity's propensity for disorder combine to yield the axiom of modern politics: Disputed questions must not be allowed to linger undecided.

The experience behind this axiom includes the religious warfare and political uncertainty that accompanied the breakup of the medieval European order and the emergence of the early modern state, but the argument is theologically reinforced by what Jürgen Moltmann has called a "negative anthropology." Political life requires a strong center of authority because human nature is invariably selfish, eager to assert itself in conflict and domination over others, and in need of protection both from the aggression of others and from its own misguided impulses. This assessment is often justified by appeal to Augustine's doctrine of original sin.[1]

Christian theology thus provides an easy way to justify the need of modern politics for a strong center of authority. Nevertheless, this modern political theology raises as many problems as it solves. Fallen human nature is prone to idolatry and self-glorification, as well as to violence. Unlimited authority tends to elicit false worship from its subjects, while at the same time deluding those who hold it into forgetting their own mortality. This, too, is an axiom of political order, well known to Christians long before the modern world began: Too much power corrupts the ruled and ruins the ruler (Acts 12:18–25). Political order seems like a good thing, but every experience with absolute authority raises anew the question whether such a *Christian* political theology is possible.

In the twentieth century, these questions became urgent, both for theology and for political theory. One paradigm of twentieth century political authority is the sovereign right, delineated by Carl Schmitt, to determine "the exception."[2] Under conditions of external threat or internal disorder, which the government itself discovers and makes known, normal procedures, rights, and guarantees must be suspended, until such time as the government again determines that the threat has passed. The regime thus takes upon itself both absolute power and exemption from accountability. When this paradigm was enacted by the Third Reich, the immediate political effects were morally debilitating, and the human tragedies that followed were beyond calculation.

No wonder, then, many concluded that if there is a place for Christian theology in modern politics, it must be a new role, quite different from the legitimation of absolute power that theology provided at the beginning of the modern era. Theology must instead interpose itself in a way that cuts off this recourse to absolute power that is central to modern political theology. Christianity must proclaim that all human authority is limited and contingent, subject at any moment to dissolution by the reality of divine judgment. That was the theological *krisis* that Karl Barth announced even before the European political crisis made the theological judgment urgent.[3] In the face of twentieth century political authority, Barth argued, the church must rise above the history and interests that bound it to nations and proclaim a judgment that falls equally on all powers in every time.

Political theorists arrived at a similar assessment of the lessons of global war and revolution, though perhaps somewhat later. The revival of political theory after the Second World War provided a sustained defense of liberal democracy on premises quite different from the Hobbesean assumptions that required absolute authority to support social peace. From Isaiah Berlin's essays on liberty to Rawls's magisterial theory of justice, these political thinkers sought to undermine the conceptual foundations of absolute power.[4] Their aim was to describe constitutional governments in a way that precluded a sovereign with the right to determine the exception.

Thus, modern political thought ended the twentieth century by formulating more explicit and more demanding theories of liberal democracy that set out the terms for legitimate political claims and asserted strong rights against political authority, and Christian theology rediscovered the eschatological, even apocalyptic, language of its own origins.[5] Political authority of all sorts belongs to an age that is already passing away. Whatever authority an exceptional situation may confer, it cannot deny that more basic truth. Political authority cannot make necessary that which is contingent or make permanent that which can only be transitory.

The development of this new approach to political theology—stretching from Barth's *Epistle to the Romans* to the more recent work of Oliver O'Donovan and Stanley Hauerwas—has taken several forms that are not always compatible with one another. In more radical versions, the distinction between the church and the world is drawn so sharply that Christian identity is defined wholly by the church and Christians have no role in the world. They are strangers and exiles, transients who happen to be stuck here for the moment. Other versions draw upon a social theory, such as Marxism or critical theory, to disenchant the claims of political authority. According to these accounts, politics is nothing more than the exercise of power in pursuit of self-interest. Claims about authority and legitimacy have a greatly diminished role in these new political theologies. In various ways, then, these new political theologies reduce political authority to an instrumental good whose purposes can only be rendered coherent in light of God's saving work, so that the self-contained systems of meaning proclaimed by various modern ideologies all become unbelievable.

Finally, and quite recently, this recovery of Christian apocalyptic theology has taken the form of exposing the theological language in which the modern state makes its claims to an exceptional role for itself.[6] Ironically, as the political grounds for claiming absolute authority have been taken away by liberal theory and human rights legislation, governments seeking to free themselves from limits and accountability have adopted an apocalyptic language of their own, discerning ultimate threats which change the terms of politics and require an unlimited scope for response. Apocalyptic language allows those who already have power to claim that in the ultimate conflict between good and evil, events have reached such a pitch of danger that there is no longer any basis on which their actions might be evaluated by conventional legal and moral standards. In this situation, it becomes the task of a counter-apocalyptic political theology to remind everyone that the message of the in-breaking of God's power is good news to the poor, to whom it was first delivered.[7] The dissolution of established orders can never be a mandate for those who now hold power to write their own ending to history.

The importance of this theological transformation is hard to over-state. After several centuries in which post-Reformation theology—both Protestant and Catholic—built connections between sovereign power and political authority and counseled that the divine will was at work even in bad rulers, historical events prompted a radical rethinking that discov-ered again the uniqueness of divine sovereignty, utterly different from its human imitations and independent of human aims.[8] While many of the theologians who formulated these ideas would recoil from the thought that their work served any political purposes, they have provided models for confessing churches, for nonviolent movements, and for base com-munities, all which stand between the extremes of passive obedience and violent resistance. Any regime that contemplates a totalitarian reordering of life around a single political idea must now know that there are mul-tiple ways for a Christian community to thwart that aspiration, simply by continuing to exist on its own terms.

2.

Less clear is whether these accounts of political life, designed as a defense against totalitarian exceptionalism, provide a theological understanding of ordinary, unexceptional, democratic politics that would be recognizable to those who participate in that kind of government, and whether this theol-ogy provides any encouragement to Christians for that kind of participa-tion. The reservation Reinhold Niebuhr voiced about Karl Barth's theology just after the Second World War often seems applicable today across a broader range of pacifist, liberationist, or counter-apocalyptic theologies: They make clear the distinction between God's sovereignty and ours, but we are left wondering whether that is all they have to say.

Niebuhr suggested, "Perhaps this theology is constructed too much for the great crises of history. It seems to have no guidance for a Christian statesman of our day. It can fight the devil if he shows both horns and both cloven feet. But it refuses to make discriminating judgments about good and evil if the evil shows only one horn or the half of a cloven foot."[9] He hoped, of course, that statesmen and theologians would begin talking to one another again and arrive at a more realistic understanding of human nature and human conflict without deceiving themselves into thinking they could eliminate evil. That, in turn, would free their energies for the achievable tasks of containing totalitarianism abroad and rendering proximate justice at home.

In many ways, Niebuhr achieved that political dialogue personally, but he has had no successor and few successful imitators. From our present vantage point, we can see that Niebuhr was a rare exception. Generally speaking, political theorists and political theologians have responded to the ideologies of unchecked power in ways that are mutually incompatible. Both agree that unlimited authority is unacceptable and should be rendered conceptually impossible, but they attempt this objective in quite different ways.

Liberal political theorists have sought to restrain appeals to "the exception" by establishing rules for public discourse. In a liberal democracy, the rules are supposed to be neutral between competing comprehensive beliefs. No one is forbidden or required to make claims about ultimate reality, but no such claims are admitted to discussions about legislation, adjudication, and choices between candidates for political leadership. If these rules are followed, no one can claim the exception by offering an apocalyptic interpretation of political choices that reduces them to a choice between good and evil. But no one can oppose the seizure of power in those absolute terms, either. For liberal political philosophers, any truth claim stated in religious terms is politically suspect. As John Rawls put it, "The zeal to embody the whole truth in politics is incompatible with an idea of public reason that belongs with democratic citizenship."[10] Politics, not to put too fine a point on it, is the realm of half truths, where people affirm just exactly what they have to share in order to come to agreement, demanding no more of their fellow citizens and offering nothing more by way of argument for their own choices. Confident in both the neutrality of public reason and the adequacy of partial truths to political purposes, liberal political theorists offer a public discourse that is open to anyone who will play by the rules and work within those limits.

Notice, then, that liberal political theorists are trying to do the same thing by excluding theological language from politics that the theologians were trying to do by introducing it. Both intend to prevent political leaders from claiming a kind of authority that is not subject to criticism and scrutiny, but the political theorists look at the world and conclude that the way to do that is to exclude the sort of move that the theologians want to make. Appealing to ultimate truths would allow would-be authoritarians to bypass the political process.

By contrast, many theologians fear that it is the partial truths that are most subject to distortion and exploitation. Vague ideas of citizenship and duty can call people to many different purposes, while the summons of the Triune God who makes all things new in Jesus Christ is not easily restated in terms acceptable to public reason. In a time of moral uncertainty, political language that lacks a distinctive Christian witness can be bent to any purpose, and so accepting the requirements of public reason may actually be worse than remaining silent in the face of evil. What is required is an unapologetic witness that clearly proclaims God's judgment, with or without permission, and whether or not the proclamation is understood.

Once again, liberal political theorists and unapologetic theologians agree that "the whole truth" cannot be embodied in politics, but political theorists try to protect the integrity of politics by excluding comprehensive doctrines; absolute power cannot be legitimated if there is no language in which to claim it. Theologians, by contrast, insist that unlimited political power can be resisted only if there is language in which to say clearly that the whole truth belongs to God alone. But having said that, there is little more that they can say, because they have thus rejected the terms that political theorists offer for engaging specific political questions.

Nevertheless, political choices are made and political questions are discussed in religious terms. That is inevitable in a democracy where many of the citizens are also people of faith. The dialogue that Niebuhr hoped would happen does go on, with or without the permission of political theorists and theologians.

3.

Any political theology that can engage the problems of everyday politics must move beyond the repetitive assertion of claim and counterclaim on behalf of public reason and unapologetic theology. The mutually incompatible strategies that have divided political theory from theology have reached the limits of their usefulness. The question for the future is whether there is a political theology that gives us a framework for understanding democracy without compromising the integrity of either politics or theology.

We might begin by noticing that the history of theology provides ways of understanding politics more broadly than we usually do today. We confine politics to the work of government. We think that people are engaging in politics when they are trying to acquire or to exercise the power of the state. Other uses of the word are, for us, metaphorical, analogical, or ironic—as when we speak of "office politics" or "academic politics." The real thing goes on in the halls of government. That understanding of politics goes back to the beginning of the modern era, when emerging modern states consolidated power in the hands of secular, territorial rulers, hoping to provide security against other rulers who were doing the same thing and striving to maintain order during a time of religious conflict and rapid social change.

This restriction of politics to the work of government was justified by the "negative anthropology" outlined by Moltmann.[11] In this anthropology, nothing of value is to be expected from sinful human aims and desires. Politics is about limiting the damage caused by conflict between those desires. People have to live in communities to survive, so maintaining a life worth living for people is a matter of bringing their impulses under control through law, backed up by force. Since people following their selfish impulses are bound to disagree, the law had better also provide for someone whose word is sufficient to end all argument.[12] It was in this way that the idea of sovereignty became central to the political theory of the modern state and to modern political theology.

Theologians, however, have another way of thinking about politics that was in use long before modern politics centered on the sovereign state began. In this way of thinking, it is human aims and desires that make politics possible. People form communities and cooperate with one another because they want things that they cannot secure on their own. We recognize our common human nature in these shared desires, but we understand that the goods we want are not completely natural. Unlike the territory and food supplies for which other animals compete, the things we want are the products of organizations and institutions. We must cooperate with one another if the goods we desire are to exist at all. The sum of those institutions is our human "city," our polity, and the various activities that keep those institutions going are our politics. Government is an important part of this, but it is not the whole of it.

This understanding of politics can be traced back to Aristotle. It was adapted to Christian political theology through the more positive anthropology of Thomas Aquinas, who, in contrast to Hobbes, did not believe that human life was only "a perpetuall and restlesse desire of Power after power."[13] People are also joined to one another through the goods they can create together, and the basis for their agreement with one another is inherent in the goods themselves.[14] This understanding of politics also represents more adequately the thought of Augustine, who likewise recognized that there is a limited, temporal reality to the human commonwealth, even though it is not united by the love of God.[15]

This Christian political theology is older than the modern state. It is also broader than its Aristotelian origins, including within its scope many goods of family and economic life that were beneath the notice of Aristotle's politics. Households and families, schools and cultural institutions, associations of workers, corporations, and churches are all part of it, alongside the institutions of government that we ordinarily call "political."

The goods that human beings pursue seem to be irreducibly multiple. No one institution can provide all of them, and political conflict seems to be as much about how we balance the claims of one kind of good against another as it is about our competing interests in the goods themselves. The family makes claims against the workplace, the workplace resists the claims of government; the church seeks a space of freedom within the state, but then has its own conflicts over freedoms claimed by schools and families. Aspects of all those questions end up back in the courts and the legislature, but that is only part of what is going on politically, and few citizens in an open society expect that government will settle those larger issues with the finality expected from Hobbes's sovereign.

These loci of political activity receive various names in Christian theology. They are "orders," or "spheres," "orders of creation" or "orders of preservation," "divine mandates," or "subsidiary institutions." Their variety reflects different judgments about the nature and value of these plural human goods, disagreements over how human goods participate in God's goodness and about the extent to which desire for them falls under God's judgment, and issues of how far our common objects of love reflect our fallen human nature and what place they have in the true good to which God would restore us. I have elsewhere called them "contexts," to choose a neutral term that avoids taking sides in the theological controversies.[16] I do not mean to imply that the theological issues that separate, say, Emil Brunner from the papal social encyclicals are insignificant, but I want to call attention to the shared features of a pluralistic political theology that emerges when theology affirms the pursuit of human goods instead of focusing on the control of human desires. Those goods may be affirmed as the first step on the path that leads to God, or they may be received as divine mercy toward our human weakness. They may even be viewed with suspicion as objects of inordinate love that constantly have to be put back in their proper place. But if the goods human beings pursue have any meaning at all, the political arrangements that are necessary to those pursuits will be theologically important, and they will reflect the variety of the goods themselves.[17]

What these pluralistic political theologies have in common is the idea that the contexts where human goods are sought are relatively independent of one another. That does not mean that any of them could exist alone, without the others. All of them must, in fact, be present to create a whole society. To speak of their autonomy, or even of their "sovereignty,"[18] does not isolate them from one another. It means, rather, that none of these institutions needs anything beyond the human goods it creates and maintains to justify its existence as part of society. It makes claims on persons and on other institutions to secure the continuation of its purposes, and it needs no authorization from sources beyond itself to do so.

In relation to the power of the modern state, it is of special importance that these contexts do not exist simply because the government recognizes them, nor do they derive their authority from the state.[19] The ways in which they are organized follow from their own imperatives, and they cannot be conformed to any ideology that happens, for the moment, to be driving the politics of government. This is yet another way to curb the "zeal to embody the whole truth in politics" that troubled Rawls and other liberal political theorists. Someone will always claim to have the final word around which family life, religious faith, and economic order must all be organized. The politics of government is perhaps particularly tempted to make those claims. We may, as liberal theorists do, reduce the risks of authoritarianism by ruling that such comprehensive claims are inadmissible in the public forum where choices about government are made. But we may also resist tyranny by reminding government that whatever ideology it adopts, this does not determine the truth for politics as a whole.[20]

Nevertheless, the modern alternative, focused on the politics of government and the state, is now deeply embedded in our thinking. We have already noted the ironic usages of "office politics" and "academic politics," which call attention to bad behavior that takes itself too seriously in the pursuit of self-interest or the manipulation of intelligence. We assume that this behavior is ridiculous precisely because it is so "political" in a context where politics does not really fit. But the ironic scorn points to a deeper truth. People playing office politics and people pursuing the politics of government behave in similar ways because they are engaged in the same activity. They are part of an institution that is essential to the creation of a good in which they want to share, and they are trying to direct the operation of the institution so that the resulting good is more like they think it ought to be. The activity is politics in either case. When we object that someone is bringing "politics" into a place where it does not belong, what we usually mean is that they have set aside the rules of normal and acceptable politics that apply in the place where they are and have instead tried to act according to politics borrowed from some other place, usually a part of government, whose political behaviors can be learned by paying close attention to the evening news.

It is appropriate to discourage that sort of behavior but mistaken to think that eliminating it gets rid of politics. Rather, it eliminates a distraction and allows people to get back to genuine politics, appropriate to the context. Society as a whole depends on good politics in each of its parts. Government, for all its unique powers and universal reach, is only one of these parts.

A political pluralism attentive to the irreducible multiplicity of human goods and institutions is thus essential to this older Christian political theology when it is applied to the conditions of modern life. Political theology understood in this way may make judgments about the limits of government, but those judgments are part of a more general affirmation of the integrity of all the institutional contexts that make up a society. The limits of government arise from the particular kind of goods for which government is responsible, not from a negative anthropology in which the state is a manifestation of sin.[21]

4.

By contrast to this earlier political understanding of human goods in human communities, the most important assumption shared by modern political theology, liberal political theories, and crisis theology stands out in sharp relief: None of these could allow the pursuit of the good to enter into the politics of the modern state. Modern political theology insisted that the result would be fatal internal weakness. Liberal political theory feared that attempts to enforce societal agreement on goods would limit individual freedom of conscience and inquiry. Crisis theology thought that an inquiry into the human good would lead to a reliance on human wisdom that would eclipse our more fundamental dependence on God. Both liberalism and crisis theology rejected the authoritarianism that modern political theology used to end disputes about the good, but they assumed that they had to solve the same problem. Liberalism sought political principles that would leave citizens free to pursue their individual understandings of the good. Crisis theology reduced political principles to such a point of insignificance that no one with an eye on the ultimate good could find much to choose from among the alternative understandings of political order.[22]

Liberal political theory has provided the most extensive and persuasive working out of this neutrality with respect to ideas about the good in political life. More recent political thinking, however, has raised questions about whether this exclusion is necessary, or even possible. John Rawls reformulated his liberal theory to make it clear that he did not rely on neutral political principles, but on an "overlapping consensus" between different accounts of the human good to provide the starting point for a carefully constructed politics based on public reason.[23] William Galston goes further, challenging the effort to formulate political theories that are "freestanding" rather than "comprehensive."[24] The claim to neutrality may have practical advantages among people who hold a wide variety of religious and moral beliefs. If the political system works well, the independence of discussions about law and policy from moral and religious convictions may come to be taken for granted. "But this," as Galston says, "is an illusion, quickly dispelled in times of internal or external crisis."[25]

When the meaning of freestanding political principles comes into dispute in ways that cannot be resolved by public reason, people turn to ideas about the good drawn from religion, ethics, and personal convictions to figure out what the political principles mean and why they are important. The abolition of slavery, extension of political rights to women, recognition of the economic claims of labor, and end of discrimination based on race, disability, or sexual orientation may all be incorporated into a politics based on public reason, but it is doubtful that they can be fully explained in those terms. When previous generations spoke of these questions, they turned to the language of God-given rights, inherent worth, and even divine judgment. People today do the same when they speak of climate change, AIDS, and the humanitarian crises sparked by genocide. They are not addressing the questions in terms of public reason, but instead are asking whether public reason is capable of grasping what is at stake in the questions.

Of course, no one of these claims, based on a comprehensive understanding of the human good, appeals to everyone. If ideas about the good were always interpreted in the same way, the issues they help us to understand would not be so controversial. A crisis always involves an argument about what an idea of the human good means, as well as how it is to be applied. After the crisis, there will still be disagreement over which ideas of the good best account for the political arrangements that now prevail and what, precisely, the implications of those ideas are for the new questions that now have to be faced. Ideas about the human good are not unanimous nor is agreement on them final. On that, at least, Hobbes and the other early modern theorists who concluded that peace and order had to rest on authority were correct. Where they were mistaken was to suppose that people locked in argument about the good could not, at the same time, sustain peace and order. Authoritarians are still dismayed by the messiness of liberal democracy and fearful that external enemies will exploit its divisions, but the modern state proves much more capable of sustaining ongoing conflict than the early modern theorists previously thought it could.

Unanimity on disputed questions proves to be unnecessary for the survival of a modern state. Indeed, the recent history of states where one supreme authority has decided all disputed questions—in politics, economics, religion, family life, and culture—suggests that it is precisely those states that do not survive. That would have seemed absurd to Hitler, Mussolini, and Stalin at the height of their powers, nor was it, at the time, obvious to the leaders of the democracies that opposed them. But few theoretical generalizations seem more secure at the beginning of the twenty-first century than this one: Modern political theology rested on a mistake. A political theology for the future rests in large part on freeing ourselves from the assumption that a successful modern state cannot tolerate moral and theological arguments in its public squares. In the effort to formulate that new political theology, we may be best served by an earlier understanding in which such disputes were at the center of politics.

5.

A pluralist political theology thus makes a place in political theory for the discussion of human goods at the same time that it expands the scope of

politics beyond the discussions that are specific to the work of government. Whatever rules of public reason may prevail there, public life cannot be insulated from the ideas about human goods that people bring to
every institution in which they seek to create and maintain those goods.[26]
Because disagreements about the human good are an ongoing feature of
political life, pluralist political theology is also realistic about political conflict. Limited resources and limited knowledge are permanent features of
the human condition. Even people who share a commitment to economic
development, social justice, and their common society will envision these
goods in different ways, assign different priorities on them in relation to
other goods, misjudge their own power and the intentions of their opponents, and exaggerate the importance of their own contributions to the
outcome of common efforts. As Reinhold Niebuhr observed, the difficulty
of transcending self-interest in these calculations increases with the size
of the group.[27] Transcending the self-interest of nations becomes practically impossible.

For just that reason, the half-measures, compromises, and conflicts of
interest that make up ordinary politics in every political context have to
become part of our political theology, if we are to have any human goods
at all. Crisis theology rightly emphasized the critical judgment that must
be made on every political claim. The economic power that lies behind
property rights, the self-deceptions of the rich, and even the illusions of
the poor must be relentlessly exposed, lest any set of political claims take
the place of the judgment of God. But in the end, that is only half the story
of human politics, precisely because politics is not the judgment of God,
not even the "Mortall God" that Hobbes saw in his Leviathan.[28]

We are human beings and not God, Niebuhr wrote, some years after his
initial deconstruction of the self-interest hidden in every claim to justice.
"We are responsible for making choices between greater and lesser evils,
even when our Christian faith, illuminating the human scene, makes it
quite apparent that there is no pure good in history; and probably no pure
evil, either. The fate of civilizations may depend upon these choices of
which some are more, others less, just."[29]

Political theology must include the approximations, intermediate steps,
and partial solutions by which greater and lesser goods are measured. It
must also concern itself with political structures that balance power so
as to ensure that controversies about the human good continue. The fate
of civilizations depends, we now see, not on enforced unity, but on the
ability to revisit our choices and to strike a different equilibrium between

the forces of liberty and equality or security and freedom. The greatest
threat is not the unresolved question, but the power to end dissent and
impose a single answer that is supposed to last for all time. Those who
seek the good through politics must sometimes settle for less power than
they might otherwise have, in order that politics may continue. They must
be less concerned about prevailing over their enemies than about erecting
the structures of balance, containment, and deterrence that ensure that
their enemies will not prevail over them.[30]

A pluralist political theology will trace this realist attention to a proximate justice and balance of power in all spheres of politics, not just in the
politics of nations. Especially in the global realities of the twenty-first century, this implies a political realism concerned with the balance between
the various contexts where the human good is sought. Both within nations
and between them, threats to human good often flow from powerful institutions that extend their claims into all areas of life and overwhelm the
genuine diversity of the goods that persons require. Notably, the success of
market systems in solving the problems of economic production and distribution propels the logic of the market into decisions about culture and
education, and into decisions about working conditions and wages that are
intricately bound up with the possibilities for secure family life. In other
places, certainly not all of them in the Islamic world, religion makes a bid
to settle all questions about the human good, from the least to the greatest
of them, on its terms. Against these contending spheres of economic and
religious power, the power of the state, which is always supposed to have
the last word in questions of politics, often seems strangely silent.[31] A pluralist political theology must therefore give attention to the powers of com-
merce, religion, and culture that now compete with the power of the state.
This expansion of the meaning of politics among nations is seen as hope-
lessly unrealistic by confirmed political realists like Robert Kagan, who see
it as a naïve extension of the political euphoria that greeted the end of the
Cold War. Optimists who anticipated a new era of political freedom and
global cooperation must, according to Kagan, yield once again to the harsh
law of global politics that Hans Morgenthau announced in the middle of
the last century: Nations pursue their interests in the form of power. This
is the only reality that counts in global politics.[32] Political realism should
be recalling us to Morgenthau's rigorous attention to the objective realities of power, not just tempering our optimism by identifying the ongoing
conflicts structured into these new global systems. The resurgent power
of Russia is a warning that global systems are still subject to the power

of competing states. Reinhold Niebuhr, especially, would have seen that these realities did not change in 1989, Kagan argues.[33]

Kagan's warnings against post–Cold War euphoria are well taken. We must be on guard against assumptions that any set of global political changes is permanent, comprehensive, or even fully comprehensible. We must be on guard especially when the changes in question seem to favor our own interests. But Kagan and his fellow political realists may be too convinced of the objective, unchanging reality of state power that on which Morgenthau based his scientific approach to international relations. Certainly, he is more convinced of it than Morgenthau, Kenneth Thompson, and Reinhold Niebuhr were. Morgenthau put it this way:

> What is true of the general character of international relations is also true of the nation state as the ultimate point of reference of contemporary foreign policy. While the realist indeed believes that interest is the perennial standard by which political action must be judged and directed, the contemporary connection between interest and the nation state is a product of history, and is therefore bound to disappear in the course of history.[34]

Political theology seeks to be realistic about the pace of these large, long-term historical transformations but also to be alert to the reality that they do happen.

Political theology has an account of the fundamental forces that shape political life, an account that is older than the modern state and independent of ways that power is pursued in the modern state. Political theology can therefore deal with new global realities, and it is disposed to expect them. At the same time, political theology has had, from Augustine forward, a healthy respect for the enduring power of self-interest in every political formation. In a world where people with limited knowledge and limited resources pursue different goods that are often in competition with one another, the rise of the modern state does not mark the beginning of self-interest, nor would its passing from the center of power be the end of history. Political theology seeks to be realistic about our place in history by offering an account of politics that transcends that location. That broader perspective may occasionally prove a temptation to excessive optimism, but it is not clear that a realism that knows only the objective law of nations pursuing self-interest is sufficiently realistic to grasp the changes that are happening in global politics more broadly conceived.

6.

A pluralist political theology would allow the convergence of political realism with critical theological assessment of human aims and institutions. Theology would no longer be identified with a final judgment that reduces all relative measures of better and worse to insignificance. Citizens of modern states would have theological guidance that is relevant to the proximate tasks of constitutional government and democratic participation.

Nevertheless, the transcendent point of reference remains important. A pluralist political theology that acknowledges the variety of human goods and gives a realistic account of the multiple contexts in which they are created and maintained would be less tempted to the idolatry of the state that was characteristic of modern political theology, but it will not be a political *theology* unless it can also give some account of the ultimate unity of the good. In this, the pluralism of political theology differs from the political theorists' "value pluralism," which accepts the irreducible multiplicity of human goods and resists all attempts to order and unify them in any scheme that could be given political effect.[35]

It was perhaps Dietrich Bonhoeffer who best understood the importance of this point of unity for political theology. He saw the moral crises that were precipitated when a totalitarian state destroyed the differentiated structures of loyalty that made a good life possible, and his idea of multiple "divine mandates"—church, government, work, and family—formulated a theological pluralism to protect each of these centers of human activity from incursions by the others, especially from incursions by the state.[36] When the differences between the mandates are ignored, the order of human life is destroyed. Nevertheless, these distinctions that protect one part of life from incursions by the others are not the last word.

Bonhoeffer's reflection on the personal crises of life in a totalitarian state, which pits loves and loyalties against one another in order to secure its hold on all of life, convinced him that this disintegration of society was only a more extreme form of the conflicts, forced choices, and divided loyalties that afflict all of modern life. The successful citizen of the successful modern state has many choices, but all too often they result in fragmentation, not in satisfaction. If we cannot allow the state to unify the good for us, neither can we live with the tensions which result when each area of life is free to make its own claims on us—work against family, faith against culture, culture against state, state against work, and on and on in endless combination and variety. "Value pluralism" is not so much a solution to this problem as it is a description of it.

Finally, then, the multiplicity of human goods must come together in a human person. Otherwise, we are simply instruments of the goods we help to create. Yet an astonishing number of persons who enjoy the freedom of modern life and have the resources to take advantage of the choices it offers nonetheless live their lives in submission to the imperatives of work and family. They conform to the expectations of culture or religion. They thank God that they are citizens of a free country. But they have no idea who they are in themselves.

For Bonhoeffer, it is God who provides this unity without which the multiplicity of human goods simply continues the social disintegration that can be seen clearly in the totalitarian state. Without this unity, the diversity of mandates provides no protection for the integrity of the person.

> This is the witness the church has to give to the world, that all the other mandates are not there to divide people and tear them apart but to deal with them as whole people before God the Creator, Reconciler, and Redeemer—that reality in all its manifold aspects is ultimately *one* in God who became human, Jesus Christ. The divine mandates in the world are not there to wear people down through endless conflicts. Rather, they aim at the whole human being who stands in reality before God.[37]

Instead of subjecting each person to the duties of separate and distinct mandates, as happened in some older theologies of the created "orders," the person is now where multiple goods, with different and possibly conflicting imperatives, come together. "God has placed human beings under these mandates, not only each individual under one or the other, but all people under all four."[38] The irreducible variety of human goods makes possible a wholeness of life, in which all goods can be enjoyed in appropriate relations to each other and in relation to God.

This unity of human goods in the person before God is clarified in the example of Bonhoeffer's life as well as in the text of his *Ethics*. The person before God has an integrity which cannot be violated by the state, but which also must not be sacrificed by too complete a personal devotion to any one good, nor taken away piecemeal by the multiple demands of institutions that see persons as good only insofar as they contribute to the economic, cultural, political, and religious goods they can help to create.

The person before God has a freedom in relation to all these competing claims and forces, but it is quite different from the freedom of the "sovereign self" that emerges from our postmodern disillusionment with the sovereign state.[39]

Whatever directions developments in global politics may take, the future of political theology appears to lie with an affirmation of the integrity of the person that finds its theological grounding in the unity of human goods as a "whole human being who stands in reality before God." This political theology will be realistic enough to comprehend the degrees of good and evil that are available for human choice, but it will abandon the suspicion of human goods that shaped both the absolute authority of modern political theology and the rejection of that authority in the theology of crisis. The politics of a future political theology will be a flawed and limited human pursuit of human goods that find, in God, a unity that is not available in politics itself. In that unity, what politics seeks is ordered and made whole, fulfilled, and not condemned.

Notes

1. Jürgen Moltmann, *God for a Secular Society: The Public Relevance of Theology*, trans. Margaret Kohl (London: SCM Press, 1999), 38.

2. Carl Schmitt, *Political Theology: Four Chapters on the Concept of Sovereignty*, trans. George Schwab (Cambridge, MA: MIT Press, 1985), 5.

3. Karl Barth, *The Epistle to the Romans*, trans. Edwin Hoskyns (London: Oxford University Press, 1933). German original first published in 1918.

4. Isaiah Berlin, *Two Concepts of Liberty* (Oxford: Clarendon Press, 1958). John Rawls, *A Theory of Justice* (Cambridge, MA: Harvard University Press, 1971).

5. André Dumas, *Political Theology and the Life of the Church*, trans. John Bowden (Philadelphia: Westminster Press, 1978), 5–7.

6. William T. Cavanaugh, *Migrations of the Holy: God, State, and the Political Meaning of the Church* (Grand Rapids, MI: Eerdmans, 2011).

7. See, for example, Duncan B. Forrester, *Apocalypse Now?* (Aldershot, UK: Ashgate, 2005), and Catherine Keller, *God and Power: Counter-Apocalyptic Journeys* (Minneapolis, MN: Fortress Press, 2005). These recent developments occupy an interesting mediating position between Christian political realism, which is thoroughly engaged in concrete political choices, and postmodern political theology, which sometimes offers comprehensive judgments that cover all political options and refuses to make theological choices between them.

8. On this point, see especially Jean Bethke Elshtain, *Sovereignty: God, State, and Self* (New York: Basic Books, 2008).

9. Reinhold Niebuhr, "We Are Men and Not God," *Essays in Applied Christianity*, ed. D. B. Robertson (New York: Meridian Books, 1959), 172.

10. John Rawls, *Collected Papers*, ed. Samuel Freeman (Cambridge, MA: Harvard University Press, 1999), 574.

11. See note 1.

12. Cf. Thomas Hobbes, *Leviathan*, ed. Richard Tuck (Cambridge: Cambridge University Press, 1991), 117–121.

13. Ibid., 70.

14. Cf. Thomas Aquinas, *Summa Theologiae*, I–II, Q. 90, Art. 3.

15. Augustine, *The City of God Against the Pagans*, ed. R. W. Dyson (Cambridge: Cambridge University Press, 1998), 960. See also Oliver O'Donovan, *Common Objects of Love: Moral Reflection and the Shaping of Community* (Grand Rapids, MI: Eerdmans, 2002).

16. Robin Lovin, *Christian Realism and the New Realities* (Cambridge: Cambridge University Press, 2008), 100.

17. See James W. Skillen and Rockne M. McCarthy, eds. *Political Order and the Plural Structure of Society* (Grand Rapids, MI: Eerdmans, 1991).

18. Cf. Abraham Kuyper, *Lectures on Calvinism* (Grand Rapids, MI: Eerdmans, 2000), 91.

19. John Neville Figgis, *Churches in the Modern State* (London: Longmans, Green, 1913), 49–53.

20. This is the political theology of a confessing church, used effectively in Germany to resist the reordering of all social institutions according to Nazi ideals, and in South Africa to defeat the ideology of apartheid.

21. Moltmann, *God for a Secular Society*, 38.

22. See Karl Barth, "Letter to a Pastor in the German Democratic Republic," in Karl Barth and Johannes Hamel, *How to Serve God in a Marxist Land* (New York: Association Press, 1959), 45–80.

23. John Rawls, *Political Liberalism* (New York: Columbia University Press, 1993), 133–172.

24. William A. Galston, *Liberal Pluralism: The Implications of Value Pluralism for Political Theory and Practice* (Cambridge: Cambridge University Press, 2002), 8–9.

25. Ibid., 41.

26. Lovin, *Christian Realism and the New Realities*, 84–116.

27. Reinhold Niebuhr, *Moral Man and Immoral Society* (Louisville: Westminster John Knox Press, 2001), 9.

28. Hobbes, *Leviathan*, 120.

29. Reinhold Niebuhr, *Faith and Politics*, ed. Ronald Stone (New York: George Braziller, 1968), 56.

30. See Andrew J. Bacevich's new introduction to Reinhold Niebuhr, *The Irony of American History* (Chicago: University of Chicago Press, 2008), for an account of the relevance of this Niebuhrian lesson to contemporary American diplomacy.

31. See Robin Lovin, "Christian Realism and the Successful Modern State," *Studies in Christian Ethics*, 20 (April 2007): 55–67.

32. Robert Kagan, *The Return of History and the End of Dreams* (New York: Knopf, 2008).

33. Robert Kagan, "Power Play," *Wall Street Journal*, August 30, 2008, W1.

34. Hans J. Morgenthau and Kenneth W. Thompson, *Politics Among Nations: The Struggle for Power and Peace*, 4th ed. (New York: Alfred A. Knopf, 1966), 9. I am indebted to John Carlson for first calling this passage to my attention.

35. See Galston, *Liberal Pluralism*, 3–11; also Isaiah Berlin, *Liberty*, ed. Henry Hardy (Oxford: Oxford University Press, 2002), 212–217; Lovin, *Christian Realism and the New Realities*, 185–192.

36. Dietrich Bonhoeffer, *Ethics*, Dietrich Bonhoeffer Works, vol. 6 (Minneapolis, MN: Fortress Press, 2005), 68–75, 388–408.

37. Ibid., 73.

38. Ibid., 69.

39. Elshtain, *Sovereignty*, 159–180.

9

Doing Political Theology Today

David Novak

1. The Task of Political Theology Today

Many people today, even many who are otherwise religious, are suspicious of political theology as an active project in the modern world. This suspicion is not only because of the infamous use made of the concept of political theology by the Nazi theorist Carl Schmitt.[1] It is also because of what many people today endorse, what Mark Lilla has called "the Great Separation"—namely, the modern emancipation of politics from the control of theology.[2] And they fear any return to what they think is the *status quo ante*, when theology did control politics.

Theological control of politics seems to be for the sake of *theocracy*, that is, a *theocratic polity*, which theology is presumed to foist on the political scene either all at once or incrementally. Theocracy is taken to be the perennial antithesis to democracy. The task, then, of those of us who "do political theology"—that is, we who advocate for political policies from a decidedly theological perspective—is to rescue the project of political theology from the suspicions of Lilla and those in sympathy with him, let alone from Schmitt's identification of theology and politics.

Lilla argues on behalf of the type of democratic polity that almost all of us who now do political theology would not want to exchange for any other kind of polity available today. His challenge to political theology cannot be dismissed as having been refuted by recent history, in the way that we could easily dismiss Schmitt, who argued for the kind of polity that almost all of us today correctly detest. That means that overcoming Lilla and those in sympathy with him is a more pressing challenge than overcoming Schmitt. Most of us would not admit to having anything in common with Schmitt, neither theologically nor politically, whereas most of us do have politics in common with Lilla and those like him.

Clearly, we need to see the relation of theology and politics differently from the way it is seen by Lilla, let alone Schmitt. But before that can be done, one needs to clarify what he or she means by "theology," a word whose referent is harder to locate than that of the word "politics."

2. Theology and Politics

There are two fundamentally different ways of doing theology, a difference that goes all the way back to how Greek philosophy spoke of God and how God was spoken of in biblical revelation. Nevertheless, for both Greek philosophy (primarily, but not exclusively, that of Aristotle) and biblical revelation, human nature is essentially political (that is, the human is inescapably related to other humans in a society) and essentially theological (that is, the human is inescapably related to God in the universe). Thus the positive relation of theology and politics is central to both traditions, despite the fact that each tradition constituted that relation quite differently.

The difference between the two traditions can be first seen in the way each tradition understands theology, or "God-talk." Even though the actual term "theology" is Greek—*theos* meaning "God" and *logos* meaning "word"—the same two terms appear in Hebrew in the biblical term *dvar adonai,* or "God's talk"—*adonai* meaning "God" (literally "the Lord") and *dvar* meaning "word of." It is my task in this essay to explicate that great difference in the meaning of "theology," to understand this difference between the way the two traditions constituted the relation of theology and politics, and to argue for the greater cogency of the Hebraic constitution of that relation over the Hellenic one.

Even though Aristotle, who coined the term "theology" (theologiké) did occasionally refer to the gods of the *polis* respectfully, he clearly did not invest them with any ultimate moral authority[3]. At most, citizens owed their gods some ritual attention in gratitude for their beneficence. Popular piety is the form justice takes in the religious relationship between citizens of the polis and their gods.[4] However, political justice is mostly concerned with interhuman relationships. In that form, justice is the business of the totally human authority society exercises over its members for the sake of maintaining public peace, and even more importantly, for the sake of attaining the overarching *telos*, or goal of the society, which is to form persons with definite character traits (*aretai*, or "virtues," which are to be recognized as what makes one "a good *X*." In Aristotle's particular situation: "a good Athenian").[5] The business of forming good citizens who have these admirable habits is considered to be too good, too important, to be left to each citizen's private taste. It is most definitely a matter of public or political interest.

Morality, though, is considered too mundane to concern the gods who transcend the city.[6] That is why Aristotle famously said that to live outside a city is to live the life of either a beast or a god.[7] Beasts are sub-verbal beings, hence confined to live in hives or herds. They cannot establish cities as arenas of rational public discourse. As for the gods of the city, they are only different from ordinary humans by degree. But Aristotle is not talking about these local deities in his metaphysical theology; instead, he is talking about the gods who fill the heavens (according to ancient Greek tradition).[8] Only these celestial deities are the intellectual exemplars for humans, whose feet are still stuck on earth, even though their heads can occasionally peek in on what is going on in heaven and overhear the celestial harmonies.[9]

Truly intellectual demands, though, which we would call *metaphysical*, are also *metapolitical*, concerning objects that are beyond ordinary or earthly physical or political interest. These objects only make their demands upon humans when humans can think beyond their own physical and immediate concerns. These transcendent objects are gods, but they are unlike the ordinary gods of the *polis*, not only insofar as they are not objects of ritual attention, but even more importantly insofar as they are intelligent ciphers of the one absolutely intelligent Being, to which all lesser intelligent beings (of which humans are the lowest kind) aspire to come as close to as possible.[10] And, whereas ordinary gods, like ordinary persons, make their demands in explicitly verbal commandments, the God of Aristotle only "commands" by not hiding the very attractiveness of his perfect Being, something he could no more choose to do than choose to reveal it. Being above time and its inherent changeableness, this God is thereby above the choice between self-presentation and absenting oneself, a choice that could only take place when selecting one temporal possibility over others. This God is all-present—never having revealed himself and never having absented himself. The God of Aristotle is eternal—both everlasting and immutable. Accordingly, this God cannot command anyone else because he speaks to no one but himself. Human attraction to this Absolute Being is, in effect, due to apprehending his (or "its") inner monologue. To then say that this God commands us is to speak only metaphorically. This God is not, indeed cannot be, the subject of a transitive verb like "command" or "create" because he does not engage in the type of external relations such verbs describe.[11]

For ordinary people in the city, the gods of the city suffice for their "spiritual" needs, which usually turn out to be nothing more than nostalgia for the prehistoric, mythical time of the city's emergence in the world. Their moral needs, it will be recalled, are handled by the city's laws that it enforces publically and by the virtues the city attempts to inculcate in each citizen. Only those in whom philosophical *eros* irresistibly arises strive to make contact with the God far above the members of the city, whether they are human (*anthropoi*) or even divine (*theoi*). This being the case, is there not a total separation here of politics from theology? After all, from the perspective of most of the people in the city, this kind of metaphysical theology (there being no difference here between "first philosophy" and theology) might seem to be either a harmless diversion or a threat to the type of religion that confined the role of the gods to the city's mythology. If this theology is a threat to the city, then the city is likely to do to its theologians what Athens did to Socrates. However, if theologians (qua metaphysicians) do not openly challenge the official religious ideology of the city, being more circumspect in their intellectual activities than Socrates was, and if they abjure political power as Plato famously did not, then there is a good chance that the city will not regard them as bringing new gods in place of the old ones.[12] That is, these circumspect philosophers will not be considered either troublemakers or revolutionaries.

Since theologians are still human, and have physical and political needs (however minimal) like all other humans, they need to affirm the political order in which they must live during their time on earth. Furthermore, they need to keep a constantly watchful eye on the politics of the city, making sure that the city is not taken over by antiphilosophical forces, which inevitably want to make the mythology of the city the absolute measure of all virtue and all truth. Unlike Plato, who (at least in the *Republic*) wanted the city to actively sponsor philosophy that would culminate in metaphysics, Aristotle seemed content with a society that simply left philosophers alone because it did not entertain metaphysical pretensions for itself. Hence, a philosopher can, in good faith, affirm a society and its politics when it provides an atmosphere that is encouraging of philosophy/theology. This affirmation can be made if for no other reason than that this kind of city does not make absolute claims for itself and, by so limiting itself, implies that the Absolute might be found elsewhere. Maximally, such a society can be looked upon as a political means to a philosophical end, even if only philosophers can appreciate this teleology. Minimally, such a society will leave philosophers alone; that is, it will not try to actively impede the theology that can only be done by philosophers.

The modern appeal of this correlation between theology and politics can best be seen in the political philosophy of Leo Strauss, even when it claims to be antiquarian. The fact that Strauss began his philosophical project with a study of Spinoza's political theology is significant.[13] For Spinoza was not speaking of the irretrievable Greek *polis*, but rather of the newly emerging nation-states, in which he envisioned one role for *civil* religion and another role for philosophy as authentic God-talk. In fact, philosophy is nothing but God-talk because God includes in himself everything we know and everything we don't know and couldn't know since we humans are finite entities (*particula*) in the overall, infinite divine reality. In Spinoza's scheme, ordinary theology turns out to be akin to a kind of Unitarian anthology of the moral teachings of Judaism and Christianity, something useful for making good, law-abiding, obedient citizens of an otherwise secular, liberal polity. This goes hand in hand with Spinoza's bringing down the metaphysical pretensions of Jewish or Christian theology so that at least some perceptive adherents of this civil religion can rise to the level of true philosophical reflection on God/Nature (*deus sive natura*). This civil religion is to be a department of the state, under the complete control of the sovereign.[14]

It is plausible to say that due to his disappointment with the political impotence of the Weimar Republic and the liberal religion that was willing to play its cultural role therein, a disappointment both Jewish and philosophical, Strauss became interested in the more traditional theological politics of Maimonides (who he seems to have thought was really a metaphysical philosopher at heart), which was based on the authority of biblical revelation.[15] Thereafter, Strauss seemed to regard the best political order, the most socially beneficial order that is the least threatening to the philosophical life, to be based on a revealed, authoritatively constituted religion, and that this nonphilosophical practical theology can subtly serve philosophy.[16] This seems to imply that one can separate biblical moral-political doctrines from biblical ontological doctrines. But can one then cogently constitute a viable relation of theology and politics after there has been

this fundamental separation? Such a separation is surely problematic for
the following reasons.

First, no one who lives by such a biblically based morality/politics, and
who appreciates its ontological foundations, could possibly accept this
"instrumental" view of their morality/politics (as Nietzsche made clear).
Surely, no one in the West who does theology could do it in a way that
wasn't biblically based in some way, and that includes philosophical theology. Theology seems to be an empty pursuit without it being the *theory*
of the religious *praxis* of a real historical community. As such, then, it
seems rather artificial to make biblical theology, even when only its praxis
is employed, the "handmaiden" of a philosophical theology (*ancilla philos-
ophiae* instead of philosophy being *ancilla theologiae*) devoted to a God
apprehended above revelation.

Second, whereas Plato, Aristotle, and Spinoza—and even Maimonides—
constituted a positive metaphysical realm to which philosophers could
aspire to reach and thereby transcend the political realm, I fail to see any
metaphysical constitution in any of Strauss's philosophical reflections.[17]

Finally, I fail to see how Strauss's thoughts on the theological-political
question offer something that could be accepted by either theologians
or philosophers. These profound thoughts on the theological-political
question have a dialectical brilliance and historical resonance to them,
to be sure, but I fail to see them making the type of truth claims that
are made by authentic theology or by authentic philosophy. In fact, without an authentic ontology underlying these thoughts, how could Strauss
make any such truth claims at all? Surely Strauss, being the "classicist"
he was, would not want to confine the ontological question of truth to
epistemology alone. If so, isn't his constitution of the theological-political
reality ultimately antiquarian as Jürgen Habermas has argued?[18] Indeed, it
would seem that just as one cannot retrieve the philosophical theology of
Aristotle after Galileo and Newton, so one cannot retrieve the philosophical theology of Spinoza after Kant. But without the onto-theological com-
ponent of the relation between theology and politics being constituted,
how can one attempt to constitute a politics connected to anything higher
than human invention?

3. Theology as the Word of God

The biblical term *dvar adonai* contains the same two terms as the Greek
term *theology*, as we saw earlier. Nevertheless, the two terms are correlated

differently in the two different languages. For the Greek philosophers, *theo-logy* is talk *about God*. It comprises the efforts of humans to at least apprehend what God is and appreciate what God's being means for humans who stand far below him. That overall theological effort contains moral-political efforts within it, as we also saw earlier. To be sure, in the biblical view, humans can and do say some things about God, yet humans cannot say anything more about God than God has already said about himself—*to them*.

What God says about himself is always about God's active relation to the created world in general, his special relation to humankind made in his image, and his singular relationship with his elect, covenanted people. The medium of that communication of God to man is verbal revelation.[19] Accordingly, *dvar adonai* does not mean "talk about God" but, rather, it means "God's own talk." And that is not God's talk about himself to himself but, rather, God's talk about himself to those he has elected to continually commune with. And since the human addressees of this divine communication are wholly addressed by it, whereas God always transcends any finite context in which he chooses to be present, biblical revelation tells us more about its human addressees than it does about the God who addresses them. As my late, revered teacher Abraham Joshua Heschel noted, biblical revelation is "God's anthropology rather than man's theology."[20] Thus, only because God has first spoken to us about himself can we speak back to him in the language of worship, language that is taken from what God has communicated to us about himself. Theology is merely the conceptualization of the language of worship (*lex orandi est lex credendi*). We can only *talk back to* God because God has first talked to us, and only then can we engage in theological reflection *about* the deeper meaning of that ongoing communication. Nevertheless, only in the case of prophets is that God-human communication mutually conducted as a dialogue. For the rest of us, this God-human communication is asymmetrical: we regularly speak to God, whereas God might sometimes speak to us. We speak to God directly; God speaks to us less so. Most often, we have to overhear what God has said to our prophetic ancestors.

God's communication to us is primarily prescriptive and only secondarily descriptive: God's primary mode of communication with us is commandment (*mitsvah*). Thus when the Bible describes the world, it is always, in one way or another, representing the world as the background of God's commandments to particular people "wherever they might be" (Genesis 21:17). Creation is the context of the covenant, and the covenant is the *telos* of creation.[21] God's first contact with humans is stated as "the Lord God commanded [*va-yitsav*] man" (Genesis 2:16), which the Talmud interprets to mean that God commanded humans how to treat or not to treat their fellow humans. In other words, "the human" (*ha'adam*) is both the subject and the object of this initial contact of God with the pinnacle of his creation, the human persons made in his image and likeness.[22] Indeed, it could be said that whereas the human *being*, like the rest of being, is the inert result of a divine command addressed to no other person, human *persons* only gain their personhood when they actively respond to the command of God whenever and wherever it reaches them.

According to this understanding of theology as God's word, theology is not where the moral/political realm ought to make room for philosophers to pursue on their own time as it were; instead, theology—*the commanding word God speaks to humans*—is hearing God's word and carefully applying it to the interhuman realm known as politics. Thus politics gains its legitimacy only by how well it fulfills God's explicit commandments. Politics must be grounded in theology. Whereas in the world envisioned by Greek philosophy, theology and politics are to be correlated by philosophers, in the world established by biblical revelation, that correlation is the work of prophets—and later the work of Torah sages (*hakhamim*).

4. Priests, Kings, and Prophets

In contemporary political discourse, the theological-political question always suggests what has come to be known as the "church-state" question. But how are "church" and "state" related in fact, and how are they related in principle? There are those who would like to reduce the church-state relation to the relation of the public and private spheres: the state is by definition public; religious communities are seen as private corporations, as associations of like-minded individuals. Yet there is an inevitable tension in this arrangement when it comes to questions of morality or social ethics. Who is the arbiter of these questions: the state or the church?

If religious communities are, in essence, private realms, and if *social* ethics (and which ethics are not "social"?) necessarily concern the public realm, how can these religious communities (and their respective revelations and traditions) possibly claim any public moral role other than simply endorsing what has come to be accepted as public morality? The only other option for them, in this political scheme, is to remain silent on questions of public morality. But when that happens, these religious communities are taken to be so private to the point of being eccentric or "sectarian" and thus politically irrelevant. Or, perhaps even worse, these religious communities all become subsumed within one governmental ministry of religion (or religions), thus taking on the roles of *civil servants*.

Surely, those loyal to and governed by the revelations and communal traditions cannot in good faith accept such a politically obsequious role or such a politically irrelevant role for what they believe to be nonnegotiable. So, it seems the only way out of this conundrum is to regard church and state as different public realms, with morality being what the church teaches the state and expects it to publicly enforce. However, doesn't this arrangement suggest "theocracy," which in contemporary parlance means the rule of a cabal of clerics, manipulating the resources of the state in the interest of their own religious communities? In other words, doesn't this lead to the state becoming an extension of the church, something like the situation in Iran today, where the politicians seem to be front men for the ayatollahs, who really make the fundamental public policies from their interpretation of Islamic revelation and tradition, with the inevitable result (if not the actual goal) of enhancing their own power?

The question now is, since political theology can only be done in the West from biblical sources, does ancient Israel, as represented in the Bible, provide us with any model of political theology better than this purported theocracy? (As it would be called by many adherents of democracy.) In other words, was the political situation in ancient Israel, which Josephus famously called *theocracy*—meaning a state governed according to God's law—anything more than a "theocracy" run by oligarchs or tyrannical, self-serving clerics?[23]

In ancient Israel, "the state" after Saul, and especially after David, eventually became a "kingdom" (*mamlakhah*). The "church" was located in the "Sanctuary" (*miqdash*), and after Solomon, the Temple (*bet ha-miqdash*) became its locale. The monarchy (*melukhah*) as an institution was under the control of the royal family, headed by the king. The Temple was under the control of the institution of the priesthood (*kehunah*) headed by the High Priest. Under normal circumstances, these two institutions, governing one people (*ha`am*), maintained a distinct balance of power between each other. The business of the monarch was to maintain public order, both internally in terms of domestic policy and externally in terms of foreign affairs, for example, making treaties and waging war. The business of the priesthood was to administer the people's relationship with God, a relationship that was primarily centered on the sacrificial altar (*mizbeah*).

In a strict sense, the business of the monarchy was political administration, and the business of the priesthood was ritual administration: to conduct public and private ceremonies. These lines of demarcation were to
be maintained at all times. Kings were not supposed to usurp the priestly
role; priests were not supposed to usurp the kingly role. If and when that
did happen, however, such usurpations were explicitly condemned.[24]

But what about moral questions, that is, questions involving interhuman relations outside the Temple itself? Who was to adjudicate these
moral questions? It would seem that such matters fell to the authority of
the priests, for both questions of internal Israelite affairs and even matters
of foreign affairs.[25] That is because the standard of judgment (*mishpat*) is
the law of God (*torah*). The people, in all parts of their life, whether political or domestic, were to be governed according to what the people would
readily recognize to be the everlasting law of God: the law that constituted
their singular covenantal relationship (*ha-berit*) with God, the law they had
accepted unconditionally for perpetuity at Sinai. And the repository of that
law is the Sanctuary, the domain of the priests.[26] Thus *political theology*,
understood as *covenantal praxis*, comes from the Temple; it is to be explicated by the priests, especially in their role as judges (*shoftim*) adjudicat-
ing cases that need to be decided by a standard not made by any human
being, even by priests descended from Aaron. Moreover, it is important
to note that even though the people all heard the initiation of that law at
Sinai, the specific contents of that law had been delivered to the people
by the prophet Moses.[27] The question became, though, whether prophets
(*nevi'im*) or the prophethood (*nevu'ah*) had, in effect, fulfilled their historical task by bringing the law to the people in a way that could not have been
done either by kings or by priests, let alone by the people themselves. Or,
did the prophets have any further theological-political function once the
law had been delivered to the people?

In Deuteronomy, where we find the most political teachings of the
Torah, we read:

> When a matter for judgment [*la-mishpat*]...matters of dispute
> [*divrei rivot*] in your courts, is too difficult for you, then you shall
> rise up and ascend to the place chosen by the Lord your God. And
> you shall come to the levitical priests and to the judge [*ha-shofet*]
> who will be in those days. And you shall enquire that they tell you
> the just verdict [*dvar ha-mishpat*]...According to the law [*ha-torah*]
> which they shall instruct you out of...you shall not depart from

the verdict they will tell you, neither to the right or to the left. (Deuteronomy 17:8–9, 11)

Furthermore, even the king is subject to the same law, of which the priests are the guardians, as well as the teachers of its practical meaning, and the judges who apply it to real situations, especially cases involving interpersonal and political disputes.

> And when he [the king] is sitting on the royal throne, he shall write for himself a copy of this Law [*mishneh ha-torah ha-z'ot*], based on a scroll [*sefer*] under the supervision of the levitical priests. It shall be with him and he shall read from it all the days of his life, so that he learn to fear the Lord his God, to keep all the words of this Law and these statutes to practice them…lest he deviate from the norm [*ha-mitsvah*] either to the right or to the left, so that his kingdom might endure, his and his descendants, in the midst of Israel. (Deut. 17:18–20)

Thus the people of Israel are led by kings who they have accepted (if not actually appointed) to rule. And both people and king are under the moral governance of a law that seems to be, in effect, a priestly code: not given *by* priests, but, nonetheless, imposed upon priests first and then *for* the king and his people thereafter.

Despite this seemingly rational political arrangement, looking at the biblical record after the Pentateuch, the priesthood as a political institution was incapable of providing true moral governance for the people or their kings or, for that matter, themselves. Instead of doing political theology, the priests seemed more engaged in theological politics, that is, protecting their sacerdotal privileges and providing ceremonial confirmation of the political and economic privileges of the monarchy and its wealthy and powerful supporters.[28] In other words, the very institutionalization of religion inevitably turned the priestly practitioners of religion into agents primarily serving their own institutional interests and the interests of their royal and plutocratic patrons.

The reason for this theological-political impotence is obvious: the institution of the priesthood could only function when the Sanctuary was a viable political institution, that is, when this institution was protected militarily, and when it had sufficient financial support. But, to satisfy both conditions, the Sanctuary and its priestly ministers were dependent on the support of the expanded and expanding monarchy. Kingship was instituted in Israel *ab initio* for military reasons: the king was to lead and maintain a standing army. As for economic dependence, the Sanctuary depended on taxation, and taxation—like military power—quickly became a royal monopoly. Almost as quickly, then, the Sanctuary became the royal chapel; the priests (*kohanim*), royal chaplains. And in this political arrangement, the prophets and their acolytes (*bnei nevi'im*) became little more than priests or quasi-priests having some politically useful charismatic talents. Religion, whether ceremonial or charismatic, became a department of state. As such, it lost any Archimedean fulcrum with which to move the world, that is, with which to independently judge the society that now employed its ministers as civil servants—and well-paid ones at that.

This situation emerged in one of the most famous confrontations in the Bible: between the prophet Amos and the priest Amaziah.[29] "Then Amaziah, priest at Beth-El, sent word to Jeroboam king of Israel: 'In the midst of the House of Israel, Amos has rebelled [*qashar*] against you; the land cannot bear all his words'" (Amos 7:10). Accordingly, Amaziah as the king's good servant was quick to tell Amos: "Seer! Flee to the land of Judah! There you can eat your bread and there you can prophesy. At Beth-El you may not continue to prophesy, for it is the king's Sanctuary [*miqdash melekh hu*], and it is the royal house [*u-veit mamlakhah hu*]" (Amos 7:12–13).

Amos, a Judean himself, was sent by God to admonish the people of the now separate kingdom of Israel, and especially their royally led power establishment, to repent of their sins. The sins of the people, especially the rich and powerful, were twofold: one, they had sinned against God by their idolatry, especially its orgiastic violation of domestic sexuality; two, they had sinned against the people by their cruelty, especially their cruel oppression of the vulnerable poor.[30] And these two areas of iniquity overlap: idolatry denies God's sole right to the full devotion of the people; injustice denies the God-given rights of the people to be treated justly. Here lies the true intersection of theology and politics: God-given rights only have true ontological grounding when they are rooted in God's all-inclusive covenant with his people, and since the relationship with God is with a "covenanted people" (*brit am*—Isaiah 42:6), no one can isolate his or her relationship with God into some sort of private realm as a refuge from public moral responsibility.

Amaziah cannot understand Amos's position. By telling him to return to Judea and prophesy there, Amaziah assumes that Amos is a political hack like himself. In fact, Amaziah might have even thought that Amos is some kind of political provocateur, sent by the Judean king to make trouble for his Israelite rival. And, since the prophets in Judea were often no less subordinate to political power than were the prophets in Israel, Amos strikes out for the true transcendence of royal or moneyed control of prophecy by asserting his nonprofessional status anywhere and stating that he "eats his bread by the sweat of his brow" (Genesis 3:19), which is the lot of every ordinary man. It is precisely because prophecy, as done by Amos—and others like him—is not beholden, politically or financially, to either king or priest neither to the palace nor to the Temple that makes it possible for Amos to exercise true moral authority on God's behalf. He is able to do political theology that transcends theological politics. "Amos answered and said to Amaziah: 'I am not a prophet or a disciple of prophets (*ven nvai*), but I am a cowherd and a dresser of sycamore trees'" (Amos 7:14).

5. Prophecy, Political Theology, and Social Critique

The prophets as moral critics did much more than many today who call themselves "social critics" do or could do. The prophets as political theologians did three things that most of our contemporary social critics seem unable and unwilling to do. First, the prophets admonished the people to return (*teshuvah*) to God and to God's law to whom and with which the people were already irrevocably related in an interminable covenant.[31] Most social critics today only admonish the masses to adhere to or to adopt their "values" (which are rarely any kind of ethical system but more often than not the taste or "lifestyle" of a self-selected elite group that the social critic is a privileged member). Second, the prophets admonished the people to whom they themselves were bound covenantally. For that reason, the prophets were just as eager to plead for God's mercy on their people as they were eager to warn the people of God's justice.[32] Many social critics today, conversely, see themselves superior to the very people whom they chastise. Even if they regard themselves bound to their fellow citizens in some sort of social contract, these social critics clearly have the advantage in the negotiation of this contract since their values are taken to be those already presupposed by the social contract. Everyone else's traditions, coming from heteronomous sources, have to be given up as the price of admission to the social contract proposed to them by truly autonomous moral agents. That is why so much of their criticism is interpreted as condescending or patronizing. Three, the prophets would rather have been wrong in their dire predictions of political upheaval than right. That is because the prophets were not prophesying about what *necessarily* was to happen in the future.

The prophets were not soothsayers.[33] Instead, they were speaking to their people (and in some cases, neighboring peoples as well) about future events *contingent* on the acts of the people in the present. That is, *if* the people would repent, *then* the dire events predicted would not take place; but *if* the people did not repent, *then* these events would indeed take place.[34] Conversely, most social critics today simply condemn those whose political views they do not share. And, it seems, the only "repentance" they ask of anyone is to come around and support those whom they think should be in political power, replacing those who currently hold it. Furthermore, the justifications made by most social critics for their political positions are at best ideological (usually capitalist or socialist), lacking the rigor of either classical, ontologically grounded philosophy or biblically based theology.

The question is whether this kind of prophetic political theology qua social critique can be done today, especially in a pluralistic, multicultural, democratic society.

The first problem we have today with prophets is that Judaism and Christianity (at least the orthodox kinds), the two Western religions that base their theo-politics on biblical revelation, have clearly denied any role to prophets, political or otherwise.[35] As such, the moral admonition of their sages, *sans* historical prediction (however contingent), has less of the rhetorical and psychological punch of those who could declare, "Thus saith the Lord," even though the actual content of what they say is the same. The sages can only reiterate what God's law requires; unlike the prophets, they cannot predict what will happen to those who disobey it.

The second problem is that until modern times, the church-state question was a question of one state interrelated with one church, one traditional religious community. Thus it could be assumed that everybody in that overall society was a member of both that one state and that one church. However, those who were not members of the state church were not citizens of the state either. At worst, they were driven from the monolithic, mono-cultural society, as was the case with the expulsion of the Jews from England in 1290, the expulsion of the Jews from France in 1394, and the expulsion of the Jews from Spain in 1492. (Is it any wonder that the vast majority of the Jews of Europe welcomed the French Revolution in 1789, with its destruction of the *ancien régime*, a regime in which Jews could only be pariahs?) At best, they were tolerated as resident-aliens, as inferior second-class strangers. Furthermore, wasn't the end of the church-state symbiosis supposed to end the "wars of religion," when rival religious communities fought each other over which community would be the sole partner with the state in this societal hegemony? So, isn't the privatization of religions (plural) the best way to prevent one religious community from attempting to dominate the state at the expense of all others and leaving those without any religious affiliation without any cultural legitimacy at all? Yet, as we have seen, no religious community can accept being so privatized, except in the areas of ceding to the state its right to have its own civil and criminal law. That being the case, might we look forward to, if not already witness, the modern or postmodern version of the wars of religion, this time manifested as the "culture war" between those whose worldview is ultimately based on biblical revelation and those whose worldview is not?

I think there is a way out of this conundrum, and there is a way to do authentic political theology in a pluralistic, multicultural society (and a more globalized world). That way is a revitalization of natural law theory that Jews and Christians (and, perhaps, Muslims as well) can represent in good faith not what comes from biblical revelation (which they can only do for their own respective faith communities), but what biblical revelation presupposes in order to be morally intelligible.[36] And those without religious traditions can still participate in this theoretical discourse as equals due to their moral earnestness, only having to regard a divine grounding of a common morality as plausible, even if they cannot affirm it in good faith.[37] But that means secular people can appreciate the need to find some presuppositions for their moral commitments beyond the mere fact that they happen to hold them.

What natural law has in common with the revealed law of the Bible is that it governs the entire community equally: rulers as well as those whom they rule; theorists as well as ordinary folk. Yet natural law differs from revealed law insofar as it only governs the communal life of humans as they are *ultimately capable* of a relationship with God, whereas it is through revealed law that God *directly realizes* that relationship between Godself and humans.

Notes

1. For Schmitt, modern political theory, when done properly, functions like political theology functioned in premodern times. In other words, such politics restores

the notion of a sovereign who can excuse himself from the ordinary norms of law. See Schmitt's *Political Theology*, trans. G. Schwab (Cambridge, MA: MIT Press, 1985), esp. 36–37. Cf. Leo Strauss, *Natural Right and History* (Chicago: University of Chicago Press, 1953), 4, n. 2.

2. See *The Stillborn God: Religion, Politics, and the Modern West* (New York: Alfred A Knopf, 2007), esp. 55–70.

3. *Metaphysics*, 6.1/1026a19.

4. Richard Bodéüs, *Aristotle and the Theology of the Living Immortals*, trans. J. E. Garrett (Albany: State University of New York Press, 2000), 141–148.

5. Aristotle, *Nicomachean Ethics*, 5.1/1129b20–29.

6. Ibid., 6.7/1141a20.

7. Aristotle, *Politics*, 1.1/1253a28–29.

8. *Metaphysics*, 12.8/1074b1–15. Cf. Plato, *Apology*, 26D.

9. *Aristotle and the Theology of the Living Immortals*, 154–158.

10. *Nicomachean Ethics*, 10.7–8/1177b26–1178b24.

11. Thus Aristotle's comparison of God to a general (*Metaphysics*, 12.9/11–20) only means that like a general, who is the ultimate epitome of the order by which the army operates, God is the ultimate epitome by which the universe operates. Unlike a general, however, the God of Aristotle does not personally issue orders to, i.e., command, his subordinates.

12. Plato, *Euthyphro*, 3B; *Apology*, 24C.

13. *Spinoza's Critique of Religion*, trans. E. M. Sinclair (New York: Schocken Books, 1965).

14. See *Tractatus Theologico-Poilticus*, esp. chap. 20.

15. *Philosophy and Law*, trans. E. Adler (Albany: SUNY Press, 1995), 60–79.

16. See his *Persecution and the Art of Writing* (New York: Free Press, 1952), 126–141.

17. Strauss himself seems to admit this in *Natural Right and History* (Chicago: University of Chicago Press, 1953), 7–8: "We are all in the grip of the same difficulty. Natural right in its classic from is connected with a teleological view of the universe...The teleological view of the universe, of which the teleological view of man forms a part, would seem to have been destroyed by modern natural science...An adequate solution to the problem of natural right cannot be found before this basic problem has been solved." As far as I know, Strauss never overcame this metaphysical impasse, and whether he even attempted to do so is arguable.

18. *Communication and the Evolution of Society*, trans. T. McCarthy (Boston: Beacon Press, 1979), 201–202.

19. E.g. Exod. 3:13–15; 6:2–8; 33:17–34:7.

20. *God in Search of Man* (New York: Farrar, Straus, and Cudahy, 1955), 412. See his *Man Is Not Alone* (Philadelphia: Jewish Publication Society of America, 1951), 129.

21. *Babylonian Talmud*: Pesahim 68b re: Jer. 33:25.

22. *Babylonian Talmud*: Sanhedrin 56b.

23. For the coining of the term *theocracy* by Josephus, see his *Contra Apionem*, 2.164.

24. For the condemnation of a king usurping the priest's role, see II Chron. 26:16–21. For the condemnation of a priest who attempted to play a monarchic role, see I Kings 2:26–27.

25. E.g. Num. 17:21; Deut. 33:8–11.

26. II Kings 22:8–13.

27. Exod. 20:1516; Deut. 5:19–28. Cf. Num. 16:1–5.

28. E.g. Jer. 2:8.

29. Shalom Spiegel, *Amos versus Amaziah* (New York: Jewish Theological Seminary of America, 1957).

30. Amos 2:6–8; also, Isa. 55:5–8.

31. E.g. Jer. 26:4–6.

32. E.g. Exod. 32:11–34; Jer. 18:20.

33. I Sam. 9:9.

34. E.g. Jon. 3:1–4:11.

35. As such, prophets may only make exceptional, ad hoc rulings. They may not institute permanent norms as did Moses. See *Babylonian Talmud*: Yevamot 90b re: Deut. 18:15.

36. David Novak, *Natural Law in Judaism* (Cambridge: Cambridge University Press, 1998).

37. David Novak, "Law: Religious or Secular?" *Virginia Law Review*, 86 (2000): 586–96, reprinted in David Novak, *In Defense of Religious Liberty* (Wilmington DE: ISI Books, 2009), 141–182.

Augustinian Christian Republican Citizenship

Charles Mathewes

Introduction

The essays in this volume aim to explore the manifold relations between the Abrahamic religious traditions and contemporary political citizenship. It is either too easy or too difficult to proceed descriptively because, speaking descriptively, the relationship between Christianity and democratic politics is all over the map. So I will not attempt such a project.[1] Instead, I will provide one normative account of how one kind of Christian religious identity can fruitfully flourish with one kind of liberal-republican citizenship.

I take up this task because we face not only descriptive confusion on the issue of the relation between traditional religion and contemporary political life, we face normative challenges as well. The most obvious problem is the still too prevalent assumption that liberal society requires non-religious modes of engagement, a view promoted by Mark Lilla from the secular side and John Milbank from the religious side.

In recent years, many have argued that no such principled opposition exists. Much of my work has explored examples of how that opposition can be happily violated. That work continues here. I want to show how one tradition, using conceptual, symbolic, and institutional resources that it recognizes as organic to itself, can generate and sustainably cultivate a type of civic engagement and a model of citizenship that is authentically liberal; albeit a liberalism deeply ambivalent about the liberal situation itself, in much the same way that some of the best and most profound liberal thinkers were.

Christians' resistance to these sorts of commitments has troubled many political thinkers since the Caesars. And, from Rousseau to Nancy Rosenblum, many modern political theorists have doubted Christianity's political domesticability. Aren't Christians ultimately more committed to their God than to the civic order we all share? Won't they impose their faith on everyone? Don't they inevitably try to use this-worldly activity for their other-worldly aims?

In reality, of course, in the most thoroughly liberal state in the world— the United States—Christians are *very* civically engaged, and usefully so, but they are not always so engaged on the polity's own terms. Study after socio-logical study shows that church attendance leads to deeper civic engage-ment—voting, volunteering, political knowledge—these metrics and more are strengthened by joining a church. Indeed, religion is looked upon by some as a source, and perhaps the most powerful source, of civic commit-ment. Thinkers who urge this case have argued, at least since Tocqueville, that liberalism's typical strategy of resistance to polities' absolutist ambi-tions is to instill in citizens' souls an oscillation between confidence and self-doubt. But, to be very quick and telegraphic, while this oscillation helps leaven any political movement with suitable self-criticism, it will likely hin-der liberal citizens' moral energies that are necessary to defend liberalism itself against enemies, both foreign (such as totalitarianism) and domestic (such as "apatheistic" vapidity). Because of this, liberalism needs strong communities of people who have languages that vigorously resist liberal-ism's characteristic kind of corrosive self-criticism.[2] Such thinkers perhaps agree with William Galston when he argues, "The greatest threat to chil-dren in modern liberal societies is not that they will believe in something too deeply, but that they will believe in nothing very deeply at all."[3] In this context, and for such thinkers, religion is seen as useful for civic cohe-sion and churches are viewed as schools of moral and civic virtue, helping to create the kind of rich and strong moral character that liberal societies require and that they may find hard to produce on their own. To thinkers like Galston, a wise liberal polity will recognize that it needs communities that propagate fundamentally nonliberal (or even illiberal) forms of faith.

The point is both valid and significant. Liberal states have recognized these facts and established institutional responses, typically in ways that insulate traditional religious institutions from the too warm embrace of the state, such as the exemption of religious organizations from taxation and the historical practice of recognizing conscientious objection as fundamentally deriving from one's religious convictions. The state can, in some relatively direct way, acknowledge and even honor religious institutions for such civic benefits. We might call this the "Eisenhower strategy," for its general attitude is encapsulated in U.S. President Dwight D. Eisenhower's (in)famous claim, "Our government has no sense unless it is founded in a deeply felt religious faith, and I don't care what it is." This sentiment has not gone away since Eisenhower; in a poll conducted in January 2001, of those who wanted religion to have a more influential role in the United States, 76 percent said they didn't care which religion it was. Empirically, then, Christianity and civic commitment in liberal politics seem quite compatible.[4]

Nonetheless, there is a tension between them that cannot be gainsaid. Whether it is "liberal," every state remains a jealous God, structurally suspicious of Christian political engagement, regarding its citizens' extra-political allegiances with tacit animus. And Christianity always condemns as idolatrous the inevitable tendency to make our political identity our essential, existential identity. After all, the political dimension of our identity is typically a crucial determining factor of our overall identity; the nation-state is a remarkably powerful force for telling us who we are. But theologically, for Christians that is just the problem: Christians claim to be citizens of another polity, and their care about earthly politics seems to have roots that run to other sources of nourishment than the rich soil of the homeland. In Christ there is neither Jew nor Greek and that prophetic moment qualifies our contemporary political categories' application to our lives. Political powers often tempt us to see ourselves exhaustively in political categories, and thereby to reenact in our lives what Christians should see as the factitious divisions, however pragmatically valid they may be, that scar the face of the earth.

Jason Bivins has coined the term "political illegibility" to describe the problem with some Christian political activity; on his reading, such activity may seem not intelligible within the received political categories, and hence is menacingly opaque for those working with the received political vocabulary.[5] When some believers sneak onto military bases and destroy vehicles or weapons or others vehemently protest outside abortion clinics and attempt to enter their doors screaming "holocaust!"; when believers destroy art they feel is sacrilegious or refuse to perform at an Olympic event for their country, because that event falls on a holy day—in all these situations, and many more, their decisions, their actions are liable to be met by many of their fellow citizens, who do not share their creed, with hostility and incomprehension. To nonbelievers, such acts may look less like legitimate expressions of religious freedom and political opinion but more like dangerous incursions into the realm of the political by strictly religious views. As such, they can seem to threaten the coherence of the "political realm" altogether, and polities and states do not like to be threatened in that way. Thinkers like Rousseau are right, at least in this: an ineliminable tension, sometimes an outright conflict, exists between Christian faith, or any vibrant religious faith, and totalizing civic commitment of the sort that is the gravitational tendency of political states. Neither readily allows its demands to be subordinated to the other.[6]

I do not think that this tension can be resolved, nor do I think that we should even try to resolve it. It is not a problem, it is our condition, and running from it to false solutions will help no one. For reasons particular to Christian faith, as well as other reasons particular to liberal convictions, both sides should recognize it as healthy tension. By properly living into that tension and not attempting to evade it, Christians can seek, as Reinhold Niebuhr put it, "To do justice to the distinctions of good and evil in history and to the possibilities and obligations of realizing the good in history; and also to subordinate all these relative judgments and achievements to the final truth about life and history which is proclaimed in the Gospel."[7] The liberal nation-state can legitimately request of citizens a genuine degree of commitment, and Christian faith should allow, and indeed encourage, its adherents to be committed. But such commitment is neither simple nor easy. Offering one account of this commitment is my aim here.

This essay attempts this in three large steps. First, it offers one interpretation of a Christian approach to the question of relating civic and religious fidelity. It then offers an account of how developments in political thought and institutions over the last three centuries, gathered under the name of "liberalism," offer an opportunity for a fuller and less conflicted exercise of that Christian account. Third, and finally, it sketches the practices of faithful commitment that this account, in our setting, enables.

1. Rendering unto Caesar

Do Christians owe something to the polities they inhabit? Today in Christian thought there are two very vocal positions, a too simple collaboration or a too facile opposition. At times they seem between them to exhaust the options. But they do not exhaust them, and it is a good thing too, for both are deeply flawed.

On the one hand, there are those who say, yes we do, because our civic identity is as fundamental to us as our religious identity; we are created to worship God and to live in political society, and this latter facet of our lives underwrites our obligation to whatever polity we inhabit. For such thinkers, the two identities are essentially complementary, each needing the other for its own fulfillment.

On the other hand, there are those who answer with an essentially unqualified "no." The state, on their view, is a demonic entity that cannot but rival God, and it sets itself up as a power in institutionally direct opposition to God. For such thinkers, "Christian" is an identity that contests much of the same space—politically, psychologically, and existentially—as "Canadian" or "American." We cannot serve two masters, so inevitably and ultimately, we must choose between them.

Obviously, both sides have strong arguments and solid evidence from both scripture and tradition to support them. But both affirm half-truths, so neither is fully adequate.

Those who offer an unqualified yes recognize that our world needs ordering between ourselves as believers and God. For them, God works through the found conditions of our world to govern our world as best it can be governed. But they make two missteps. First, they threaten to naturalize the given political structures, an act that always stands in danger of baptizing the status quo as God's ultimate will. That is, they fail to take sufficient account of the fact that such forces and institutions are not simply superficially inflected with sin; in this world, states inevitably participate in the entropy of self-love and come to expect to be worshipped. Furthermore, these thinkers make a theological error in assuming that states were part of God's prelapsarian order—so that, had Adam and Eve not sinned, mankind would still have developed states.[8] This allows too little seriousness about the moral calamity of the Fall, and the distance between where humanity is, religiously and morally speaking, and where humanity should be. For such thinkers, sin complicates life and makes it more difficult, but life itself remains largely continuous with what it was meant to be. Here the Fall is essentially a consoling doctrine—humanity has screwed up, to be sure, but that works mostly to excuse our mistakes. The cosmos as a whole is not radically flawed, and our received patterns of thought and behavior can proceed without a too radical transformation.

Those who offer an unqualified "no" recognize the moral calamity of the Fall. But they go too far, and yet again, ironically, render it a kind of consolation. They wisely see that a world governed by violence is in some fundamental way in opposition to God's will, and that the Fall has had a devastating effect not just on our individual agency, but on our relationships with one another, and thereby on the whole human world wherein the human race lives, moves, and has its being. But they then preemptively conclude that any and every collusion with such forces of violence can serve no other end than the further rebellion of humanity—that there is no way in which humans or God can use this system for other, more wholesome ends. If those in the first camp offer a consolation based in complacency, partisans of this latter camp suggest a consolation based in despair. The world as a whole is just wrong, and any involvement that colludes in its existence is quite literally bad faith.

Before I sketch a view of the relation between Christian faith and civic commitment that I think is superior to these two visions, I want to note some dangerous theological assumptions that I think these two share. Many find such views politically problematic. I also think there is good reason to find them unfaithful to the religious traditions they purport to profess. As one task of this essay is to engage in an intramural theological debate with such views, I should say why I find them so troubling: Both views are consoling, in the sense that they imply that Christian believers in the world needn't worry that their faith will yet grow and be radically challenged. Neither will accept that believers may, in quite profound ways, change their understandings of the meaning of their faith. These two views offer a deluded response to our condition, a pose of "knowingness," which is deeply inimical to true faithfulness.

By "knowingness" I refer to our presumption—a presumption believers and nonbelievers alike share—that we understand fully, and finally, what we say we know, or rather (because "presume" invests our act with too much self-consciousness and agency), that we never think about what we know or how we know at all.[9] We refuse to see the depth of mystery "behind" our various confidences. Most of what we understand as "knowing" or "doubting" is really strategies of *avoiding* thinking about faith, avoiding the riskiness central to it. There is an enormous tension between what we tell ourselves we know and the realities to which our "knowledge" refers, a tension we tacitly acknowledge by frequently changing our opinions about things, deepening them, or simply tossing them overboard. But we avoid confronting the fact, or investigating the implications, of how frequently our beliefs change, and so those changes do not become significant; they are not incorporated into a rich narrative of growing in wisdom about the flimsiness and shallowness of our knowledge.[10] We do not admit we live in history and are thus ongoing projects; we would rather die than change, so we try to avoid having real beliefs rather than confront what it means to have faith—especially its implications for who we are. We cannot stand live questions, and because such questions are part of life, we try hard not to be alive at all. We presume epistemological purity, a condition of having fully realized one's goals, no longer needing to question, no longer needing to live in time.[11]

The sin here lies in humanity's warped desire to be a certain kind of thing—to have a certain kind of identity, a final, definitive, and *apocalyptic* identity, one that will render us (at last!) impervious to the imperative of history to keep changing, to never be the same. Yet this desire is not just an illusion, it is also a reactionary understanding of agency. Not only is it not what we are at present, it is not even an accurate picture of what we will be; rather, it is an expression of our resentment at the fact that we want to rival God and cannot do so. The problem of political idolatry, then, is part of the larger problem of idolatry, which is the problem of our apocalyptic impatience to *be* the people we will only be at the End of Days. Our knowingness, then, has apocalyptic pretensions, tempting us at every moment to think we know, at last, the way we will at the end of history. This fantasized apocalypticism is spiritually dangerous and should be resisted. We are implicated in politics, in history, and in the world, and we cannot escape from them. Yet on the other hand, the presence of authoritarian political structures and the necessity of force are not natural in the sense of being part of the prelapsarian created order, and hence our enmeshment in them always goes forward in history, under a judgment we cannot escape.

So much, for the moment, for my theological complaints about these views. I will return to these later. But now we should return to the direct question of the relation between religious faith and civic commitment. And on that, instead of the two views sketched above, we should affirm something like the following: Christians do owe something to their polities, but the conditions under which Christian faith warrants this political fidelity are qualified. These qualifications will leave the secular authorities unsatisfied and possibly a bit nervous. Polities exist to provide order, or to restrain disorder. Part of order, indeed, internally essential to order, is justice. What is justice? Justice is the condition in which all get their due—what we may call, at least in part, respect. Christians participate in God's work by supporting the goals of order and justice, primarily (though not exclusively) *through* the political institutions they inhabit. Yet Christians do this neither on the polity's terms nor for the polity's reasons. For Christians, the polity is not its own final cause, and it serves God's purposes, not its own ends. Hence, Christians' civic fidelity is anchored in religious fidelity; it is not a matter of separate sources of legitimacy, such as God's "natural will to create and sustain" and God's "supernatural will to redeem and sanctify." Christians seek the welfare of their cities, so to speak, out of fidelity to God, not primarily through fidelity to their cities.

The tradition has often appealed to the story of Caesar's coin as a scriptural basis for this fidelity. When Jesus replies to the Pharisees, "Render to Caesar the things that are Caesar's, and to God the things that are God's" (Matt. 22:21), one can understand this statement as, in part, challenging the terms on which the question is put. It is crucial to distinguish, Jesus seems to say, between what is *rightfully* Caesar's and what is rightfully God's. This may at first sound impious, as if they are on the same level, but then, secondly, Jesus implies that they cannot be. Caesar is and always will be subservient to God (and it was because the Christians believed that, and acted on it, that the Romans persecuted them), yet it is Caesar's face upon the coin; hence, Christ allows some secondary and subsidiary voice wherein Caesar may make claims on us, within a certain realm, if Caesar is willing to inhabit that realm and no other. The key here is Caesar's *relative* autonomy and legitimacy, expressed by counterpointing the two obligations in one sentence. As Oliver O'Donovan puts it, the story means to reject "the view that Jesus assigned Roman government a certain uncontested sphere of secular right."[12] Any claim to authority that Caesar puts forward is open to contestation and challenge. Jesus' saying injects instability into politics; there is no easily solved equation, no fixed proportion between them, no settled percentage to be doled out to each. The relationship between them, so clear in theory, must be continually readdressed and reconfronted in practice.

Extending this reading of the story, we may say that while the state may be a tacit rival to God, claims it makes on our fidelity can be resisted, and the state can be a force for good, for order, and for decency; this is so at least as the state exercises a restraining justice, and occasionally it can serve the more constructive purpose of promoting some good.

It took quite a while for this vision of politics to become visible for Christians. The New Testament writers, it seems, were caught up with apocalyptic expectations and almost exclusively concerned with cultivating the eschatological community of believers. Their attitude toward the state was either quietist acquiescence, as in Romans 13 and 1 Timothy 2:1–2 (pray for government, "that we may live a quiet and peaceful life"), or apocalyptic renunciation, even resentment, as in the Book of Revelation. Here, the New Testament writers seemed to say, we have no lasting city, so we should look for the city to come; more reflection on the details of this passing age, they imagined, was a waste of what little time they had left. Later, as these apocalyptic expectations receded, thinkers reincorporated the Old Testament's vision of sojourning in a foreign land and seeking the welfare of the city into a new vision of Christian citizenship that was best articulated by Augustine. This deepening Christian political vision was part of a wider appreciation of the goodness of God's creation and a recognition of our obligations for its sustenance. Christians accepted the call to love God without reserve, and in loving God they are to love the world.

This reading is contestable, of course, and rival readings have always existed. For an Augustinian like Luther, it could still eventuate in a fairly quietistic proposal, while for others, like some medieval representatives of what was called "political Augustinianism," it could veer toward the fusion of church and state. There are no guarantees that these theological resources will be mobilized in a civically enriching way. Furthermore, the kind of commitment it suggests can sound tepid and inadequate both politically and theologically. Does this provide a political community's members with sufficient motivation to fight, kill, and die for their polity? Don't you need more vehement, more absolute forms of commitment than this allows? Many political thinkers, as different as Jean-Jacques Rousseau and Carl Schmitt, would agree. And to be sure, political rulers in earlier eras may have been unquestionably right, by their own lights, to be disappointed with the insistence by Christian churches that God grants a merely provisional and contingent authority to them. But on its own self-understanding, the modern liberal-democratic state can properly ask for no more than what the Christian churches are, at their best, willing to offer. The next section explains why.

2. The Distinction of Church and State

Political communities may be inevitably possessed by pretentions toward presenting themselves as *final* and absolute communities, implicitly expecting their inhabitants a willingness to see their individual good as inextricably associated with, then indistinguishable from, and finally subservient to, the good of the "larger" institutional order. This tendency is an old lesson in political life—as old as the Israelite prophets (think of Nathan before David) and the Greek tragedians (think of *Antigone*). So far we may say, nothing new under the sun.

But perhaps, once in a long while, there is something new. And if modernity has a claim for genuine novelty, it lies not in technological advance but in its political innovations. For over the past few centuries, first in Europe and then beyond, institutional forms have arisen that resist, in important ways, the pretentions gripping previous political institutions. We name these institutional forms "liberal democracy," and they are worthy of our attention because they develop and institutionalize the politically valuable, albeit theologically problematic, concept of privacy and create a viable political environment for such a concept to flourish.[13] An appreciation of the institutional structures and the politico-moral "cultural ecology" of liberal democracy may usefully orient Christian political engagement within our setting in a way beyond simplistic stances of unadulterated affirmation or blanket condemnation. Here I explain how Christians should understand this setting, and why they should, in this dispensation, provisionally, if critically, support it.

Liberalism embodies a genuine advance in our political imagination in modernity—the political idea that the state is a stopgap, not a failed church (or even less a successful one). This idea has a much older theological provenance, going back to the New Testament anxieties about empire, but it is only in the eighteenth century that we see it emerge in explicitly *political* discussions. Liberal democracy recognizes and is troubled by the absolutist claims that most political structures throughout history have made upon their inhabitants and acknowledges the deepening of this problem due to the intensification of state sovereignty in the centuries since the Treaty of Westphalia. Out of this recognition, liberal democracy takes as one of its main tasks to resist the state's encroachment on human identity.

Now, in talking about "liberalism" in this way, I appreciate I am taking sides in a very long and ugly battle and employing a word commonly used in diverse—indeed, incompatible—ways. There are some who think "liberalism" is structurally and essentially hostile to human flourishing. There are others who think that everyone should be a liberal, as it is the inevitable destiny of humankind. I tend to agree with thinkers such as Lionel Trilling and the John Stuart Mill of the essays on Bentham and

Coleridge (and perhaps of *On Liberty*), who recognize that what they call "liberalism" can be a good thing, but that it cannot, even on its own terms, be allowed a complete and uncontested imaginative and psychological sovereignty over our souls. I suggest that, while we may accept liberalism as a political reality, with its own blessings (and challenges), it cannot become our sole cultural reality.

There is a complicated story to tell about the interaction between the emergence of liberal-democratic theories and vocabularies, on the one hand, and the institutional emergence of the modern nation-state, on the other; I will not be so foolish to properly attempt to tell it here.[14] The modern nation-state is a remarkably powerful and unprecedented institutional reality in the world history of politics. It both encourages nationalist sentiments, thus tightening the bonds among its inhabitants, and strengthens the state structure by extending its reach across society and centralizing sources of power and legitimate authority within its hierarchical aegis. The sixteenth and seventeenth centuries saw the condensation of previously dispersed and fragmentary forms of political sovereignty into extremely concentrated centers of power.[15] In this situation the nation-state necessarily relied on free markets, which inevitably gave other nonstate actors wealth and power that in turn emboldened them to resist the sovereign. This led to a complex series of "negotiations" between these rival powers, in order to work out the rights and duties of all the parties. These "negotiations," which were anything but literal negotiations, constitute in large part the history of modern Western polities as well as the history of political thought. They lasted centuries, with diverse outcomes, one of which, in some places, was liberalism, or more precisely, the liberal state.

Despite the unprecedented power the liberal state holds, it is self-limiting in two ways. First, it is structurally self-limiting via its general constitutionalism, its belief in the importance of having a written constitution, and its cultural commitment to the "rule of law," to the idea that all are properly subject to the constitution. This constitutional form permits an externalized legal basis for sovereignty against the state's potentially limitless claim to absolute rule. Second, the liberal state is self-limiting in its express insistence on the inviolability of the individual person. This is conceptualized differently—for example, in terms of conscience or privacy—but it is essential. This has condensed over the past century into the liberalism of privacy, the idea that each person has at their core the right not to be controlled by another, that who they are is radically—not just politically but in more extreme formulations meta-physically—to be left alone to create themselves.

The upshot of all this is a salutary suspicion at the root of liberalism: the suspicion that any and every political (and by extension, cultural) system has the potential to reduce people to a role in some immanent system of political or cultural power—that is, to say that people are "nothing but" the role they play or the place they occupy in some system. Liberals call such reductionisms "totalitarianisms," and from its beginning, liberalism has set itself against them. Whether it has taken the form of the nascent and primitive totalitarianism of the divine right of kings, the wholly modern and awesomely powerful totalitarianism of communism and National Socialism, the narrow, but dagger-sharp, totalitarianism of fundamentalist terror, or the thin and dimmed-down totalitarianism of absolute marketization, totalitarianism is what liberalism fears and sets itself up to oppose.

If we think about "liberalism" in this way, those who believe that liberal states need religion find powerful arguments in their favor inherent in the terms of liberal political thought. For on this account, what liberalism fears is precisely the absolutization and theologization of the state. To counter that, liberalism requires strong citizens able to resist the state's siren song of absolutization, and clearly, despite all its faults, religion has been *the* source of such rival energies.

Yet Christians cannot simply support such intraliberal arguments for their propriety in liberal thought. To do that would lead inexorably to the absolutization of the language of political liberalism itself, something Christians should not permit (nor, on its own best lights, should political liberalism). Furthermore, any such straightforward support would effectively accede to the political institutions "placing" Christian communities and believers under (and therefore making them subservient to) the political institutions' understanding of the world. This would be anathema for Christianity, as it would undercut the faith's claim to offer something like the "ultimate" or "absolute" language within which to understand the world. If Christians are good citizens, they can do great good for the liberal state, on the state's terms, but while their motivation to be good citizens should include such considerations, it must not be determined by them. Rather, they should be good citizens because it is part of God's calling to them in this time and place to be such.

Given that, how should Christians stand vis-à-vis this tradition of liberalism? After all, the Christian account can very well be totalizing in just the way that liberals fear. But the totalization is crucially different, because it injects an eschatological leaven into the mix, insisting on the "not yet" character along with the "now." So Christians stand in a complex relation with this liberalism, supporting its suspicion of and hostility to apocalyptic determinations by worldly powers, yet insisting on the ultimate truth of one such determinism, albeit one whose final application is eschatologically deferred.

There are good reasons to be critical of much of what passes for political thought and language today. Some thinkers have attacked the modern notions of privacy, individualism, and associated ideas as conceptually incoherent, morally pernicious, and theologically impious.[16] They complain that these categories seduce their users into accepting a radically autistic interiorism, encourage a moral egoism, and insinuate an essentially Pelagian picture of God's relation with the world. I think these charges convey a great deal of truth; after all, the concept of privacy is related etymologically to *privatio*, privation, which for much of the Christian tradition is the defining ontological mark of evil. But I think the attacks can be pressed too far, leaving Christians bereft of the valuable work these resources perform, or—as is more likely—leaving Christians unable to acknowledge how they rely on these resources even if only provisionally, and so plunge them into a situation of bad faith, which is always to be avoided.

So, strategically it is better to exploit liberalism, for it can be practically quite useful. First of all, liberal democracy shifts the locus of political sovereignty from the ruler or the political community to the individual humans who populate that community. Complaints that in modernity, humans have been taught to be fundamentally selfish, to not think beyond their own parochial good, may be true, but this was not the intended effect of the transposition of the locus of sovereignty, of the fundamental political subject, from the ruler to the people. The intended effect—and one effect accomplished—was to undercut the sovereign's claim to be the fundamental, integral building block of politics. Individualism has many pernicious effects, but no one today will deny that it had the rather large benefit of acknowledging the selfishness of the many is at least superior to the selfishness of one. (The fact that we universally agree with this sentiment is itself part of its success—it provoked a revolution in our values as much as, if not more than, in our institutions).[17]

Secondly, liberal democracy teaches that the nation is not the *summum bonum*, nor should it be the final frame of any human's moral identity. Liberal states explicitly and intentionally resist the tendency toward theo-political idolatry, a tendency that can only end in a state's conversion into a "failed church." The reach of our moral vocabulary has historically been at odds with the reach of our political identity (so that we could have obligations to those who were not part of our polity, for example), but liberalism was the first to pay explicit attention to this disjunction and to make it a foundational part of both its political institutions and its political imagination. Liberal states implicitly recognize in their institutional structures that they are fundamentally designed to manage wholly mundane problems and projects; they are the first political institutions explicitly to acknowledge the peril of the (perhaps necessary) theological pretentions of politics, and they seek structurally and institutionally to eschew the theo-political ambitions inevitably latent in political life.

Of course this acknowledgment is a theoretical one, often violated in practice. While citizens and governors of these states may have more theological or eschatological ambitions for their political communities, the institutional structures are designed to stymie the implementation of those ambitions, to vex their political development in the first place and, if they develop, to block their implementation. This means that built into liberal political institutions is a negative, critical function at least as fundamental as the positive and constructive functions they possess. Ian Shapiro put it more sharply: liberal democratic states are not so much institutions designed to *achieve* goals as they are designed to *hinder rule—* the subordination of some by others.[18]

Historically, these institutions and civic-cultural developments first appeared in the seventeenth and eighteenth century, in the Netherlands and Great Britain. But the United States is the first state that was designed from the beginning to be less than the sum of its parts, designed *not* to be a failed church but a device for managing the complexities and conflicts of life, allowing us to get on with the pursuit of flourishing life and giving us a way of participating in public life that would be part of a flourishing life with many more parts. The United States was designed to restrain sovereignty and thereby to short-circuit any messianic hopes. As James Madison said:

> The great desideratum in Government is such a modification of the Sovereignty as will render it sufficiently neutral between the different interests and factions, to control one part of Society from invading the rights of another, and sufficiently controuled [sic] itself, from setting up an interest adverse to that of the whole Society.[19]

This is why, for example, the Constitutional Convention refused to make George Washington king, when that was what many of the people—including some of the founding fathers—wanted. This is what Abraham Lincoln was urging on his audience when he called America the "almost-chosen people." The aim is to resist the all too human desire to worship something palpable and large—something like the idea of America itself.

The United States may be the first state so conceived, designed to honor individuals in this distinctly liberal way. It is of course true, as some of its critics complain, that this liberal order does more nakedly endorse individual selfishness and downplay the value of distinctively political goods. So it is an ambivalent site for genuine political action. It is also true that America's culture works against its liberal institutions' anti-apocalypticism and has been doing so almost from the beginning. Even in the founders' time, few shared their elite vision of an enlightened and moderate citizenry informed by intellectual reflection rather than primitive passions. And since their age, the civic life of the United States has become far more populist, religious, and vigorously polemical—more like a punk rock festival than a minuet. Even with these changes, some of the preliberal understandings of politics in nationalist, jingoistic, and partisan apocalypticism have remained. Much of the history of the United States has been about a struggle between the institutions and the people living within them, with both sides changing and neither wholly in the right. In no way, then, am I saying that the American experiment is perfect; there are profound flaws and tensions latent herein.

Nonetheless, the traditions of Christian political thought and American liberal republicanism provide us with some helpful conceptual and institutional resources to understand how to be a citizen without putting absolute faith in the political order. Yet we have so far only identified the possibility of and rationale for a Christian inhabitation of this political condition; we have not yet detailed its contours. I next offer a theological account of citizenship that hopes to do just that.

3. Confessing Citizenship

So we see the problem of politics and identity that faith confronts, and the general Christian attitude toward worldly polities that Augustine encouraged (in section 1). We see how liberal democracy, as an ideological and institutional arrangement, creates more space for such an attitude or approach than other, earlier, visions of politics allowed (in section 2). Now we must see how Christians can inhabit this, *both* to the benefit of the polity *and* to their own benefit.

Both Christian and liberal political thought recognize that civic life is fraught with deep and abiding tensions, and both traditions, at their best, refuse to offer false pseudo-resolutions to those tensions. Christian faith goes further than mainstream liberal political thought, I would argue, in suggesting that those tensions are not only deep and abiding, but also potentially productive. Through living within their rival theological and political fidelities, Christian citizens can both enrich their political life and deepen their faith. Furthermore, contemporary civic life in liberal democracies is surprisingly structurally welcoming to those who wish to live in that tension.

How, then, should Christians inhabit it? We need a theological account to enable Christians to seize this opportunity and to be the sort of citizens that modern political life enables. This part explains to Christians in what way and to what degree they may be committed to their local civic orders, and how they can interpret such civic commitment theologically. First, it talks about how to be a Christian citizen; second, it talks about how Christians ought to think about identity more broadly still, and how their civic activity can help in their ascetical practices of identity-constitution. As we will see, central to both is the practice of confession, and the concomitant recognition that the citizen, *qua* citizen, exists "under judgment"—under a certain kind of judgment that should qualify their actions in important ways. I explain what that means in what follows.

3a. Faith's Ascesis for Politics: How to Be a Citizen

Hannah Arendt once said that Augustine was the last ancient thinker to know what it meant to be a citizen. This may be true, but it has nothing to do with Augustine's understanding of his own political world. "Citizen" is not a category Augustine would apply to the politics of his age. Historically he knew about citizenship, but he thought its age had passed. He thought in terms of subjects, not citizens. Because of this, we cannot apply his political thought directly to our world. Yet there is a way in which his thought helps us grasp the full meaning of liberal citizenship and for Christian citizens, connect it to deep theological and ascetical practices intrinsic to their faith. For to be a liberal citizen, as I will soon explain, means to exist *under judgment*, and the Christian narrative, as exegeted by Augustine, enables the recognition of that judgment in a rich and valuable way. This section explains how.

First of all, Augustine fundamentally understands politics—which he took to be the complicated ordering of public life, at times by force—to be a consequence of the Fall. It is not a vehicle for building the kingdom of God on earth, and if it is not that, it can be nothing more than a remedial structure for securing some modicum of peace and relative justice in a fallen world, until Christ's return inaugurates the only truly just polity, the reign of God. Because of this, the core civic virtues for Augustine are pretty passive: they revolve around instrumental commitment to the stability of the civic order, for the sake of the goods that that order directly provides, which are basically structure, security, and last but not least, stability for the sake of the continuance of the churches' liturgical life. Whenever he speaks of this, he continually returns to the dangers inherent in political life: the dangers of pride, idolatry, glorying in power, all of which are summarized for him by the phrase *libido dominandi*. All in all, Augustine's picture of the moral promise of politics is at best grimly minimalist.

But there is another side to Augustine's views, for the civic virtues are themselves, in a way, the theological virtues of a strange land. Life in this world can be led as a form of training in virtue for the life to come. Engagement in civic life—just like every other part of our ordinary, mundane lives—is fruitful for cultivating our character; engagement in the earthly city helps fit us for the heavenly city to come. This is the aspect of Augustine's thought that I wish to develop further here.

We can begin to do so by thinking about the precarious way in which we, believers and nonbelievers alike, ought to inhabit the role of "citizen." Even today, on the terms of the liberal state itself, we should see it as an unstable or provisional category—one that enables some things and disables others. On this understanding—admittedly one that not every self-professed "liberal" would sign on for, but one that is not too controversial—liberal citizenship is not a kind of quasi-religious identity, not a total and absolute commitment to some political community, outside of which one cannot imagine one's life. That would be a picture of citizenship where the person "within" the citizen is wholly, exhaustively identical with their political identity, but the liberal state wisely shuns that reduction of the human to the citizen. Liberal citizenship is more a negative reality than a positive one, as liberals see politics as a necessity, not an intrinsic good. A liberal citizen has as one of her duties the obligation to be a watchman, jealously guarding her rights and independence against the monarchic tendencies of the state and, indeed, against her own wholesale reduction to the identity of "citizen" itself, by a too total "politicalization" of her identity. Liberal citizens are citizens only in part—they insist that they are more than, and not just other than, citizens. (This is why politics can seem of secondary import in liberal societies.) The irony here should not be missed: The idea and reality of "liberal citizenship" uses a category that has historically been used in a totalizing and absolutist manner, but it uses it to resist the totalizing and absolutist tendencies in modern political life.

It should be no surprise, then, that liberal citizenship is a complicated kind of commitment, requiring watchfulness on the part of the individual. The liberal citizen is in an endlessly tense relationship with the state, other citizens and even herself, as all these entities act vigilantly upon and sometimes against the citizen: the state seeks to encroach upon her by asking for her legitimate service; other citizens alert her to the state's potential encroachments upon her; and she herself checks constantly to see if we are all doing right by protecting our individual existence from the state's tendency to make absolute claims on us. There are standards of behavior and commitments that the liberal citizen is held to, by others, by the state, and by herself. In short, the liberal democratic citizen exists *under judgment,* politically speaking, and cannot hide from that fact, because she knows she will be held to account in explicitly liberal democratic terms, for the quality of her vigilance against the enemies, foreign and domestic, of liberal democracy.

But if she is a Christian citizen, she lives under *theological* judgment as well, and she understands why; because, in the role of citizen, she claims to share in sovereignty, to share in the absolute and bottomless well of the power to decide. The hubris of the citizen, in claiming such sovereignty, is not often enough recognized. Theologically, however, it is hard to avoid, and religious citizens' particularly emphatic recognition of this hubris, among other traits, can make faithful citizens especially beneficial for a polity in several ways. These individuals, and the churches they populate, remind the polity that the state's claim on them is not the highest claim that a human should feel. They will exist in an unsettled but relatively stable truce with the liberal condition of society as a whole. Healthy liberal societies will not disdain them for it. As the Eisenhower strategy rightly suggests, Christians will understand themselves as necessarily drawing strength from those nonliberal, even illiberal, traditions and will not try to draw them into liberalism's too warm embrace, because in the long run, that would mean death for them and for liberalism as well.

Furthermore, Christian citizens not only complicate and enrich the liberal polity as individuals, in their communal life they do so as well. After all, they have another community to which they ascribe real (indeed, ultimate) political import, one that also claims their allegiance, and that does so in a higher and more total way than the liberal state. And so Christian citizens appear not only as citizens but, in an indirect and complicated way, they may also appear, at least in civil society, assembled in churches, which are a standing rebuke to every state's ambition—spoken or unspoken—to offer a complete community for its inhabitants. In this way, faith constantly disrupts and disturbs the polity's tendency toward narcissistic idolatry. In civic terms, we can say that by *splitting* Christian citizens' loyalties, refusing to allow them to slothfully resettle on one worldly axis of value and privileging a radically different end over patriotism, Christian faith constantly disrupts the polity's tendencies toward absolutism.

But there is another, better way to put this that is harder for the state to affirm: The churches are social bodies whose existence is tacitly subversive of the human's institution-building desire in general. In theological terms, we can see such absolutism as setting up a false idol. In some sense, even the liberal state still smacks of Babel for the church—an effort by humans to organize their lives in profoundly self-contained, self-regarding, and self-mastering ways. Tacitly, for those who cannot directly hear its good news, and hopefully explicitly for those who can, the churches are always a standing rebuke to the hubris at the heart of the human endeavor to live together without direct and immediate governance by the one true Sovereign.

In properly theological terms, the churches do this by understanding themselves as not something that has begun by humans *ex nihilo*, but as things begun by someone else—namely, God. The churches' Declaration of Independence is the Gospel, and their Fourth of July is Easter morning; but God gave the churches (indeed, the world) the Gospel, just as God gave them the savior Christ. And the churches as the Church—the churches as an eschatological community living proleptically on earth—are not most fundamentally an enactment of human will, but of an enabling power that then gives the church the will to go on, to continue to be the Body of Christ on earth.

One way of saying this is that the church is a body that is self-consciously *under another's judgment*, namely, God's. And this is no stillborn God, but a living one. The church is a dynamic community whose dynamism and community consist in receiving this living God's judgment and hearing this living God's word, spoken against its illusions and spoken for its improvement. The church is a community where dynamic human beings learn that their dynamism considered on its own, as a kind of frenzied activity, is not all there is—that dynamism is enframed and enabled by its participation in God's gracious dynamism, a dynamism so profound that it even creates the conditions of its own reception in humanity. Part of what it means to learn to be the church is to learn to be a community standing under judgment and to hear that judgment for what it is: both a condemnation of the community, for its arrogance and straying from God, and for its indifference and cruelty (which are the same thing) to all humanity and all creation; and an affirmation of the community, despite its sins, as the place through which God has chosen to inaugurate the redemption of God's creation as a whole. To hear that judgment, negative and positive, God's condemning wrath and God's loving mercy, and to discover that wrath as the "alien" face of that love, is to be the recipient of God's constitutive act of creating an audience for the divine word, in all the theological senses that the term connotes.[20]

In itself this is a powerful thing. But it is also the case that the church exemplifies something that may be powerful in new ways. In a recent book, Jennifer McBride has argued that the churches can serve as a powerful example in contemporary societies of a community that accepts moral responsibility, while most are fleeing it at all costs.[21] The churches can demonstrate the right way of being human by modeling what it means to be fallen, what it means to beg for forgiveness, and by doing so, rendering the community it inhabits graciously capable of redemption. In our culture—a culture so powerfully terrified by moral fault that even Nietzsche would be surprised to see it—such a model could serve no end of good.

But as "locations," or events, of receptivity more fundamentally than activity, the churches are not simply rebukes; they serve as a positive alternative as well. For their existence says that the polity's fantasized destiny, its teleology, is in fact a misunderstood theology—a real longing, but not in the way that our political vocabulary can let us express. The churches say, that is, that politics expresses extra-political longings. So Christian faith, lived vigorously in community, keeps politics honest, because the eschatological dimensions of such a faith oppose the apocalyptic dimensions of politics, which must inevitably move in the direction of false (that is, idolatrous) consciousness. Faith lets us see that there are no "final solutions" in politics, that there is no end to politics.

By doing this, faith keeps politics properly "political" and playful. The playfulness of politics is very important and easily lost. One of the dangers of politics is its ineluctable tendency to draw people in and suffocate their belief that there is anything beyond or outside politics. Such suffocation causes two things to happen. First, people lose the sense of joy, the sense of depth and richness of life. Existence becomes a joyless struggle to defeat others, out of fear that lest you do, they will do the same to you—a kind of vicious inverted parody of the Golden Rule. When life becomes nothing but getting and spending—or worse, seeking to obstruct another's getting and spending—all joy disappears. Second, if politics is all there is, then anything becomes legitimate in order to get one's way. The collapse of all into politics means, inevitably, the collapse of any sense of a higher moral order, which would serve to hold our more ruthless tendencies in check.

This sense of playfulness can also be cultivated beyond the centrally political dimensions of our lives, of course. And yet politics seems a distinctively important sphere for this playfulness, because in politics we find that our commitments and positions are not and cannot wholly and honestly be identified with ourselves. As *The Godfather* would have it, they are not necessarily "personal," they're "business." The distance this distinction gives us is useful for learning more from public life, allowing us to secure ourselves from total absorption by the public sphere, while remaining close enough that we can learn from it. Because of this, politics can serve as a useful forum for self-improvement, because we do not care about it as much as we do the immediate contours of our immediate interpersonal relations. Indeed, it can deepen our faith. The next section explains how.

3b. Politics' Ascesis for Faith: Confessing our Identity

Politics benefits faith because, if it is openly and honestly undertaken, the vexations of public life constantly remind us of our real condition, and the distance separating that present state and the condition that Christians aspire to attain in the kingdom of heaven. Faith, expressed publicly and nondefensively, tries as best as possible to be honest about its origins, confessing the contingent and fragile path whereby we got to where we are. This honesty may, one hopes, provoke others to recognize the contingent and hence fragile character of their own beliefs and lead to a more civilized dialogue. But such political consequences are not to be counted on; we should do this rather for the way it makes us more humble about our own situation. Honest assessment of one's beliefs can make one aware of the deep precariousness of some of those beliefs—and also, and always, make one aware of how narcissistic it is to imagine that one has gained these beliefs by one's own effort. Through this, we may realize the gift-character of one's beliefs and indeed, of one's entire mind.[22]

Furthermore and more important, the experience of confessing faith gives us an inescapable reminder of our tragic condition. While such public expressions are meant to bring us together, to put us more in communion with one another, they also estrange us in significant ways. They teach us again that what I see as a suitable reason for believing in a policy, or a position, you see as noise, and what you see as evidence for a program of action, I do not see as real at all. Public expression of belief teaches us over and over again the inescapable idiosyncrasies of our minds. It reminds us that each of us is irreducibly ourselves.

Finally, in these ways and others, confessing faith reminds us that, whatever our faith may be, we are not *wholly* faithful, that we have a long way to go before we can claim confidentially that we genuinely possess, and therefore truthfully represent, the faith which we purport to proclaim and confess. Our beliefs are far more fragile than we imagine and marked by our own quirkiness in surprising ways. We cannot imagine that we have reached decisive resolution on these matters at any time. This is civic life's deepest ascesis for faith.

By cultivating a sensibility that seeks out dialogue, humility, and awareness of this tragic condition, this *ascesis* has powerful effects on the formation of character and helps faithful citizens honestly live out their lives. Genuine engagement in public life promotes frank recognition of our condition—our need to discern our stories, yet our inability to do so without having lived our full stories, hence never properly in a situation to do so short of our final "determination" in death (and arguably not even there). Christians should inhabit this condition gracefully, by acknowledging that determination and faith is their inescapable condition, yet not one over which they are their own masters. Christians' saving grace is that true faith, genuinely inhabited, is relational, faith in something outside ourselves. True relational faith directs, orients, and opens humans in a way that will be resolved only eschatologically. In the meantime, Christians must learn to face the terror of an open, yet-to-be determined identity, and they will face this perhaps most obviously and immediately in the political realm. As children, we go where we will, but when we have a mature faith, we will be girded and taken where we do not want to go.

How can Christians do that? Part of the answer that Augustine urged on his own congregation was to understand their faith as *in Christ*. When one has faith in Christ, they put their faith "in" another: in a person whose story they affirm, whose story is determinate for them, though they do not fully know yet how it is determinate. This is both subjective and objective, an active investment and a passive acknowledgment. They *participate in* Christ's "faith," Christ's relation to the Father, and so it is not finally their own wholly private faith, nor even the communal faith of the church. It is a genuine, achieved relation that the church can rely on, can *trust*. It is not *one's own* faith but Christ's faith—not one's own identity but the identity Christ enables one to have that is crucial. Here is how to talk about the sacrifice of Christ as the key to one's identity. One's identity is not one's own sacrifice, but rather a mimetic reproduction, in the Spirit, within one's own life of that earlier sacrifice and is thereby a participation in it. What Christ gave up was not only life, but a whole self-understanding which was shown to be the wrong one—the false messianism expected by many of his disciples. To be properly faithful is to continue in the path of discipleship, of following Christ, and this means moving from epistemological questions to Christological ones. Christian faith is Christ's faith, and the core and primordial sacrifice of this faith is Christ's sacrifice, which Christians reenact by sacrificing the idea that believers properly possess a final "true" identity even now. Christians' faith and identity will be redeemed only through faith in Christ's resurrection; this is how Christian faith has an eschatological dimension.

So understood, faith (and the identity that faith both confers and expresses) is only properly possessed in the eschaton. In the meantime, faith offers only the promise of a self, of an absolutely stable and secure identity, and serves as a control on other fidelities. Christians should go about their lives with a kind of "now and not yet" confidence: knowing they have been called into a new being, and feeling that they have some provisional apprehension of what that new being is, but with a sense, ever-deepening as they strengthen that apprehension, that eye has not seen nor ear heard the fullness of that new mode of being. Most pragmatically, this attitude serves as a check on other loyalties, ensuring that believers do not expect them to stay the same, to remain unshriven, in the new creation into which we are entering. And Christians can do this, they believe and confess, because of Christ, the first fruits of that New Creation, wholly accomplished, securing for humankind the promise of what will be. In grace, believers can have confidence in a stability outside the immediate "self" that they possess. This keeps their self-understanding open to quite serious revision, without jettisoning the idea of a real self altogether.

This practice of self-exposure, and ascetically enduring our own openness—a practice of witness, if you will—is what Augustine described with his word *confessio*, or confession. Confession is a complicated term. First of all, it is a double confession—both a confession of one's sin and of praise of God—given to a double audience—composed both of God and of one's fellow humans. The primordial theological activity of confession, then, is profoundly public and political, "vertical" *and* "horizontal." Yet this is not simply a new technique for political life. Augustine aims for an affective revolution that would transfigure politics. "Confession" here does not mean exhibitionism; it is more an orientation than any communication of autobiographical data. In confession we find ourselves decentered, no longer the main object of our purposes, participants in something not primarily our own, a turning to and openness to being transformed by the other.

But "confession" also has a second duality about it. On the one hand, it means to find yourself in Christ's story, so that your narrative gains meaning in the Gospel narrative, and your life finds a role in the story that the Gospels recount. Maybe you are like Peter, faithful but clueless; or Matthew, corrupted and knowing (and hating) it; or Martha, burdened with having a better sister; or Paul, holier than thou. Probably, we are all these people and then some. But no matter: In finding a "place" in the story, you find a route to uncover deeper parts of yourself, revealed in the various characters' lives and responses to Jesus' call. On the other hand, it means to find Christ in your own story—to come to understand your life story as marked by Christ's mastery of your story, not only as an event in your story, but as the frame of it. Here you find the story as a God-haunted one, and you come to understand your desires, your struggles, and your failures as all shadowing a larger pursuit: Christ's pursuit of you, a pursuit that has revealed some tentative conclusion in the very act of finding this story as your own—but which also can now truly be lived and truly begun.

A confessional identity has several relevant components. First and most basically, a confession is not a triumphalist genre. Originating in Roman law, the term *confessio* designated the act of publicly giving witness, before a court; it then gained the connotation of a martyr giving evidence of her faith, where this "giving evidence" goes beyond words to the actual act of undergoing martyrdom. To confess, then, is to give testimony, witness; it is a humble act and a humbling one. You do not pretend to know what your confession ultimately amounts to or how it will count. You are simply trying to be as honest as possible about what was involved in your life. It is also an incomplete act of self-offering, for it elicits and waits upon the response of another.

Confession is thus a distinct mode of self-understanding. It works to resist, on multiple levels, our presumption of knowingness that I discussed earlier—our humanly inescapable (after the Fall) desire to judge and ultimately to *be* the judge, to be the author of our own story, to be God. This presumptuousness is, in Christian terms, perhaps the deepest and most pernicious form of sin that we possess (or that possesses us). We presume we are our own authors, because we presume that we are the root cause of ourselves, our own explanations, our own creators.

A confessional approach attacks this presumptuousness at its heart and teaches one to see one's life as much less intelligible than one would like. It teaches Christians to see as sinful the absolute unintelligibility of their sinful lives. They must unlearn the false explanations they give their corruption and learn how to be shocked that they are as corrupted, as messed up, as they are, then learn how to be humbled and mournful about it. And it teaches them to be bewildered by the sheer gratuitousness of their bare existence, by cultivating their recognition of their inability to explain their existence as "merited" by anything else. We must unlearn the false explanations of our existence and come to see our lives instead as a great gift, wholly unmerited by anything we did or could have done, in order to help us come to wonder in gratitude at the sheer gift of our existence. In undertaking this quest for greater self-understanding, instead of a deeper consolidation of knowledge about one's life, believers discover instead that they gain, in a certain way, a deepened *in*-comprehension of their lives: not a total disorientation, but an orientation toward mystery. In this new orientation, they meet the surprises that invariably attend life not fundamentally as threats against which they must be armored, but as gifts they must learn to receive.

Many worry that such a confessional mode of life simply provides theological legitimacy to the narcissism that seems so pervasive in our lives today, and thereby reinforces a tendency that is already too widespread. There is danger of such misuse. But, as ever, something's *misuse* does not speak at all to its proper use; and I think this confessionalism, with its emphasis on humility about the self and openness to others' views about the self, is actually such narcissism's greatest enemy.

Conclusion: A Republic, If You Can Keep It

Dr. James McHenry, one of Maryland's delegates to the 1787 Constitutional Convention, recorded in his notes a scene that occurred at the close of the Convention, on September 17 of that year. As Benjamin Franklin left the hall in Philadelphia, a woman waiting outside asked him, "What kind of government have you given us, Dr. Franklin?" He replied: "A republic, if you can keep it."[23]

This exchange should be taught in every school's civics class and inscribed above the lintels of every public university, first of all my own. For Franklin's reply is addressed not only to the woman who asked the question but also to all the citizens who have come after her. (Franklin, after all, knew the government he had helped design would not be for him; he lived in it for only one year, dying on April 17, 1790.) The challenges and obligations of citizenship in a republic are manifold. Most of the challenges are, in fact, the obligations. Most of the time, we take too little cognizance of them. We are happy to get by with a minimal attention to our civic duties; most of us are content—proud, even—if we vote. But voting is not the fulfillment of our duties as citizens. In fact, it is one of the easiest duties. There are many more. Being a citizen of a republic is a difficult challenge.

Religious faith, at least of the Christian kind, does not relieve those difficulties. If anything it magnifies and adds to them, for it renders commitment to our common republic complicatedly ambivalent. It is not simply a matter of antagonism, as if faith is necessarily reflexively hostile to political commitment. Nor is it simply a matter of chastening, as if faith's job is akin to the proctor at a high school dance in the 1950s, keeping a prudent open space between the dancers' bodies. Nor is it simply a matter of reinforcing or amplifying that commitment. It can be any of these at any time. At all times it is at least one of these. Almost all the time it is more than one.

And yet that complicated, even dialectical, ambivalence is not all bad, even from the wholly secular perspective of the republic. After all, the great danger, historically speaking, of republican government is idolatrous self-love, which creates in its adherents an unquestioning fanaticism, which leads to imperialism, which leads to moral decay and eventually, societal collapse. And this fanaticism was caused by the state asking too much of its citizens, and its citizens willingly, even eagerly, providing it. Republicanism may not be unique in having its vices be defects of its virtues, but it is especially susceptible to those virtues' straightforward reversal into vices. It was the genius of liberal republicans in the eighteenth century, James Madison perhaps foremost among them, to urge a certain ambivalence be leavened into the republican spirit, lest it too easily curdle into a simple will-to-power of one's own community against all others—what Augustine called the *libido dominandi*, the lust to dominate that becomes the dominating lust. And it was those liberal republicans' great good fortune to possess in the religious consciousness and institutions of their fellow citizens a collection of energies and convictions that met their needs.

The challenges for religious believers in liberal republican polities, and for polities that are populated in part by such religious believers, are manifold. In both directions misunderstandings are likely to occur. Religious believers' actions may from time to time seem not properly "political" to the state and to their more secularly minded fellow citizens; this genuine incomprehension on the part of their secular neighbors and the modern state may seem incomprehensible, in turn, to those religious believers. Inevitably, such misunderstandings will lead, from time to time, to tragedy. Such failures will obstruct the efforts on both sides to live in genuine political community with one another, to see one another most fundamentally as partners and not opponents. In such situations—which is to say, in very many situations in which Christians are likely to find themselves today—Christian citizens should try to live by Reinhold Niebuhr's earlier quoted words: "To do justice to the distinctions of good and evil in history and to the possibilities and obligations of realizing the good in history; and also to subordinate all these relative judgments and achievements to the final truth about life and history which is proclaimed in the Gospel."[24]

Of course, how this command is lived out will differ depending on the setting. In our setting, I think there are three obligations, or challenges, that Christians have especially to undertake—one fundamentally affirmative, one fundamentally critical, and one that is both. I list them in that order.

First, the fundamentally affirmative obligation is simple. Christian citizens must always agitate for, and publicly demonstrate their recognition of, the infinite value of the individual, as bearing the weight of the *imago Dei*, the image of God. This is something that churches do practice today, albeit not entirely in concert with one another; concerns about abortion, about torture, about the treatment of prisoners and the poor and the weak are all manifestations of this primordial affirmation of the faith. It is not just a matter of affirming this in private. Christians must *show it forth*, as

Augustine said: "Restore to God the image of God in the human being, just as the image of Caesar on the coin is restored to him."[25] Establishing the appropriate mode of "showing forth" and the appropriate ranking of causes to agitate about are and will continue to be disputable, but that such affirmative agitation is required is undeniable.

Second, the fundamentally critical obligation is less clear but still relatively straightforward. Christians must be Orwellians against "moral clarity." It is not that Christians should be against real moral clarity, of course. But we should recognize that real moral clarity produces a true approximation of the situation, and after the Fall, the situation is always morally ambiguous. Real moral vision does not make things clearer, but rather more vivid, in all their ambiguities. The danger all of us, believers and unbelievers alike, face here is the ruthless simplifying energies of our own egos, amplified by the ideologies and identity politics of the day; the danger is what I earlier described as "knowingness." A true hermeneutics of charity slows you down, makes you resist too easy a judgment in any case. What Christianity, as Augustine sees it, offers is *moral obscurity*, moral difficulty. Life, after all, is not easy, nor is it simple, and most of the clear choices we must make are clear only because they are trivial. Christians should be known for their capacity to be, from time to time, confused and uncertain.

Third, and most complicated, is the question of pluralism. How should Christians address the fact of pluralism? What virtues should Christian citizens cultivate to confront this? The problem of pluralism, of course, is one that many people have been thinking about for a very long time, and the sense that we today confront it in a wholly unprecedented manner says as much about our ignorance of history as it does about our ignorance of the distinct shape of our conundrum. (In the past three or so decades, an enormous literature on religious pluralism has developed which speaks to these matters as well). In general, I think, Christian citizens have a certain set of challenges given to them by living in a pluralistic society, challenges with their own dangers, to be sure, but with a certain set of benefits as well.

A pluralistic setting undercuts religious belief's "taken for grantedness" and makes such belief no longer an unquestioned background assumption, but something that one is reflectively aware of as contingent. If one is to affirm one's beliefs in this setting, then, one must *actively* affirm them. (This is what some call "reflexive modernity" and others call "the heretical imperative"). Religious believers, some would say, should cultivate the ability to see their own belief in alien guise, as it were—to see it from the perspective of one who does not share it, perhaps. This demands a great deal from any human being, but it has benefits. Most important, having this skill gives believers a crucial principle whereby they can judge the extent to which hypocrisy or idolatry has entered their convictions. It is hard to overestimate the value of skeptical challenges to one's beliefs. Believers should welcome such challenges as a healthy scouring of their convictions.

On the other hand, I would argue it is morally and epistemologically equally useful for unbelievers in a pluralistic society to learn to see things from a religious person's perspective, and to try as best they can to understand what the religious person is seeking to say. Part of the reason for this is simply the value of enlarging one's mind, enlargement that comes from encounters with those with different convictions. But another part has to do with the particular path that secularism has traveled in our era. The secularism of modernity is quite different from the secularism of late antiquity—of Augustine's own age, for example, which had its share of secularisms (and certainly was quite pluralist). It seems to me that the loudest voices of contemporary secularism are marked by a more drearily reductionist materialism than the secularists of earlier eras. This materialism reduces humans to something far less than what we seem to be. Another way of saying this is that modern secularism has been entwined with a certain kind of modern scientism, in a way that late antiquity would find incomprehensible. And because of this, modern secular thinkers are often under-equipped to think about the breadth and depth of human experience. The religions can remind them of the full scope of human existence, the multiple dimensions of human life—not simply for matters of political significance, but also for all matters of human significance in its full existential shape—and challenge them to find structural analogies in a secularist vernacular for these missing dimensions. This may be a fairly romantic vision of the secular significance of the religions, to be sure, but one should not discount it for that. To be acquainted with the religions is to be acquainted with a dizzying array of ways of being human, and even on secularists' own terms, such acquaintance is to be sought— dare we say—devoutly.

Finally, one of the best things about genuine pluralism is how deeply it confuses the categories we try to use to manage it. For after all, these categories of "believers" and secularist "unbelievers" are far too fixed. Most of the things believers and unbelievers believe are the same: that any two newspapers from a pile of fresh newspapers will contain the same news; that you can put letters in mailboxes and, if they have stamps, they will be picked up and delivered to where you said it should go; that if you turn the car key, it will start the car. And most of the time, all of us are at some point on the continuum of belief and unbelief. (The exchange between Felix Frankfurter and Reinhold Niebuhr, after a sermon by the latter, nicely captures this: Frankfurter, a lifelong atheist, said, "Reinie, may a believing unbeliever thank you for your sermon?" Niebuhr replied, "May an unbelieving believer thank you for appreciating it?"[26]) Recognition of these facts will be encouraged by life in a pluralistic society, and that offers yet one more opportunity for growth by Christians who inhabit it.

Religious citizens, if they remain faithful, can still successfully contribute to their polities today. Theirs is a difficult task, to be sure. But all republican citizenship is difficult, and at least they will be a bit more alert to the challenges than some others might be. And, as no one ever said the vocation of a believer was easy, so no one can say that the vocation of a believing citizen should be simple. If faithful Christians are to be citizens, something like this complicated minuet with Caesar sketched here is required. Difficulty, if truthfully explicated, is no reason for foregoing the effort; and Christian faith asks no less of its adherents, and their polities can expect no more. After all, on their own terms, to accomplish this difficult task, all such citizens will need is what they always and everywhere need—the grace of God, shed abroad in their hearts, to give them the ability to delight in God's will, and walk in God's ways, to the everlasting glory of God's most holy name.

Notes

1. For more on this, see Thomas Banchoff, ed., *Democracy and the New Religious Pluralism* (New York: Oxford University Press, 2007).
2. Whether those communities' languages can engage in self-critique—a necessary virtue of any community—is a different, though no less important matter, which must be settled by looking at the concrete resources available within each community.
3. William Galston, *Liberal Purposes* (New York: Cambridge University Press, 1991), 225.
4. For Eisenhower see the *New York Times*, December 23, 1952. For a wonderfully puckish source-criticism of this quip, see Patrick Henry, "'And I Don't Care What It Is': The Tradition-History of A Civil Religion Proof Text," *Journal of the American Academy of Religion* 49, no. 1 (1981): 35–49. For the 2001 statistics, see Steve Farkas, Jean Johnson, and Tony Foleno, *For Goodness's Sake: Why So Many Want Religion to Play a Greater Role in American Life* (New York: Public Agenda, 2001).

For a powerful and acute exploration of the ironies and paradoxes of this view, see Patrick Deneen, *Democratic Faith* (Princeton: Princeton University Press, 2005).

5. Jason Bivins, *The Fracture of Good Order: Christian Antiliberalism and the Challenge to American Politics* (Chapel Hill: University of North Carolina Press, 2003), 10.

6. The fact that in the U.S. setting, churches get along so well with the state system is not evidence against my point, but rather evidence of certain failures of the American churches and certain (proper) kinds of restraint on the part of the U.S. state and other liberal states—as I will explain later in this essay. Again, see Deneen, *Democratic Faith.*

7. Reinhold Niebuhr, *The Nature and Destiny of Man,* vol. 2: *Human Destiny* (New York: Charles Scribners Sons, 1943), 198.

8. Not to mention, as a point of exegesis, it was Cain who seems to have built the first city after murdering his brother Abel (Gen. 4:17).

9. For more on this "knowingness," see my essay "The Liberation of Questioning in Augustine's *Confessions,*" *The Journal of the American Academy of Religion 70,* no. 3 (Sept. 2002): 539–560.

10. See also Vaclav Havel, *The Art of the Impossible: Politics as Morality in Practice,* trans. Paul Wilson et al. (New York: Knopf, 1997), 238: "The primary origin of hope is, to put it simply metaphysical...hope is more, and goes deeper, than a mere optimistic inclination or disposition of the human mind," and is anchored in "humanity's experience with its own Being and with the Being of the world."

11. Of course, this development can happen outside the political realm. But I am restricting myself to this realm here.

12. Oliver O'Donovan, *The Desire of the Nations: Rediscovering the Roots of Political Theology* (New York: Cambridge University Press, 1996), 92.

13. While some have recently deployed the notion of "illiberal democracy" (most famously Fareed Zakaria), the idea is implied in the notion of liberal democracy itself. See also John Courtney Murray, "Are There Two or One?" in *We Hold These Truths: Catholic Reflections on the American Proposition* (New York: Sheed and Ward, 1960), 197–217. More recently, see Pierre Manent, "Modern Democracy as a System of Separations," *Journal of Democracy 14,* no. 1 (2003): 114–125.

14. For one good attempt, see Charles Tilly, *Coercion, Capital, and European States AD 990–1992* (Cambridge, MA: Blackwell, 1992).

15. See John Brewer, *Sinews of Power: War, Money, and the English State, 1688–1783* (Cambridge, MA: Harvard University Press, 1990).

16. See the work of John Milbank, Stanley Fish, or Paul Griffiths for examples of such attacks. For a vigorous and useful defense of the concept of privacy, though ironically one not too different than the approach urged here, see Jean L. Cohen, "Rethinking Privacy: Autonomy, Identity, and the Abortion Controversy," in *Public and Private in Thought and Practice: Reflections on a Grand Dichotomy,* ed. Jeff Weintraub and Krishan Kumar (Chicago: University of Chicago Press, 1997), 133–165.

17. Albert O. Hirschmann, *The Passions and the Interests: Political Arguments for Capitalism Before its Triumph* (Princeton: Princeton University Press, 1977), and John Dunn, *Western Political Theory in the Face of the Future* (New York: Cambridge University Press, 1993). See also Ernst Kantorowicz, *The King's Two Bodies: A Study in Medieval Political Theology* (Princeton: Princeton University Press, 1997).

18. See Ian Shapiro, *Political Criticism* (Berkeley: University of California Press, 1990), 266. See also Shapiro's *The State of Democratic Theory* (Princeton: Princeton University Press, 2003).

19. James Madison, "Vices of the Political System of the United States" (the confederacy, pre-Constitution), The Founders' Constitution, http://press-pubs.uchicago.edu/founders/documents/v1ch5s16.html.

20. See Paul de Hart, *The Trial of the Witnesses: The Rise and Decline of Postliberal Theology* (Cambridge, MA: Blackwell, 2006).

21. See Jennifer McBride, *The Church for the World: A Theology of Public Witness* (New York: Oxford University Press, 2011).

22. Here I have been much illuminated by Michele Dillon, "Can Post-Secular Society Tolerate Religious Differences?" *Sociology of Religion* 71, no. 2 (2010): 139–156, esp. 149–150.

23. The papers of Dr. James McHenry on the Federal Convention of 1787 can be found in Charles C. Tansill, *Documents Illustrative of the Formation of the Union of the American States* (Washington, D.C.: GPO, 1927); the exchange between Franklin and the woman is recorded on page 952.

24. Again, Niebuhr, *The Nature and Destiny of Man*, vol. 2, *Human Destiny*, 198.

25. Augustine, *Political Writings*, ed. E.M. Atkins and R. J. Dodaro (New York: Cambridge University Press, 2001), *Sermon* 13.4, quote at 122.

26. Elisabeth Sifton, *The Serenity Prayer: Faith and Politics in Times of Peace and War* (New York: W. W. Norton & Company, 2005), 75–76.

Islamic Political Theologies and International Relations

Jocelyne Cesari

Introduction

Since September 11, the debate over the compatibility of Islam and secularism has become an increasingly public one, and has come to bear many similarities to the "culture talk," described by Mahmood Mamdani in his book, *Good Muslim, Bad Muslim.*[1] The foundation of culture talk is the essentialization of both Muslims and Islam. Islam is presented as a powerful ideology uniting Muslims from London to Kabul, and Muslims are presented as "ossified historical specimens," neither able to address the current challenges of political and religious progress nor able to abandon their obsession with the past. This approach is continuously reinforced by political events such as the cartoon crisis in 2006 or the protests against the anti-Muhammed film in 2012. *It also informs scholarly literature* on Islam and politics, which is most of the time built on the artificial division between secularism and Islam.

In this perspective, secularism is often seen as a product of post-Enlightenment thinking. It is thus designated as both "modern" and "Western," an ideal beyond the grasp of Muslims and other "non-Western" groups. In this sense, Talal Asad rightly warns of the normative dimension of various discourses on secularism, more specifically noting that secularism is sometimes rendered a mere mimicry of Christian theology. In presenting Muslims as "religious others" such discourse reinforces notions of eternal irreconcilability between Islam and modernity, secularism, and human rights.[2]

Such ideas permeate also the domain of international relations theory (IR) and can be found in the most prominent interpretations of Islamic radicalism—which explain violent forms of political Islam as a consequence of the Islamic religion turned into ideology and the lack of or failure of secularism. Overall, this approach presents two major faults.

The first fault is one of definition. Many scholars within the IR field apprehend Islamic manifestations in politics as a "return" or "resurgence" of religion within the past fifty years. This return is seen as a challenge to the separation of religion and politics that was supposedly at the foundation of most Muslim nation-states. The second fault is one of classification. Within IR, religious manifestations are categorized almost exclusively as ideological phenomena, that is, identified and studied primarily as ideas or beliefs. Such an approach reduces religion to a rhetoric that is used in political mobilization and hence gives the illusion that the knowledge of concepts and symbols of religious traditions is the major way to understand their role in politics.

Both faults have led to major misconceptions about religion within the IR field. By simultaneously accepting the idea of a "return of religion" and the dichotomization of religion and politics without critique, the appearance of religion generally, and Islam more specifically, presents a direct challenge to the presumed religious/secular dichotomy IR theorists assume present throughout state actors in the international system. Additionally, once religion has been classified as an ideological phenomenon, most mainstream scholars of international relations dismiss it as a philosophical issue that cannot and should not be integrated into the larger framework of international relations.

This article questions the taken-for-granted division between religion and politics that makes any forms of interactions between religion and politics illegitimate or signs of anti-modernity. As I show in the first part of this chapter, Islam is easily *essentialized* within the domain of international relations, due mainly to the long-standing construction of both Islamic religion and polities as the typical Eastern "other." In the second part, I offer an alternative to this model, by analyzing secularization in Muslim-majority countries through the dialectics between religion and politics at both local and international levels.

Islam as a Cause of International Conflict: The Weight of History and External Influences

The reason why "culture talk" is so influential among IR theorists is because religion has long been absent from most IR discourse. Since the 1960s and

1970s, IR discourse has consistently set up an opposition between modernization, on the one hand, and religion, on the other. However, by the
1980s, since the Iranian Revolution and the rise of the Religious Right in
the United States, theorists had to reassess the place of religion in international relations theory. For instance, in the introduction to his book
Religion in International Affairs: The Return from Exile, political scientist
Pavlos Hatzopoulos speaks of the recent resurgence of religion within the
field of international relations. He claims that "the global resurgence of religion confronts IR theory with a theoretical challenge comparable to that
raised by the end of the Cold War or the emergence of globalization."[3] At the
same time, many scholars of modernization and social change have begun
reformulating their approaches by showing that modernization can also be
responsible for the rise of religion, rather than its decline.[4]

Nevertheless, Islam, as a nonsecular and antimodernist tradition, is
persistently seen as a cause of international conflict. In the field of IR,
the interest in culture as a factor in international conflicts is a relatively
recent phenomenon, stemming from a growing heterogenization of the
world stage and the end of conflicts fought exclusively on the basis of the
nation-state interests. The post–Cold War era has effectively compelled
a reevaluation of traditional approaches to IR and has forced analysts to
address cultural and religious factors, previously absent from most theories. Barry Buzan was one of the first to examine the consequences of the
disappearance of the communist enemy. In a 1991 article in *International
Affairs*, he predicted that the new situation would inevitably create a shift
in the central relationships of power and precipitate "the collision of cultural identities."[5]

But it has been the work of Samuel Huntington, first presented in a
1993 article in *Foreign Affairs* and subsequently elaborated in a 1996 book,
which has dominated the discourse on culture as an element in international conflicts.[6] Huntington argues that Islam is uniquely incompatible
with and antagonistic to the core values of the West (such as equality and
modernity). This argument resurfaces in most current analyses of international affairs and globalization, notably in terrorist studies since 9/11.
However, as abundantly proven by the social sciences, civilizations are not
homogenous, monolithic players in world politics with an inclination to
"clash," but rather consist of pluralistic, divergent, and convergent actors
and practices that are constantly evolving.[7] Thus, the "clash of civilizations" fails to address not only conflict between civilizations but also conflict and differences within civilizations. In particular, evidence does not

exist to substantiate Huntington's prediction that countries with similar cultures are coming together, while countries with different cultures are coming apart.

In all these analyses, the answer provided to the question, "Why do they hate us?" rarely takes the wider context of competition for political influence, regional dynamics, and historical sequences into account. Rather, it is almost always based on discussion of textual and ideological use of religious references by Muslim actors.

The cultural divide is thus envisaged as the primary cause of international crises. Admittedly, the "Huntingtonian" position is based on a premise that cannot be simply dismissed: that identity and culture play a decisive role in international relations. Additionally, Huntington's argument can be situated within the current trend of researchers attempting to understand the scope of the political revolts against the Western-dominated international order.[8] But *what* culture and *what* Islam are being spoken of here? The idea of a monolithic Islam leads to a reductionism in which the conflicts in Sudan, Lebanon, Bosnia, Iraq, and Afghanistan are imagined to stem collectively and wholly from the domain of religion. It is, moreover, ironic that the role of religion, so long ignored or neglected in terms of international politics, is now exaggerated and decontextualized in an ahistorical perspective, which has elicited its fair share of criticism from scholars of Islamic cultures.

Seen in this light, the clash of civilizations thesis represents an attempt, albeit a consistently inadequate one, to shift international politics away from an exclusively nation-state-centric approach, only to immediately re-create and legitimate the view of a fixed world of cultural agents participating in predetermined conflicts of interest.[9] This is to say that any attempt at an analysis of culture and global cultural conflict is an admirable one, but it must not be done through a reification of both culture and civilization.

This ahistorical approach to Islam's global role can be explained by the persistence and constant reinvention of the Western political imaginary, which, at least since the age of Enlightenment, has fashioned itself in opposition to Islam.[10] Mustapha Kamal Pasha accurately describes the West's modernist-liberal imaginary, based on the concepts of progress, nation, the rational individual (à la Robinson Crusoe), secularization, and the power of law.[11] Encounters between the West and other parts of the world were shaped by this imaginary, and it was brought to bear in IR as the only legitimate form of political interaction. In this way, the modern liberal order became normalized throughout the world, forever defining the terms of relations between the West and other societies. The concept of secularism is a crucial aspect of this international liberal order. It is based on the fiction of a clear-cut border between public and private space and state and religion, borrowing from a romanticized interpretation of the European and American history. Therefore, it is not a very useful tool to account for any form of religious expression outside the private sphere. In this context, any manifestation of religion on an international scale is seen as something opposed to modernity and a form of resistance to the secularized liberal order. The location of religion outside the public sphere has thus become a touchstone against which to judge other cultures or societies in which such separation is imperfect or nonexistent.[12]

Of course, Western political concepts have been imposed upon all cultures, not just that of Islam. Nonetheless, unlike other worlds and cultures, Islam has played a central role in the construction of this very political imaginary. The liberal-modernist story that constitutes Western identity has effectively adopted Islam as its foil in order to create itself. Such mirroring has a history which reaches much farther back than September 11, dating rather from the Ottoman Empire's political domination of Mediterranean lands during the eighteenth century. Europe's relationship to the Ottoman Empire has been set down in the gradual establishing of the East/West binary. This binary, present as early as the writings of Machiavelli, would come to have a decisive impact on the eighteenth and nineteenth centuries by influencing the building of the major political concepts of the Modern West: equality, human rights, and balance of power. More than simply a product of religious differences, the opposition of East and West was a reflection of political opposition. "The orientalization of the Orient," as Edward Said put it, was above all the effect of a European cultural crisis linked to the advent of modernity.[13] It was the expression of a particular conception of a political and cultural destiny, defined in opposition to the Ottoman system.

Examples of this identity-formation through the relationship to the Muslim "other" appear as early as the sixteenth century, for example, in the writings of Guillaume Postel, considered to be the forerunner of the dialogue between Islam and Christianity. Postel's attitude was indeed innovative, in that he expressed a desire to understand the other through the study of language and literature. Nevertheless, the ultimate goal of his understanding was to incorporate the other into an integrated, universal perspective, and in this sense, Postel can also therefore be said to be the precursor of Orientalism. At this time, examination of foreign cultures led to relativism, one of the central concepts of Enlightenment philosophy. By creating a relationship with the distant and the unfamiliar, the journey, be it real or imagined, allowed for an increased knowledge of one's self. Two stock figures were pressed into service for these transformations: the "Egyptian Sage" and the "Mahometan Arab" (according to a typology described by Maxime Rodinson).[14] Early modern political cosmology is thus a product of this relationship with the absolute, Oriental other. This image appears in many political reflections of the time such as Jean Bodin's 1566 *Method for the Easy Comprehension of History*. This kind of literature will build the opposition between the West in step with the natural progress of the world, and the East already stuck in the past.

Islam and Secularism: A New Take on Modernization

The narrative of secularism in the West has been constructed with an underlying opposition to an imaginary and premodern Islam. Theories of secularization converge on several common points: social and political differentiation, rationalization, and privatization.[15] Most of these approaches, however, stand in stark opposition to the actual situation of Muslim societies, past *and* present. A common example of the contradiction between rhetoric and fact is the argument that there is no separation of religion and politics in Islamic history.[16] Although historians and Islamicists, such as Ira Lapidus,[17] have demonstrated its inaccuracies, this theory is still used by political scientists to argue that Islam is incompatible with secularism. In reality though, Muslim societies went under a process of political and religious differentiation under the caliphates with the emergence of a specialized body of religious authorities. Additionally, the differentiation process between Islam and politics in its modern form was the most significant during the colonial and especially the postcolonial periods. The influence of modern ideologies like nationalism, imported from the West, transformed the balance between society and religion. The emergence of the state as a central political institution went hand in hand with a greater homogenization of the political community. This homogenization process was central to the legitimization of state rulers who utilized Islam to both bolster and ground these national projects. Such a turn of events has contributed to the politicization of Islam in unprecedented ways.[18]

Most of the postcolonial states have sought to create secular national identities that supersede religious identities. This meant that Muslim countries went through a process of secularization in almost all domains (economy, politics, welfare, etc.). The main domain that retained Islamic references was family law (with a few exceptions, like Tunisia and Turkey). At the same time though, Islam remained the religion of the state or the religion of the majority, and religious terms such as *ummah* and *jihad* became part of national narratives.

In other words, political Islam, defined as a politicized narrative within the religion, is inherently part of the modernization and secularization of Muslim-majority states. Under these conditions, the Western-centered definition of modernity cannot help explain this process because of its underlying assumption that secularization leads to the decline of religion in the political sphere. In Muslim-majority countries, modernization had an opposite effect: Islam became part of the national myth. For this reason, the concept "political religion" helps us to better understand the contemporary interaction between Islam and politics.

A myth is not only an ideology but also a narrative that is neither fable nor fiction. The content of a myth is not what makes it a political narrative. For example, the idea that the world is about to end has no intrinsic political message. Rather, a myth is politicized when its narrative is used to address the political conditions of a given group. A myth can be cognitive (a lens through which we perceive the world), practical (an image on the basis of which we act in the world), or aesthetic-emotional (a dramatic representation on the basis of which we feel about the world). For example, the cognitive aspect of Islam as a political myth will borrow the concepts of ummah, jihad, and shari'a from the religious tradition and reinvest them as elements of a narrative that defines Muslims as activists or militants for the sake of ummah, seen as a political unit that must be regulated by shari'a as a fixed code of laws.[19] Such a narrative is translated into heroic historical figures like Said Qtb or Bin Laden and concrete events like the Gulf War or the Afghan War that facilitate mobilization and activism. The aesthetical-emotional aspects of Islam as a political myth relates to the systematic connection of current human experiences of contemporary Muslim fighters with the foundational figures of the Prophet Muhammed in Medina and the Shi'a with the martyrs of the son of Ali.

Religion-based political myths have been used by the post colonial secular states to reinforce national identities.[20] In these conditions, Islamic revolutions or movements cannot be seen solely as disruptions to the State's secular order. They are actually the most recent outcome of complex inter-actions between state and Islam that started at the time of nation building. These interactions can take different forms, but the outcome is always the same: a politicization of the Islamic message as shown by the examples of Iran, Pakistan, and Turkey (presented below).

The centrality of Islam within Iranian political institutions is not sim-ply the result of the 1979 Ayatollah's revolution. Instead, it is the outcome of a long modernization process in which Shi'ism was transformed into an ideology of resistance through different political and cultural changes. The driver of these transformations was the encounters of Shi'a Islam with Western imperialism throughout the region. These encounters with the West initiated a modernization process that, at the turn of the twentieth century, transformed Shi'ism into a national ideology of resistance. It was this transformation, long before 1979, that made the Islamic Revolution of 1979 possible.

The Constitutional Revolution of 1906 was the first modern revolution in Iran that eventually led to the creation of the nation-state. It marked the collapse of medieval Persian political culture and the simultaneous rise and expansion of Iranian civil society. At the center of the identity forma-tion of the modern Iranian state was the nationalization of Shi'ism, which accompanied a Shi'ization of Persian culture. Most important, though, was the phrasing of anticolonial resistance in Islamic terms, from the begin-ning of the nineteenth century onward. The loss of Iranian territory to the Russians in the early part of the nineteenth century and the economic con-cessions made to the colonial powers toward the end of the century cul-minated in a national resistance movement in Iran. On both cultural and political fronts, nationalization of Shi'ism took a form whereby scattered symbols, institutions, and texts of faith coagulated into the iconic force of national religion, and the constitution officially recognized Shi'ism as the state religion. Such a nationalization of Shi'ism entailed an aggressive modernization agenda of the religion and its institutions, which exposed its medieval doctrinal roots to the corrosive joint projects of colonial modernity and European Enlightenment.

The Islamic Revolution of 1979 demonstrates the way in which the reorientation of Shi'ite ideology was adopted in order to reshape the politi-cal system into one that is consistent with the *ulama*'s vision of a theo-cratic mode of governance. The *ulama* found their political focus and voice in Ayatollah Khomeini's reinterpretation of the Shi'ite theory espoused in *velayat-e faih* (Islamic Governance of Jurist, or Supremacy of the Jurist) and

mobilized other revolutionary groups under the common cause of transforming the political system of Iran. This reinterpretation of Shi'ism not
only became the impetus of the Revolution, but it also provided the basis
for reconstructing the political system. Religion was no longer a separate
entity. Instead it became an integral part of politics in Iran. Shi'ite ideology played a crucial role in constructing a semi-republican state when it
simultaneously helped to end the 2500-year-old monarchy and integrated
traditional elements of religion into the new system it created.

The founder of Pakistan and leader of the Muslim League, Mohammad
Ali Jinnah, adopted an explicitly secular nationalist project to bring together
the different people that lived in East and West Pakistan. He initially envisioned no interference of the state with Islam.[21] As a consequence, the
Muslim League was regarded as overly un-Islamic by more religiously ori-
ented actors such as Mawdudi, the founder of Jamaat-i-Islami, as well as
by the majority of the *ulama*. Ultimately, Pakistan was created as a Muslim
state, with reference to Islam in the constitution. Three factors contributed to the deep entrenchment of Islamism in Pakistani identity and politics. The first was the intention behind the creation of Pakistan, which was
to build a new home for the Muslim population in the Indian subconti-
nent. The second factor comes from the political tactics undertaken by the
Muslim League in the creation of Pakistan. The Muslim League needed
the support of the *ulama* to gain the support of the Muslim-majority prov-
inces and decided to bring the *ulama* of the Barelwi School into its election
campaign. The Barelwis were not previously active in politics but soon
began to demand that Pakistan be established as an Islamic state. The
Muslim League therefore turned to Islamic rhetoric as a political strategy
to rally the support of various groups.[22]

Lastly, the conflict over the territorial boundaries of the new nation-state
reinforced the political entrenchment of Islam. The partition of Bangladesh
in 1974 revealed the failure of a state for all Muslims and therefore intensified the consolidation and unity of the population for more Islamic agen-
das.[23] Over time, Pakistan evolved into a more Islamic state, especially
under the rule of Zia Al Haqq (1977–1988) who introduced shari'a ordinances. The conflict over whether Pakistan should be an Islamic state still
continues.[24]

Turkey is a unique case: the state's control over Islamic institutions
coexists with the exclusion of Islam from the social and public sphere.
Although equal treatment of religion exists as idealized rhetoric, it is
far from being realized in the public sphere. The constitution of 1924

stipulates that the "religion of the Turkish state" is Islam, but the reference to Islam in the constitution was removed in 1980. The Tevhid-I Tedrisat (Unification of Education) Law that passed in March 1924 led to the closure of 479 madrasas and created a unified secular school system under the Ministry of Education. Although some Islamic schools, such as the Imam Hatip schools, were initially allowed to stay open under state control, they were closed in 1930, and there was an absence of Islamic education in Turkey until 1949.[25] The authoritarian policies in the domain of education and culture (forbidding Islamic dress codes and the use of Islamic signs in social interactions and public spaces) created a homogenized modern nation that excluded both non-Muslim religious groups and non-Turkish ethnic groups like the Kurds. In the Lausanne Treaty (1924), Turkish citizenship was defined according to people's affiliation to Islam, and discriminatory treatment such as overtaxation levied on non-Muslims was rampant. From 1950 on, the strong authoritarian secularism diminished with the return of Iman Hatip schools. The political victory of Islamist parties from the 1980s onward, attest to the importance of political Islam within the secular framework created by Kamal Ataturk. It shows also that the initial secularist project contributed in unexpected ways to the politicization of Islam.

Conclusion: Modernization and Secularization as Tragic Categories

Islam's multifaceted manifestations at the international level demonstrate that the opposition between Islam and liberal secular values is insufficient to account for the complex position of religion generated by cultural globalization. Nonetheless, the process of cultural globalization can promote defensive reactions in the name of Islam, or what Homi Bhabha has called forms of "contra-modernity."[26] It is not difficult to understand how and why Islam can be called upon as a resource for combating a West that has been essentialized as a destructive and oppressive entity. It is in such a context that the more conservative interpretations of the Islamic message (Wahhabism and rigid forms of Salafism) have gained many followers in all parts of the Muslim world. The Wahhabi interpretation of Islam is the official religious doctrine of the Saudi Kingdom. The followers of this doctrine connect to the first generations of the Prophet Companions or Salaf.[27] They refer back to the original sources of the religion, the Qur'an and the hadith. This return to the source texts may also be considered conservative, as it is for the increasingly popular Jamaat Tabligh or for those who draw inspiration from the thought of the Saudi Sheik al-Albani.[28]

A return to divine revelation can also produce more inclusive interpretations that adapt easily to Western sociopolitical contexts. For example, the Muslim Brotherhood movement asserts that Islam is compatible with democracy and advocates participation in political and civil life.[29] The political victories of Islamist parties in the first free-and-fair elections of the Arab Spring in 2011 and 2012 are the concrete outcomes of this position. Interestingly, it also initiated the entry of Salafi groups into politics that, until the Arab Spring, despised or rejected elections and democracy.

To summarize, the multiple forms of political Islams are the direct outcome of modernization projects initiated by the postcolonial states. Such modernization, disconnected since its inception from liberalism and democracy, will heavily influence any political transformation. With most roads to the West barred, inner resources for change have been shaped and manipulated by state actions and national narratives. It is indeed an important element of the politicization of Islam that is often neglected: the postcolonial state has made use of Islamic terms such as ummah and jihad in the forging of national identities. It has also promoted Islamization of society while barring Islamic parties or oppressing political parties based on Islam. The political evolution of Egypt from Sadat to the Mubarak regime is a relevant example of such duality of state action both domestically and internationally. Under Mubarak, praying became as popular as shopping or football, and like other popular pastimes, served as a distraction from the innumerable frustrations of Egyptian life. Indeed, Egyptian Islam increasingly caters to consumerist needs. The popular televangelist Amr Khaled mixes Quranic citations with boosterish advice of a more general kind.

Mubarak also used the West's fear of political Islam to reinforce his legitimacy in the international system. In one of his last speeches (January 28, 2011) to the Egyptian public, which was also broadcast worldwide, he explained the social upraising on Tahrir Square as follows: "There is a fine line between freedom and chaos, and I lean toward freedom for the people in expressing their opinions as much as I hold on to the need to maintain Egypt's safety and stability... I will defend Egypt's safety and stability and its people's wishes, for that is the responsibility and the trust endowed in me when I swore an oath in front of God and the nation to protect it."[30]

Interestingly, the revolutions of spring 2011 that led to the demise of the Mubarak regime in Egypt and of Ben Ali in Tunisia, as well as the protests unfolding in Bahrain, Yemen, and Syria, at the time of this writing, did not use Islamist rhetoric. The protestors demanded political freedom, democracy, and redistribution of power and resources in very secular terms. But Islamic parties have won the elections in Tunisia and Egypt and have emerged as the major political force post Revolution. The question of what kind of democracy will emerge from the unfolding transitions, remains open.[31]

As suggested by Muslim scholars such as Abdullahi An Na'im and Abdolkarim Souroush, the shift to democracy may involve the bifurcation of the state and Islam throughout the Muslim world.[32] Such voices though, are far and few between and more are needed to address many of the region's long-standing problems in a meaningful way. It is too early to draw conclusions regarding the outcomes of the Arab Spring, but equidistance between state institutions and Islam will be a key element in any successful democratic transition.[33]

Notes

1. Mahmood Mamdani, *Good Muslim, Bad Muslim: America, the Cold War, and the Roots of Terror* (New York: Pantheon, 2004).

2. See Talal Asad, "Secularism, Nation-State, Religion" in *Formations of the Secular: Christianity, Islam Modernity* (Stanford, CA: Stanford University Press, 2003).

3. Pavlos Hatzopoulos and Fabio Petito, *Religion in International Affairs: The Return from Exile* (New York: Palgrave MacMillan, 2003), 3.

4. Scholars Jurgensmeyer and Thomas point to recent backlash in developing countries against secular Western ideologies as having helped to encourage the role of religion as identity and necessitate its presence in IR. See Mark Jurgensmeyer, *The New Cold War: Religious Nationalism Confronts the Secular State* (Berkeley: University of California Press, 1993), and S. M. Thomas, "Taking Religious and Cultural Pluralism Seriously: The Global Resurgence of Religion and the Transformation of International Society" in *Millennium* 29, no. 3 (2000): 815–841. Jeff Haynes explains the backlash against modernization by the fact that it has undermined traditional, often religious, lifestyles. Jeffrey Haynes, "Religion and International Relations: What Are the Issues?" *International Politics* 4, no. 3 (Sept. 1994): 451–462.

5. See Barry Buzan, "New Patterns of Global Security in the Twenty-First Century" *International Affairs* 67, no. 3 (July 1991): 431–451.

6. Samuel Huntington, *The Clash of Civilizations and the Remaking of World Order* (New York: Simon and Schuster, 1996).

7. Brian J. Grim and Roger Finke, *The Price of Freedom Denied: Religious Prosecution and Conflict in the Twenty-First Century* (Cambridge: Cambridge University Press, 2011). Peter J. Katzenstein, *Civilizations in World Politics* (London: Routledge, 2010).

8. See A. Bozeman, "The International Order in a Multicultural World," in *The Expansion of International Society*, ed. B. Hedley and A. Watson (Oxford: Clarendon, 1984).

9. See R. E. Rubenstein and J. Crocker, "Challenging Huntington," *Foreign Policy*, 96 (Autumn 1994): 113–128.

10. See Mustapha Kamal Pasha, "Human Security and Exceptionalism(s): Securitization, Neoliberalism, and Islam" in *Protecting Human Security in a Post 9/11 World*, ed. Giorgio Shani, Makoto Sato, and Mustapha Kamal Pasha (New York: Palgrave MacMillan, 2007).

11. Ibid., 114.

12. Ibid., 115.

13. Edward Said, *Orientalism* (New York: Random House, 1978).

14. Maxime Rodinson, *La Fascination de l'Islam* (Paris: Francois Maspero, 1980).

15. Olivier Tschannen, "The Secularization Paradigm: A Systematization," *Journal for the Scientific Study of Religion* 30, no. 4 (Dec. 1991): 395–415.

16. "There was no differentiation between Muhammad's prophetic teaching, his authority in moral and spiritual matters and his role as a tribal mediator, arbitrator and organizer. No distinction was made between the realm of religion and that of state." William M. Watt, *Muhammad at Mecca* (London: Oxford University Press, 1953).

17. See Ira Lapidus, *A History of Islamic Societies* (New York: Cambridge University Press, 2002).

18. For more development on this multifaceted politicization, see Jocelyne Cesari, *Understanding the Arab Awakening: Islam, Modernity and Democracy* (forthcoming 2013).

19. Such an approach contradicts other contextualized approaches of shari'a, ummha, and jihad that are debated in the traditional religious interpretations, see Knut Vikor, *Between God and the Sultan: A History of Islamic Law* (New York: Oxford University Press, 2005).

20. The concept of political religion was forged by twentieth-century scholars to show that European political history lacks a clear demarcation between religion and politics. The concept of the European nation-state, for example, defined largely by culture and linguistics, is tied inextricably to religion. With the advent of the modern nation-state, the rules of engagement between religions have not become politically irrelevant. As a case in point, the Jacobin phase of the French Revolution and its accompanying "Cult of Reason" went beyond the notion of "civil religion" that Rousseau had defined earlier. The Jacobin cult was, in fact, the only putative form of political religion that made overt attempts to become an organized religion, perhaps because it emerged before the broader secularization of society took place. As the nineteenth century advanced, however, successors to the Jacobins abandoned any ambition to create a direct substitute to religion.

Modern secularism, as it is generally understood, has introduced substitutes for theistic religion. These substitutes have taken a bewildering variety of forms. For example, dedication to charismatic leaders such as Mao and Stalin resembles behavior exhibited by religious movements. As Mircea Eliade puts it, "the great majority of the irreligious are not liberated from religious behavior, from theologies and mythologies," in *The Sacred and the Profane: the Nature of Religion* (New York: Houghton Mifflin, 1987), 205–206.

The politicization of religion has been fundamental to nationalism. It has led to the secularization of politics as in the case of the German *Kulturprotestanismus*. Observing these developments, some German Christian commentators noted the formation of political religion in Germany and in other Western countries even before they noted the emergence of National Socialism. This politicization of religion was seen as a unique feature of modern, Western, secular, or semi-secular culture. Yet, this politicization has taken place in a diverse range of contexts outside of Western paradigms.

A new phase in the development of political religion began in the 1960s with the independence of Middle Eastern and African states that formed their own national cults. The largest new democracy of India created a more limited political religion as had the proto-democratic Kemalist Turkey before it.

The discrepancies between the current liberal narrative of religion and religion's actual function in public life, highlighted by examples above, suggest that the accurate narrative of the interplay between religion and politics remains in dispute. How, then, can scholars incorporate these discrepancies into their understanding of the relationship between Islam and politics? Scholars need to abandon the "natural history" narrative of modernization and link the vicissitudes of religion to the growing pains of the modern state. Political Islam can be seen as an unintended consequence of, rather than a conscious reaction against, the current status of this unfinished process. Therefore, an unconventional narrative sequence will need to be crafted in order to etch out the foundations for the alternate analysis of Islam as a political myth.

21. Ishiaq Ahmed, "The Pakistan Islamic State Project: A Secular Critique," in *State and Secularism: Perspectives from Asia*, ed. Michael Siam-Heng Heng (Hackensack, NJ: World Scientific, 2010): 185, 187, 194–196.

22. Ibid., 187, 192–193, 195.

23. Ibid.

24. Farhat Haq, "A State for the Muslims or an Islamic State?" in *Religion and Politics in South Asia*, ed. Ali Riaz (New York: Routledge, 2010), 122.

25. See Ahmet Kuru, *Secularism and State Politics Toward Religion, The United States, France and Turkey* (New York: Cambridge University Press, 2009), 222.

26. See Homi Bhabha, *The Location of Culture* (London: Routledge, 1994).

27. Their connection to the Salaf has to be distinguished from the reformist movement of the nineteenth century called Salafiyaa and illustrated by figures such

as Rachid Rida, Mohamed Abduh, and Al Afghani. Like Abdel Wahab, they went back to the Qu'ran and Sunna but did not reject contextualization of their interpretations, leading them to some modernist interpretations to forbid polygamy or promote equality of husbands and wives in the divorce procedure. In stark opposition, the Wahabis opted for a decontextualized approach to the Qu'ran and hadith and aim to replicate as much as possible the Medina experience.

28. Al-Albani, who died several years ago, was a specialist in Hadith and taught at the University of Medina.

29. Jocelyne Cesari, *When Islam and Democracy Meet* (New York: Palgrave, 2004).

30. Reuters, "Highlights—Egyptian President Hosni Mubarak's Speech," January 29, 2001, http://www.reuters.com/article/2011/01/29/egypt-mubarak-speech-idAF LDE70S00620110129?pageNumber=1&virtualBrandChannel=0.

31. For some responses, see Cesari, *Understanding the Arab Awakening*.

32. See Abdullhai Ahmed An-Na'im, *Islam and the Secular State* (Cambridge, MA: Harvard University Press, 2008), and Abdulkarim Soroush, *Reason, Freedom, and Democracy in Islam* (Oxford: Oxford University Press, 2000).

33. Equidistance between state and religion can take many forms and is not synonymous with separation, see Alfred Stepan "Religion, Democracy and the 'Twin Tolerations,'" *Journal of Democracy*, 11 (2000): 37–57.

Index